D0210227

HOOKED!

Stories of Obsession, Death, and Love
by Alaska's Commercial Fishing Men and Women

Edited by Leslie Leyland Fields

EPICENTER PRESS
Alaska Book Adventures™

Epicenter Press is a regional press publishing nonfiction books about the arts, history, environment, and diverse cultures and lifestyles of Alaska and the Pacific Northwest.

Publisher: Kent Sturgis
Acquisitions Editor: Lael Morgan
Proofreader: Melanie Wells
Cover & text design: Victoria Michael, Michael Designs
Printer: McNaughton & Gunn

Cover Photos ©2011 Dan Lamont, www.danlamont.com. Front cover--from top, left to right, a deck hand aboard the pollock-trawler Auriga of Anacortes, Washington awaits expected high winds and rough seas on the Bering Sea; a bosoms' mate aboard the Pacific Glacier, a Seattle-based factory trawler working in the Bering Sea, expresses his passion for his work; a deckhand aboard a tender helps deliver salmon to the Seafood Producers' Co-op in Sitka Alaska; a salmon trawler works in the Gulf of Alaska out of Sitka; back cover—a couple on their way to their favorite crab-fishing spot in Genoa Bay on Vancouver Island.

Each story ©2011 on behalf of the writer and published with permission. In Addition, "Nights of Ice," an excerpt from a book by the same title by Spike Walker, and "Let the Kid Drive the Boat, excerpted from North by Northwestern: A Seafaring Family on Deadly Alaskan Waters, by Sig Hansen, are published with permission of St. Martin's Press

Library of Congress Control Number: 2011930477
ISBN 978-1-935347-14-9

10 9 8 7 6 5 4 3 2 1
Printed in the United States of America

To order single copies of HOOKED, mail $14.95 plus $5 for shipping (WA residents add $1.80 state sales tax) to Epicenter Press, PO Box 82368, Kenmore, WA 98028; call us day or night at 800-950-6663, or visit www.EpicenterPress.com.

With great appreciation to all the fine writers and good people
in these pages willing to share
a piece of their lives on the water. May fish always find you!

CONTENTS

INTRODUCTION

IT STARTED IN 1977 on a tiny island in the Gulf of Alaska when I put on my first pair of hip boots and vaulted into a small wooden skiff full of salmon. In my previous life in New Hampshire I had written about everything, surreptitiously scribbling stanzas on restaurant napkins, fussing over line endings on index cards while in line at the store. My step into the skiff, though, was a step into silence. I was sucked under with such force, working twelve to eighteen hours a day, seven days a week, for four months on a remote island incommunicado with the rest of the world—all literary thoughts fled.

Though this world was astonishing – volcanoes spouting over the roofs of the cabins; dailt scenes of whales, seals, sea otters and sea lions daily; winds that blew eighty knots; living on a scrap of land flung onto the Shelikof Strait, sometimes hanging on for life itself. My journal, which I had kept faithfully for ten years, became the equivalent of a series of grunts: picked two skiffs of pinks this morning, worked past dark on Seven-mile in a northeastern blow, kicker broke down around the island, arms going numb at night, can't sleep. Language was a luxury. There was no place in my fishing life for literary allusion; I was body and muscle only. This was the active life, the life of doing, where salmon were salmon, the ocean was itself and nothing more, and the day's object was to pick and deliver as many hundreds and thousands of fish as possible. I wrote no poems or essays about fishing for nearly ten years.

I shouldn't have expected otherwise. Commercial fishing has rarely been viewed as the realm of the contemplative. This belongs to fly-fishing, sport-fishing – men and women at rest in the wilderness, senses awakening, losing and then finding themselves, restored for return to that other world. Fishing here is not doing but being, or some magical alchemy of their perfect merging. Books and anthologies abound connecting the spiritual and the natural with sport-fishing.

Commercial fishing, though, is a business and so the second cousin from the other side of the tracks, the world of doing and action, where the bottom line governs all activities. Tasks are done in fast forward, so repetitive and at such speeds and for such a length of time that they are best done unthinkingly, instinctively, automatically. Your worth, both economic and personal, is often measured in terms of how fast you can bait the halibut hooks, how quickly you can pick fish, how long you can work without sleep. The all-absorbing intensity of the work, coupled, with many Alaskan fishermen's schedules and lives on the water, does not allow for languid introspection.

And should a fisherman have the time for such, revelatory communication about his life's work cuts against every tradition and fiber of this occupation. In fishing, sport and commercial alike, secrecy is required and assumed. Competition is intense, even cutthroat. When any kind of fisherman, sport or commercial, speaks, gross understatement or overstatement rules the day. No one expects otherwise: there is so much that cannot be said.

The traditional Alaskan fisherman's seal of silence was broken first in 1993 by Spike Walker's *Working on the Edge: Surviving in the World's Most Dangerous Profession: King Crab Fishing in Alaska's High Seas.* National attention to the dangers and drama of commercial fishing intensified in 1997 with Sebastian Junger's *The Perfect Storm,* on the bestseller list for fifty-three weeks, followed by Patrick Dillon's *Lost at Sea.* Almost overnight, commercial fishing became popular literary territory. *Outside* magazine, noting the growing appetite for such stories, wrote wryly, "If you're a commercial fisherman, you've probably been contacted by an agent."

The cameras followed the books. In 2005, the Discovery Channel took a risk on a new reality show trailing the lives and work of men in Alaska's crab fishery. I hardly need to say more. "The Deadliest Catch" now airs in over 150 countries and is currently in its seventh season, catapulting fishermen, who normally worked in relative obscurity, to world-wide fame. In the strange mix that reality TV has perfected, a global audience now raptly follows both the life-threatening extremes of crab fishing, and the most mundane routines and interactions. Books then followed the cameras--we include one of those fishermen here, Sig Hansen, with an exciting excerpt from *North by Northwest: A Seafaring Family on Deadly Alaskan Waters.* Wherever I travel, and other Alaskan fishermen report the same, I am met with intense questions and interest in commercial fishing. The silence that long shrouded the industry has been lifted.

Why, at the turning of the first decade of the millennium, in the post-information age, when more than eighty-five percent of Americans live in urban or suburban areas, are so many turning to television shows and books about men and women who break their backs, and sometimes lose their lives, pulling fish from Alaska's seas?

It is not hard to hazard a few theories. Commercial fishing, as many know, is ranked as the most dangerous job in the nation, with a death rate from seven to one hundred times the national average. It does not require flights of imagination or verbal high jinks to create from such a setting and occupation the necessary elements of story: plot, conflict, tension, drama, and tragedy. All of this is built into the business of commercial fishing. But even story is sometimes not a large enough container. This is epic, even, the primeval, universal struggle of man against nature: men and women alone in a fifty-seven-foot boat against a twenty-foot raging sea, or wrestling a leviathan in steep waters, adrift in a suffocating fog. Yet these stories are not Odysseys or Iliads, where the Greek heroes, godlike figures, ultimately and inevitably triumph against all the malevolent forces that would keep them from reaching home and hearth. For all the courage and daring, in these recent writings and through the camera we see fishermen as thoroughly human, as beset by flaws, pride, and mortality as the rest of us. Their obituaries appear in our local newspapers; we leave their funerals weeping. Their stories read like sagas, feeding our deep human hunger to understand the ultimate battle against nature and death; but the lives are real, the losses are personal.

Yet, even for those of us who commercial fish, reading about the losses of our own, thrilling to adrenaline accounts of fishermen's rescues and near rescues at sea is not macabre; it is human and it is necessary. Scott Russell Sanders wrote in "The Most Human Art: Ten Reasons Why We'll Always Need a Good Story," published in the *Georgia Review*, that story, whether fiction or nonfiction, is essential "to teach us how to be human" and to "help us deal with suffering, loss, and death." Those who have suffered share their stories "as a way of fending off despair," and as a way of teaching us to live consciously and wisely.

There is something here, too, about our national passion for frontier and wild-ness. We are losing both the imaginative, mythical frontier, and the actual wilderness, we feel. Where do we go now to explore, to test our American mettle? Where else but out past the continents' boundaries to the oceanic plains beyond. This is our Wild West. It is not by chance that the commercial fishermen who work this expanse are often called "the last of the cowboys." At our fish camp, we speak a piece of this anal-ogy daily. Our own boat, a modest sixty-five-foot scow we bought at an auction for a song, used mostly to tender our supplies to fish camp, was bought with the name crudely and audaciously stenciled on the stern: *Cowboy*. The twelve-hundred miles of the Aleutian chain are called "Out West" by those who live and fish there. In Alaska's most wild fisheries, where fleets of wheeling boats stir a single bay to dust, reeling lines on lines, nets over nets, every boat unbridled, every set a maniacal, defiant few minutes' ride – these are rodeos, we say: one of the last Wild West shows still playing.

The mythos of the cowboy carries with it a rugged individualism we still prize, but even more we are drawn by the physicality of the fisherman-cowboy's life. Most Americans spend their work days harnessed to a screen, their wrists captive on the keyboard, their sen-tient bodies aching on uncomfortable chairs. Relaxation and leisure means more time in front of a screen, immersed in virtual worlds, some of which gain their virtue by requiring the waving of wands at digital images--as much activity as some people get in a day. As our physical interactions with the natural world atrophy, we hunger for sensual, whole-body experience with the wild forces of nature – earth, air, fire, and water. Even the agrarian culture that remains, accounting for less than four percent of the population, is increasingly distanced from feet-in-the-soil, hard-muscle extraction of the harvest, often laboring in air-conditioned computerized cabs and rounding up herds of cattle from helicopters.

It is nothing but romanticism to insist that someone somewhere still tills the earth, herds the cattle, and fishes the sea as his forefathers did. No one can compete and sur-vive as a business in this global economy with such ideals; a population of more than 300 million couldn't be fed. And yet, the fishermen remain, some fishing just as their fathers and grandfathers have fished: in fleets of small boats clustering Alaska's coasts, working in homemade vessels with crews of two or three, salmon seining in forty-two-foot Deltas, set-netting in open skiffs, hand-hauling the beach seine, pulling a living from the depths with backs, arms, ungloved hands. We are anomalies, indeed.

Some of us in this book are still fishing close to the old ways. But nostalgia, television shows, and literary trends may not save us or others here from the same fate as the small family farm and ranch. A short time ago, there were many threats on the horizon. Today they are here among us: global warming which is measurably increasing the acidity of the ocean, affecting every level of the food chain; fish farms that raise penned fish, routinely feeding antibiotics against the diseases that proliferate, risking infection and destruction of the wild stocks; increasing pressure from sport fishermen to augment their own share of the resource by reducing the commercial fisherman's catch; the threat of consolidation through the rationalizing of more fisheries, which clusters the resource into fewer, more corporatized hands, and shuts out the small, independent fishermen.

Much has been lost already. It is no longer enough to weigh anchor and risk life and health on the North Pacific or the Bering Sea or the Shelikof Strait for a hold of fish. Many fishermen have become activists, lobbyists, consultants, working off-season with the same determination as in-season to preserve the resource, or their own right to a share of it.

While fishermen are becoming increasingly vocal and public in their fight to preserve their livelihood and the natural resources, they are beginning to define themselves and write their own stories. Until recently, most books about fishing were written by outsiders, writers, and journalists who offered a peek or gaze into this other world. This is what makes this collection significant: the stories here are written firsthand by men and women who live this life. There is no filtering journalist; the writing and the events here are intense, direct, first person. They give a fuller view even beyond the camera, of the diversity, excitement, and risk of fishing in Alaska's vast seas.

Collectively, the fisher-writers here have fished cod, halibut, salmon, crab, and herring. Some writing here have fished commercially for several seasons; others have spent most of their lives on the water. The rousing sea stories are here: the dramas of near-death battles, the sickening tragedy of lovers and friends lost to the waters--but this is not the whole story. This collection represents an extraordinary holistic view of Alaskan fishing: not just the dying, but the living; not just the obsessive doing of fishing, but the passionate being as well. As you read, you'll understand why so many are hooked, unwilling, or unable to leave this uncommon life.

One word of warning: if you feel the pull of the nets, the bite of the gaffe yourself, there's room for you here. But take heed--the hook leaves an unfading mark. ⚓

> "You can't always get what you want
> But if you try sometime,
> You just might find,
> You get what you need."
> —The Rolling Stones

PAYIN' YOUR DUES IN TOGIAK

TOGIAK -- It's 9:30 p.m., late May in Alaska, and we be jammin' now. Half an hour to showtime, 'til we finally get to rock 'n' roll. We've been anchored for almost three weeks, eagerly anticipating the arrival of mega-schools of herring. Now the wait is almost over.

The crew of the *High C* is wound up, focused, intent, intense. We're jazzed. We're gonna rock. This is our year. We can feel it, we can smell it, we can almost touch it. We're due. We're gonna catch some fish. A lotta fish. Way lotta fish. We're gonna do it. We're gonna be it. Top dogs, big guns, herring honchos, the ever-lovin' rockin'-rollin' baddest of the bad, Togiak highliners of 1992!! Yeah! Yeah! Yeaaaaaahhhhhhh!

"Whoa, Doc, pull your chute!"

"What, oh yeah, standing by..."

Guess my personal stereo was a little loud. Yeah, I'm excited. It's just that I've heard so much about Togiak, and we've been waiting so long, and so many fish are expected--we just have to make a killing. Skippy and my two fellow

JOEL GAY plays a jazz riff on "the stuporous waiting followed by minutes of panic" that characterizes Alaska's most infamous herring fishery.

crewmen have had some big hauls, but not recently. They're due. Overdue. That's how herring highliners see the world--you can't score big at every stop on the herring circuit around Alaska, and not every year. But it adds up, it evens out, and this is the year for the *High C.*

This is my first trip to Togiak. Heard all about it, seen friends come back with big grins and fat wallets, but I'm the new kid on the block. Still, I'm thinking a little beginner's luck is in order. Nothing exceptional. Hundred tons. Maybe 150. The fish have been small since British Columbia, which means we could get $600 a ton. At that price, my ten percent crew share--minus my share of food and fuel, unfortunately--would give me $60 for every ton we catch. Hundred tons, $6,000. Yeah, nice little shot.

First thing, I buy a Stratocaster. Sweetest electric guitar in the world. I can almost feel its curvaceous heft, the whammy bar, the screaming power of three pickups screwed tight to a solid maple body. I'm ready. I've done the acoustic thing—Dylan, Peter Paul and Mary. Now I wanna rock. I wanna play the blues, bend some strings, Stevie Ray Vaughan, B.B. King, lord a mercy, sting me.

I don't know if hanging out in Togiak qualifies as "payin' your dues," but it should. Flew to Dillingham with Dane, our skiffman, thinking we'd be home in ten days.

"We've got it down," Skippy told us, "start to finish, ten days."

But nooooooo, it wasn't spring in Dillingham, it was winter: eighteen degrees, ice still forming in the Nushagak River. Had to buy a new jacket for $45. They don't cut you any slack in Dillingham. Spent several days in the PAF boatyard turning the *High C*, which is a typical stubby thirty-two-foot aluminum Bristol Bay gillnetter, into a Togiak seiner. As we transformed the ugly thing into something even more ridiculous, Maria Muldaur's words rang in my ears: "... If I can make a dress out of a feed sack, I can make a man outta you."

Herring fishing equates to days of stupored waiting followed by minutes of panic. So Miles, the leadman, and I brought our trumpets. We go way back, playing together in the hills above town. Not that they wouldn't let us play downtown, you understand, but rather that our special and unique blend of musical genres transcends the stifling restrictions of traditional harmonic delineation.

After hearing us, Dane kept his ear plugs handy and Skippy urged us to keep our mutes in until we were out of the boatyard. But hey, when music is your life, there's no holding back. We do it all, "Star-Spangled Banner" to the "Mickey Mouse Club Theme," rock, Dixieland, reggae. We bad.

We were just settling in to life at "Club Dead" when word filtered through the skipper grapevine—fish seen in Hagemeister Strait! How rude. Just when we had located free showers and got chummy with Ricardo the Pizza King of Dillingham, they expected us to go fish? But hey, we're professionals, no? So we loaded the seine, stowed the groceries, and set out down Nushagak Bay.

The rest of the state is pretty wild, but you're really heading for the edge of the map when your bow is pointed toward Togiak. When you think of Dillingham as "the big city" and the only thing between you and Tokyo is Dutch Harbor, you're out there.

At Cape Constantine we immediately hit six-foot seas that exploded on our stubby little bow and rained back down onto us like a million diamond teardrops backlit by the sun. Off in the distance whales rose from the sea, spyhopping--black pillars emerging briefly from a shimmering blue desert and then just as quickly gone. We passed huge factory trawlers quietly dragging for yellowfin sole, all business and monstrously hungry compared to the giddy fleet of thirty-two-footers parading past.

The western sky flooded red at sunset, then black, and we were enveloped in that world known only to mariners, defined by the cabin walls, the muffled roar of the diesel, the green glow of the instrument panel, and the polyrhythmic bobbing of the boat. After a big bowl of Skippy's garlic soup, I went out and barfed.

We anchored around midnight in the floating city that develops every spring in Nunavachuk Bay, just east of Togiak. Morning found us surrounded by one-hundred or more seiners, tenders, and processing ships. Skiffs ran around like bicycle messengers in a submerged metropolis. Airplanes and choppers zoomed in and out. Everywhere you went, exhaust stacks bellowed and belched. After a lovely walk on the beach we drove over to Togiak Bay, where life wasn't quite so hectic.

Togiak. The name rolls off the tongue easily, whether you've been there or not. Unlike, say, Iliuliuk. Togiak conjures images of, what--Alaska wilderness calendar beauty? A 5,000-year-old Alaska Native village rooted in the ways and means of its forebears? The bustling and efficient hub of a modern American commercial fishery?

Sorry, the correct answer is "D. None of the above."

There are no trees in Togiak, and in May the grass is dead, the beach littered with brown and gray ice. There is no dock, much less a harbor. To fill your water tanks, you beach your boat in front of the big red octagonal building, go find the guy with the key, and connect your hose to his water spigot. All the houses in Togiak look like they were built in Washington and barged in, and the cars, snowmachines, and three-wheelers appear to have come to Togiak to die. The store has traditional woven grass baskets, frozen pizza, and ice cream but not much in the way of fresh produce. It makes Dillingham prices seem downright cheap.

The only thing that seems vaguely old is the road, which twists around downtown Togiak as if recalling the days it was a foot path.

We anchor across the bay in the mud flats off Togiak Fisheries, Inc. So do three-dozen other boats, rafting in twos, threes, and fours. Rafting up makes life more interesting when the tide is out, but when we float it's a zoo--boats churning mud in hopes of staying off the raft next door, skippers yelling, crewmen fending off errant vessels.

That's about the only excitement, however. For the next two weeks we watch springtime come to western Alaska. Pretty thrilling, really. Birds. Ice floes. Some fishermen follow the playoffs on big screen TV in the cannery. Miles and I run daily on the beach and play duets, Dane reads a lot with his ear plugs in, Skippy and our pilot fly home. Our big thrill is watching two guys walk to shore through knee-deep mud. Sad but funny as hell.

We sleep late, eat a lot, read, play cards, and lounge. And every day, without fail, we talk about how much money we're gonna make. It's what herring fishing is all about: the possibility of making the big score, hitting the jackpot. Recounting stories of 600-ton sets, or sets so big the purse rings broke. The stories weave their way into your subconscious so that soon you start to think 200 tons is entirely possible. Hey, someone has to do it, why not us?

Miles says a fat paycheck will let him pursue his art and not fish salmon this summer. Dane wants to upgrade his setnet operation. Skippy has everything he needs. After a Stratocaster and amp, new truck, skis, trip to New Zealand and packing my IRA, my list is fairly short. We try not to be overconfident, but with a crack crew like ours and the Alaska Department of Fish and Game projecting a total catch harvest of 15,000 tons, how can we not make money?

Then one day, unbelievably, herring appear on the grounds. We pull the hook and cruise out to meet them, and to visit the ADFG management camp that sets up every year on Summit Island. Miles and I come ashore with Skippy, but keep walking until we're above the brushline. There we find heaven on earth--the tundra in aromatic bloom, sun, a warm breeze, no diesels, no bugs.

But all things must pass, and soon we're back on the boat and prowling the shore, the last of the hunter-gatherers. We fish at ten tonight. We've looked around Eagle Bay and Metervik but now we're back in Nunavachuk. Tall bluffs on the west end of the bay cast long black shadows on the water, but we're on the east side, basking in the last rays of sunshine. Mistake number one.

As Skippy drives around, Miles and I inspect the deck. Pelican hook lubed? Check. Cleats covered? Check. Tow line, wind line, breast line in order? Check, check, check. We see buddies from our hometown and laugh at how jealous they'll be when we catch 200 tons. "Maybe we better leave enough for another opening," Miles jokes. ADFG says this first period will last just 20 minutes, which everyone interprets to mean "the first of several." Mistake number two.

Being the superstitious type, I silently apologize to the herring gods for my greed. We don't need 200 tons, really. Forty would be fine. Actually, just enough to pay expenses. And a Strat. And an amp. That's not asking too much, is it? Mistake number three.

Fifteen minutes to go and we find ourselves among two dozen seiners. Not Bristol Bay "gill-seiners," but the real thing: crow's nests, seine trays. Each one has probably made one-hundred sets this year. We did three. This morning. Mistake number four.

Five minutes. The aromas of diesel, gasoline, and testosterone fill the air. An enormous school of herring--800 tons? 1,000?--fills this end of the bay and everyone seems to expect a chunk. Skippers jockey for position, idling and charging, forward and reverse, while their skiffmen hang on for dear life.

One minute. The roar is deafening, the tension palpable, the focus so intense you'd think this was war. Someone charges through the school in frustration. Spotter planes circle tightly overhead. Every engine is red-lined, every skipper amped. One skiff cuts loose, then another, and suddenly everything is in motion. Flying corks, churning water, Skippy is yelling, Miles is yelling, I'm yelling...

Mistakes five through twenty-nine occur very quickly, though it's like a dream to me now. I remember the skiff hitting another boat, letting go of the net, and feverishly hauling back five fathoms of gear by hand. There was something about a rock. Another rock. And then suddenly we find ourselves alongside a tender. Dark now. We seem to be floating in a void, a nether world created by halogen decklights and a gently lapping sea.

A tender woman with hot pink hair and a nose ring suggests maybe we ought not to deliver. Something along the lines of, "It's not big enough." We do, though-- not quite nine tons. There's a three-fathom hole in the bunt, where the other 191 tons must have escaped. Next set, we say.

But there is no "next set." The following morning Fish and Game says the fleet caught 17,000 tons. That's it. No more. See you next year.

The crew of the *High C* is in shock. My personal share is less than one ton. The Stratocaster slips away. I don't know whether to laugh or cry.

In twenty-four hours, I'm flying back to Anchorage. Back to family, responsibility, obligation. No more fantasies. No more dreaming. Back to reality. On the airplane I peruse the newspaper and flip to the want ads. But for some reason I skip "Help

Wanted" and go first to "Musical Instruments," where my heart stops. "Stratocaster," the ad says. "Good condition, with amp and case. $300."

"No way," I mutter, "That's too good a deal. Must be a mistake. Maybe $600. Even $500 would be a steal. But $300? It was gone the first day." At the airport I don't even call.

Instead I drive straight to the Fly-By-Night Club, slam down a couple of beers, and listen to a killer Chicago blues guitarist. The stage lights, the sound, the people with their fancy clothes and neat haircuts—they make Togiak seem a million miles away, and I catch myself wondering which world is real. The chilling sensation of river ice scraping the hull an inch from your head, the stinging Arctic wind, the birds and delicate tundra flowers, the helicopters and Japanese buyers, the millions of dollars invested in fish eggs--is that real? Or are these phony fingernails and spray-paint coiffeurs, these suitcoats and Italian shoes real? Beats me.

The next morning, I can't stand it any longer and I call. "Yeah," the guy says, "I still got it." I race over to his darkened apartment and there it is. My Strat. Red as Madonna's lipstick and begging to be fondled. I hand him a stack of 20s and practically run out the door, afraid he'll realize his error or I'll realize mine.

Two months later I see Skippy in town. I haven't called him because I honestly believe I owe him money--we spent more in groceries and fuel than we grossed, I'm sure. But he's a helluva nice guy and says, "Hey, I got a check for you."

"No kidding?"

"Yeah," he says, and smiles wide. "Three-hundred bucks. Whattya gonna do with it?"

JOEL GAY spent nearly thirty years living in Alaska, mainly in the fishing town of Homer. His work as a journalist led him to cover the commercial fishing industry for newspapers and magazines, which in turn led to his decision to start fishing in 1989—the year of the Exxon Valdez oil spill. He seined for salmon in Cook Inlet, gillnetted in Bristol Bay, tried herring fishing one season, and operated a salmon tender in Nushagak Bay. Gay also wrote about and photographed all aspects of commercial fishing for a variety of publications including *National Fisherman* and *Pacific Fishing*. He is the author of *Commercial Fishing in Alaska*. He now writes about fish and game for the New Mexico Wildlife Federation.

CASHING OUT ON THE BERING SEA

MY BUNK, DOWN BELOW, was my only real refuge on the F/V *Obsession*, but it was there that I brought, face-to-face before me, the most emphatic creations of danger. In one dream, I'm sorting crab and I can't keep up. I grab a shell. I yank its legs from a tangled mass, and toss it to a tank. A ton—a literal ton—of unsorted creatures, raised like a heap of slag, clicks and sloshes and dissembles around me. Dislodged crabs, unsorted, back away by the dozens across shining deck boards. I reach for another crab, yank on it, toss it in a tank. I'm waist-high in sea muck, pot bridles, tangled lines; I'm stuck in a sewing machine that won't turn off. A wave breaks, shifting the matter of the deck into a dark and vital soup. Crabs and octopi surge up my legs. Lost fish slip away overboard. A halibut, long as I am, rips and flaps from the slag, slides from my gloves. A wave slaps the back of my hood. Seawater fills my breath. I can't keep up, can't see, and can't sort fast enough.

Fear came in vivid swatches. Only yards from the boat's engine through a few wooden panels, that bunk was my

MARTHA SUTRO leaves her high school classroom to work as a deckhand on an Alaskan crabber in one of the most intensive and dangerous fisheries in the world.

only zone of privacy for several thousand miles around. Letters, crumpled editions of the *Kodiak Daily Mirror*, a ratty sleeping bag, yesterday's socks, and a sole clean sweatshirt all stuffed the edges. It was room, bed, and personal cave—all at once. I slept on top of my hardcover copy of *To the Lighthouse* and I didn't even know it.

Dream: a codfish's eyes rise into mine. A crab ticks up the edge of some close rim, the pot door, the lip of my bunk, a tangle of blankets. He stares at me, climbs like a primitive. I turn, sit up, try to sit up, try to unseal my eyes. I push my legs around and out of the bunk so they dangle, familiar, over the edge. An engine grinds on. I open my eyes—no light. The wooden bunk lip takes the place of safety, presses against the backs of my knees. We're driving somewhere, still.

Bob had the bunk above me. He was the oldest guy on board, the gentlest, most self-effacing, most enduring member of the crew. He'd been working on and off on the *Obsession* for over twenty years. Forlorn, accepted, he could drink so much in Dutch Harbor, he pickled his withered body, chain-smoked through his days, slept as if barely alive. I never knew, when I stammered awake from nightmares of crab crawling through the sleeping bag, or lurched out of the darkness because a voice was booming "We're on the gear!" whether Bob was up in the wheelhouse on watch, up having a smoke outside, or right up above me in the bunk, asleep. He had a drunken wife in Anchorage, sometimes saw his two children. Their school photos were tacked above his bunk. He fished to keep them going. He slipped in and out of the stateroom like a weary old cat, smoked behind the windbreak just outside the pilothouse, bones and skin, faded fishing shirt, the same black jeans.

If you were a mother, this might have concerned you: Your daughter was disappearing between anonymous waves, out of the reach of any reliable signal short of a Coast Guard contact, on a sea so distant the maps nearly rendered it polar. I did not know the extent of my mother's fear when I went crab fishing, but I do know that it was shapeless. There was no order, no structure for her fear, and structureless fear is the worst kind. Hers came in the form of the underground: the bottom of a well, the bottom of a coal mine.

I went to work on a one-hundred-foot crab boat with five men my mother had never known nor imagined she'd want to know. In 1992, *Forbes* magazine ranked crab fishing second only to coal mining in danger. *Forbes* measured "danger" in the industry's number of work-related deaths per year. My mother ripped the article out of *Forbes* and taped it to her refrigerator in Virginia.

Two years before I went to fish, I'd met the captain of the *Obsession*, Ted Goss, when we'd both signed on to a guided climbing expedition in the Alaska Range.

When we left Talkeetna, at the end of that trip, Ted, as if offhandedly offering me a weekend getaway, said to me, "If you ever want to crab fish on the Bering Sea, just give me a call." Ted had the worn, sturdy texture of a farmer, nothing like the men I had ever known. The pulse of his life was just as unrecognizable to me: It was determined by plane schedules, fishing openings, state Fish and Game quotas, the weather. I promised myself a trip to the Bering Sea.

In the two years that elapsed before I went, I saw Ted twice, once on the West Coast, where he lived, and once on the East, where I taught teenagers at a tiny school in northern Vermont. When he visited for a weekend one spring, he brought a pile of Kodiak newspapers and a cooler full of crab. When he left, he sent letters that read like lists. Sometimes he sent only lists: quotas, Loran readings, measurements for pot bridles, pot doors, webbing, pots. Sometimes I couldn't read the handwriting, but what I could read was the constellation of different pressures, smells, timetables, people.

There was nothing formal about my arrangement to go work for Ted—no contract, no promises, no real schedule, short of my duty to show up in Dutch Harbor at the beginning of February, ready to work. Part of Ted's appeal was his hard-working, successful, laissez-faire approach. I bought right into it. We made our plans roughly, in a couple of quick and casual phone calls. When my mother asked about Ted, I defended him unequivocally to her, without even really knowing him.

A month before I left home to fish I received a package from Ted. Inside, there was no letter, only texts: a worn copy of a book, precipitously titled *Working on the Edge*, its cover shot with a wash of orange bodies blurred against a veil of green water. There were also a few random nautical charts: Shumagin Islands to Sarak Islands, Alaska Peninsula and Aleutian Islands to Seguam Pass.

Last to fall out of the envelope was a video case, unmarked, with a tape inside. The night the package arrived I sat on the floor of the living room at my parents' house in Virginia and stuck the video in the TV set. The frame of the image on the screen floated out to a nebulous, pancaked mass, an ice pack. White and white and white against a terminally gray sky, against slivers of a shale-colored sea, rising and sinking with a sanguine, prehistoric reliability that forgave the witness of a camcorder. The frame; panned from the stern-mounted wheelhouse of the vessel, where the camera was filming, up toward the bow of the boat, showing the deck in between, a space low, rectangular, and enclosed, like the sunken stage of a theater.

Ice shagged the railings. Rusty crab pots, hoses, boxes, coils of line, equipment I couldn't recognize sat usefully but quietly in the frame, like farm equipment looks when it rests, dirt-encased, in between shifts. The shot drifted back to the ice pack. A disembodied voice outside the picture made a simple, muffled comment: "Pretty tight pack." Nobody, nothing answered. Just the nervous static of a nylon sleeve in the wind, and a granular moan, shifting and rising. Not a lot of speech in this world, I thought, but a thousand kinds of cold. No work, either, when the hull of the boat is hugged by a shoreless game board of pack ice. The image on the screen floats back to the deck, up to the bow, and the coarse wind surged, wavered, resurged. Boat to sea. Sea to boat. That's all there was.

I was sitting cross-legged on the carpet. My mother watched silently behind me in a chair, watching as if sure something astonishing would appear on screen. When nothing happened and the tape went to gray, I turned the set off.

Out of the long silence, she spoke, "Why in the world would you want to go to a place like that?"

The grandfather clock in the hall struck and rested. Outside, a mild winter breeze pushed rain across the sycamore trunks and I thought of the laced fingers of ice on the stanchions of the *Obsession*. Winter here; winter there. No contract, no promises, no schedule. Just show up in Dutch, ready to work.

"I want to see the Bering Sea in winter." I couldn't begin to fabricate anything close to a real answer for her. I had a pilgrim's importance, which felt complete only when it was charged with the possibility of this scale of transformation. Good-bye to the secure and well-laid paths, the careful civilized corridors that had molded me. They no longer suited my questions. Crabbing was an idea that only my will could realize. Still, it was just that, merely an idea—immune to details of threat or danger.

On an end-of-January day I stood at the Richmond airport, a wool sweater itching my neck, my duffel of sweatshirts, thick socks, gloves, and notebook packed and already on the airplane. Just as I'd anticipated, the dim sense of ambivalence I'd had for about a week was steadily sharpening into a crisp panic. After this, the basis for motivation was just a hunch. Mother saw this, whether she knew it or not. "I'm certain I should, of course, without hesitation or decision, cancel this plan," I started to hear myself say. Absolutely.

Not five months earlier my same mother had been putting me on the plane for Kathmandu, where I'd determined a solo journey through the Himalayas was to originate. What I'd said, at that departure, was, "See you in three months," acting out a well-kindled carefreeness. In between treks into the mountains of Nepal, I'd called home every day, sometimes twice. Mother knew the power of these hunches.

She was standing in flats and a blue overcoat, a dutiful confidence written into her eyes. She looked me over, top to bottom, even wishing, I knew, she'd scrubbed the hiking boots I was wearing. I was twenty-seven, but she, in her strained belief in me, was trying to lend a physical support, as if I, her only daughter in a family of boys, were twelve again and it was camp on the other end of this flight. I waited for a minute, hoping she could detect my sense of rising vertigo. The passengers were gone, the desk attendant called for the stragglers. Mother hugged me hard around the neck: "Call us when you get there."

Her shoulders pressed against mine and my instinct, a quick and fortuitous signal, reached me with the closest intensity. Suddenly, I felt saved by it. I was meant to stay there in the southern winter. Perhaps get a job at a sandwich shop. I spoke. "Ma, maybe I'll stay. Maybe this is just a dumb idea. Maybe I should just not go."

She hugged me again, not so tight. Was she caught off guard? Willing to believe me? Had she even heard me speak? "You've gotten yourself into this." Her eyes looked directly at mine. In my impression of the moment I cannot remember a time when I felt her as connected to me as then. "You have to see what it's for, where it's taking you."

I felt like a motor inside me had stopped. I could say nothing of course. I turned from her, the panic replaced by a vibrating emptiness that rendered me just a body that walked down the long throat of the airplane entryway, knowing she watched. Many kinds of fear, many kinds of boldness came out of the succeeding months, but nothing that crystallized, that cumulative, nothing, in action, that automatic.

Flying across the continent, past its edge and out toward its hooked and fragile tip, I realized that for the sum total of twenty days of my life I'd known Ted in person, he was not even as clear a figure in my mind as the water I'd known and the water I was expecting. I imagined the Bering Sea as snow-filled, deathly, corrugated in black. Capricious, elastic, familiar, seas and dreams of seas sank and stretched in my mind, a torrent of verb forms. The saltiest water I'd known was the Chesapeake's, an almost deciduous sort of liquid, that soft and safe, that resilient. On a capsizing Sailfish, the sail meets the wave with a little sea foam. There's a jump, an easy collapse backward over the hull, miniature bravery in righting it again, the boom at an anxious shudder and drip, the sail flickering like tin.

Fog and clouds matte the iron-streaked Gulf of Alaska and the Bering Sea all winter, and indeed, for most of the year. On a plane, looking down, nothing appears, nothing, until a grind of wheels dislodging from the belly starts. Just then, barren, barren islands—the lonely hummocks of the Aleutians—rising white and wind-scoured, not a single tree. A Russian Orthodox Church, its tips as brown against snow as burnt onions, cast the gloom of a forgotten country on the margin of the bay. This was Dutch Harbor. From above, container ships, crab boats, freighters, draggers, and a tugboat all appeared as toys. Big pickup trucks, supply trucks, and vans routed through potholed, muddy roads that ran between jetties, brown hills, and the messy shoreline of boats. At that first sight of it, the clouds slung so low, the ocean outside the harbor swelling, iron-backed, tracked by cords of foam, I let my head fall back against the seat rest and looked down from only a corner of my eye. A loose knot shifted in my stomach. I had never been on a winter sea.

On the second day there I found a pay phone in the entryway of Stormy's Pizza Place in Unalaska, the village across the island from Dutch Harbor. "This is the end of the earth," I told my mother. She could only respond with questions about the weather, the people I'd met, questions about the flight. She really wished she could say nothing. She'd already started a kind of endurance race, a daily, weekly, terror-management seminar, forcing excruciating detachment, unable to restrain intense bewilderment.

Outside the cracked glass of the phone booth the wind was ramping in off the water. A rusty pickup truck, its bed loaded with a hundred coils of line, splashed through flakes blowing exactly sideways. Someone else was waiting for the phone. I hung up, zipped up my jacket, and took off across driveways and parking lots, making my way down to a black beach where waves were crashing, a beach rimmed by clapboard houses, junked cars, and totem poles. Every so often, a big wintry dog looked my way through eyes mostly covered over in blown fur.

I got my fishing gear at Carl's General Store, in Unalaska. One each: a blue wool cap, a pair of brown steel-toed fishing boots, orange bibbed overalls, and an orange hooded slicker—the rain-gear made by a Swedish company called Grundens. Several each: rubber fishing gloves, some orange, some black, and polypropylene liner gloves to go inside the rubber. Also one jacket, called a Stormy Seas jacket, to wear all the time, even under the slicker, that reminded me of a baseball jacket, except this one zipped up in front, so high its collar covered most of my face. It was warm, lined in pile, and between the pile and the shell, was fitted with an inflatable cushion.

Inside the left chest pocket was a CO_2 cartridge and a ripcord. "If you end up in the water out there when we're working," Ted said to me as I left for Carl's, "that'll help you stay afloat 'til we can come around and get you." There was firmness, even affection in his voice, and simultaneously, a kind of aloofness. He was working, after all, dressed in navy coveralls, hands coated in grease, down in the engine room of the *Obsession*, getting us ready to "get out of town," as they said in Dutch.

I was the only new member of the crew that winter and I went alone, with Ted's suggestions, to buy the gear. I spent $300 on it and walked back to the boat, carrying it in a plastic shopping bag. Our diesel tanks and water tanks full, our cupboards stocked with groceries, our bait freezer packed to the ceiling, and our deck loaded with sixty pots ready for fishing, we drove out of Dutch the next morning at 3 a.m., motoring past other draggers and fishers silently clustered in packs and lit by sodium lights on their rigging.

Ahead of us, Priest Rock marked the entrance to the harbor. The sea, farther out, was as black and still as ink in a well. The scrubby, cold peninsulas of harbor passed behind us. I stood up in the wheelhouse, looking out, sensing a giving way, an ungrasping.

"Should be a good night out there for driving around," Ted said, the bright lights of the controls setting off his face, his hands on the toggle that steered us. I walked across the wheelhouse and looked at the Loran: 54.28.78 N, 166.39.06 W.

How was it I had come to that moment, driving out to the middle of the Bering Sea with five men I barely knew? "Martha's fishing with us," was the introduction Ted had given me. No one questioned him, or me. Bob, the old-time crew member, accepted my addition with a kind of sad friendliness. Bill, Steve, Mark, all, like me, in their twenties, formed a kind of brotherhood, taking over a cramped stateroom and sharing a style of working, a lingo, and a silent admiration for Ted. I knew they would test me on deck. Their brotherhood was in no hurry to accept an East Coast English teacher who'd never even been on a fishing boat, much less a crab boat.

After two days of driving, we reached the fishing ground, a plank of water that looked no different to me than any other part of this ocean. It was thirty degrees out on deck, and the bow of the *Obsession* was charging through swells cresting in a flinty chop. Spray, caught by a thirty-five-knot wind, slapped on the rigging and pots we were carrying. Stacked three deep as they were, they rose with a shimmering brown architecture, forty-feet off the surface of the ocean.

The whaleback rig of the *Obsession*, with its stern-mounted wheelhouse and bow-mounted forepeak, made for a vessel that initially seemed awkward in my eyes, but out at sea I could appreciate its layout immediately. From the wheelhouse windows, the entire theater of the deck, the crane, and the ocean ahead was visible.

Atop the forepeak, eighty feet bow-ward from those windows was a smaller, open deck where, when we sometimes—nervously—fished in waters covered in an ice pack, we stood with binoculars trying to sight our buoys out in the jigsaw of water and ice. Bundled in warm gear, Mark and I would climb the ladder to that forward deck, and, once we had the buoys in our glasses, we would turn and look back at the wheelhouse windows, where Ted was driving, and point in the direction of the red buoys.

The Bering Sea extends a lonely and storm-fraught sixteen-hundred miles westward from the coast of Alaska to Russia; the Continental Shelf forms its floor for the first four-hundred of those westward-reaching miles. This shelf is home to the greatest stores of king crab on the planet. Bering Sea weather—gloomy, monotonous, sometimes monstrous—is all a fisherman must endure, because the water, rarely greater than six-hundred-feet deep on the shelf, makes crab fishing relatively manageable. To the thick yellow bridle of each pot we've attached three two-hundred-foot lengths, called shots, of line tied together. At rest on the seafloor, the line will string to a pair of buoys, called a setup, which floats on the surface of the sea. Eight to fifteen pots, set in a line on the ocean floor, form a string that the skipper sets where he's historically found crab or where he hopes to find some.

Up in the wheelhouse, a computerized plotter records the location of these strings. As we set the pots overboard so they could attract crab for a day or two or sometimes more, Ted entered their location, tracked by Loran coordinates, into the plotter up in the wheelhouse. Miraculously, we could spend two days crossing a seascape as undefined as a liquid desert, and—if northern Bering Sea wind hadn't pushed the ice pack dramatically southward, covering and snarling the pots—suddenly arrive exactly at one end of a line of buoys tacked on the surface of the misty and inconsequential sea. The electronic plotter became the dictate of time, record, and action. If you were down in the galley slapping peanut butter on English muffins, or changing sweatshirts, or watching a video on the scratchy television, you climbed up the stairs to the wheelhouse to look over Ted's head at the number on the plotter. With twenty nautical miles to go to the beginning of the next set, you had time for more peanut butter. With two and a half, however, you'd better pull up your straps and stuff a candy bar in your pocket, so you were on deck and ready when the *Obsession* pulled alongside the first pair of buoys.

On the first day of my crabbing career, however, I understood this system only roughly. Part seasick, part petrified, partly in denial, I sat on the floor of the wheelhouse and pulled on my Grundens. I tugged the boots on over thick socks and the bibs on over long underwear, sweatpants, and the Stormy Seas jacket. The rollers ahead of the boat bore wind-sheathed crests of foam that broke as if combustible across the bow and the side rigging. Out the long line of windows, I could see the iron frames of the pots so thick with spray that it formed a frozen coating, barely glinting in the distant winter sun. This morning we were going to bait the pots we had on deck and set them in this stretch of ocean. Bob and the brotherhood, well sealed in their own gear and saying nothing to acknowledge my tangle, clamber around and past me, out the side doors of the wheelhouse and forward across the stacked pots to the bow. I couldn't get the straps of the bibs adjusted and Ted had to tie them in back, saying calmly and not quite convincingly, "Don't worry; you'll be fine out there. Just listen to Bob and you'll be fine." I snapped up my jacket, swearing to myself that I wouldn't be late or last or even slow.

The physical objective was clear: get across the stack and up to the bow of the boat where the boys stood, somewhat protected, between the stacks pots and the small forward portion of the vessel, where a room, called the forepeak, is tucked underneath the raised forward deck. Getting there involved a couple of tricks, tricks I'd mastered easily when the boat was tied up in Dutch Harbor, when the pots on deck seemed like nothing more than an extravagant jungle gym. Out on the open sea, on that first day of fishing, the jungle gym lurched hysterically and unpredictably. If I missed a step there was no pier to swim to, no neighboring hull to reach for. Even getting from the wheelhouse to the first step on the bars of the pots involved a maneuver outside the boat's railing, where, when I looked down between my new brown boots, I could see our churning wake thirty feet below. Human beings didn't last but about ten minutes in that water, even if they were floating in Stormy Seas jackets.

I swung out over the water and stepped up onto the pots, feeling the new armor of my bright rubber work clothes securely, almost heavily around me. Once I made it away from the edge of the boat, and chose a line up the center of the stack, I crossed from wheelhouse to bow, stepping on the pot bars as if they were ties, slowly but evenly, knowing the boys were ahead of me, somewhere down on the deck, feeling Ted's eyes on me in the wheelhouse. No falls, no crawling on my ass, all the way forward. I had no idea what I was supposed to do when I got there, except follow and obey the other orange shapes. I did know that my ignorance made me afraid. And that I had other fears: not being strong enough; not being calm, bold, or effective enough in Ted's eyes—or in my own.

That first day of work I spent at a kneel. Under the shelter deck, a kind of porch roof covering a forward corner of the deck, metal bait box, bolted down, was a place I could work with only one way, by kneeling. I sat back on my heels so I could use my lap. The red-lidded jars with holes in them were just small enough to fit in my rubber-gloved hand, but not nearly tacky enough. I jammed them against the side of the bait box, against my slippery thighs, between my knees and the box—anything to hold them while I stuffed bits of herring in them and then screwed on the lid and then screwed the jar onto a hook that fastened at the top like a giant safety pin. With a few wedges of codfish also dangling from the hook, those lank, ugly ornaments, called bait setups, weighed about twenty pounds each.

I plugged those bait jars as full as possible with the slimy fish bits. When the bait box emptied, I rose, gray and pink flecks of herring covering my orange front sides, herring somehow stuck in my hair, and tipped unsteadily across a bucking deck for several feet to the bait freezer. I dislodged a fifty-pound box of frozen herring, tore its cardboard and plastic wrapping off, and thrust the icy chunk into a chopper, where a blade, operating with a deafening clatter, made an icy mush ready for the bait jars.

The proverbial shelter deck was the salon of this dignified process, but really, it was not elaborate shelter. Spray, sometimes even spray from a portside wave coming over the portside shelter deck, spat persistently on my hood. The sound of wind in my ears, a sound I would come to recognize permanently, was one that didn't find shelter anywhere, ever, on the boat. From the kneel I worked in all day and into the dark hours, I shifted between weather systems: the one on the empty slate horizon which I looked continually toward as if expecting an appearance; the one on deck, four men I hardly knew and could barely distinguish from one another, at their tasks with the pots and crabs; and the one in my stomach, a cemented, persistent grind.

My first day, my second day, my third, my first night, my second, my whole first fishing trip, two weeks long, was not about work, it was about surviving. It was about negotiating mistakes, learning how to step forward or back on a steep and icy deck, how to stand, and even work in direct blasts from the wind, how to stay out of the way of the work that wasn't mine. Steve and the boys had each other to keep up with, and they pushed me out of the way to get where they needed to go, thrust work at me, snatched work away, and yelled at me as much as they could. I didn't have this job from walking the docks of Kodiak or Dutch like they did; I had it from a connection, from Ted's curiosity in me, from luck. I was there for the money, but not like they were, since I'd ended up somehow with the privileged option of adventure, not the requirement of it. Mixing a little resentment for me with a dim, unsuspecting allegiance to me, they kept me at a distance. Some skippers maintain that it's never good to have a woman aboard a fishing boat, especially a crabber. Ted didn't think that, but I knew already that it was tricky to sleep with the guy who was driving the boat, and work on deck with the guys who weren't.

I was what they call a half-share in the fishing wage world, and Steve, full share like everyone else, was the fiery deck boss. Knowing that I should never, ever correct a single phrase of his speech was my only sustaining intelligence on deck. Silence was not a comfortable state for me, but I moved, knelt, stuffed, stood, and obeyed, mostly with perfect silence. Red-headed, red-bearded, with an agility that sprang and popped when the deck was busy, Steve narrated: his impressions of the weight of each incoming pot, his impressions of the wind, his guess at how long we'd work that shift. He called out to me to speed the hell up on the bait. He yelled, hard and quick, at me whenever I came within ten feet of a launching pot or the lines and buoys spewing overboard after it: "Stay the fuck away from the fuckin' lines!" "Hurry up with the fuckin' tote!" "I said hurry up!" Some moments, I could do it. Fuckin' crab. Fuckin' pots. Fuckin' wind, fuckin' deck boss.

Whenever possible, Steve compared crabs to humans at a vigorous, elaborate sex act. When the pot surfaced, its webbing strained by the load, Steve calibrated the degree of heat in the wait those crab were feeding on, "like hungry men on the hottest pussy." The wave hitting over our heads was freezing, mixed with snow, enough to kill any of us, really, whether we were wearing rubber outfits or not. Steve would say he wanted some warm pussy. Warm pussy would make that frigid, stunned feeling disappear.

Bill, smart, lazy, dangerously subdued around Steve, was the hydraulic crane operator. He had a wintry, inverted spirit that seemed to place him in the faraway— even if that's where he found himself. He moved slowly, almost sufferingly around the boat. The crane operator has the joy of avoiding racing deck work; he also has a boredom that verges on peril, sitting still for hours in freezing spray. I never knew what Bill, running the crane from a deep, almost Tolstoyan motivation was thinking when he spoke out against Steve; he was guaranteed a lashing in return, but a lashing with a futile, nearly impotent ring to it.

"So how much warm pussy you been feeling these days?" Bill asked, at a pause in the work. He had a wad of Copenhagen in his mouth. He mumbled.

"What did you say, man?" Steve almost spat, wanting, more than anything, to rupture Bill's passivity.

Bob stood by the rail with a helpless-looking cigarette in his mouth. I collected bait set-ups and set them in a ready tote.

"You fuck," said Steve. "You've never even had any piece of pussy. You fuck."

I wanted to speak, to be less than a bystander—something. But the wind surged, my voice was too deep in my hood, and, by the tenets of the crab fishing world, Steve, hard-fisted and top brother on this deck, really had nothing to lose, even if every claim and narration he made felt like a provocation directed at the rest of us on deck.

When we weren't working, we were waiting to work. While we waited, we drove around the ocean. While we drove, we slept, read, rotated through watch schedules, ate microwaved pizzas, and watched *When Harry Met Sally* over and over. The boat was its own private world. If seas were calm enough, we'd take showers. If big swells were running, I'd feel green if I stayed upstairs in Ted's stateroom, and I'd retreat to the bunk down below in the little room I shared with Bob. When seas were really rough, even Ted couldn't stand that rolling up in his bunk. I would stumble out of the black air of the stateroom into the fluorescent light of the galley, and see him sleeping stretched out, a sudden, thick form in a sweatshirt and jeans on a bench beside the galley table.

Radical seas and winds had their own clear face, especially in the long nights. After a twelve-hour or twenty-hour or even sometimes longer run of work, we scrambled for the food we needed in the galley, set a watch rotation, and went straight for sleep, many times so exhausted we skipped cleaning up. Once I awakened for a watch shift, and then once awake for the two or three or four hours it entailed, I could put together the fragmented pulse of the boat. Sodium lights high on the rigging of the *Obsession* lit the equipment and the deck or stacks of pots out beyond the wheelhouse windows. In a high wind, with rain, snow, or spray flying out of the impenetrable night ocean, the space shone like an eerie clearing in a storm. Murres, so homeless and urgent far from land, flipped wildly through the chasm of our light.

Minuscule, heroic, the task of moving matter from this great fluid seemed apparent to me in those hours. Like a small and rugged noun, we seemed the very gravity that the dissonant sea required. We offered foundation, buoyancy. Sand, iron, sun, crab—they were objects in space with no stake in movement, time, or even readiness. A boat on a blank sea. A crab pot tipped swiftly off the boat and still visible, just for a moment, before coils of speed and space took it, a red buoy its only suggestion. Nouns, so many, such a quantity, became the matters of importance on a fishing boat. How many pots? How many strings of pots? How many pot bridles? How many feet in these particular shots in this particular string? How many knots, as in knots on the pot ties? How many knots, as in boat speed? As in wind speed?

How many nautical miles? How many gallons of diesel? Water? Oil? How cold? How fast? How high? How many? With the tanks full of crab, the bow iced up, the crew and the captain in their bunks asleep, we possessed every potential, every capacity for energy. In the storage yards of Dutch Harbor, huge crab pots stood rusted, stacked, and waiting for the integrity of some movement. Webbed iron, boat or land-bound, towering, imminent, replicated, looks as placid and entropic as piers sticking out across the pond of a park. We were a conduit, a completion, dissembling towers, abiding by a seafloor we could locate, smell, contact, and never see.

I pictured my mother leaning against the dishwasher in my parents' kitchen, a March sun breaking across boxwood bushes out the window, the *Forbes* article straight ahead in her gaze. The notes of a Chopin étude filtered from the background. I was at a phone booth at the fuel dock in Unalaska. We'd delivered eighty-five-hundred pounds of crab from a ten-day trip, sold at $1.92 a pound, and we were trying to get out of town in an hour. How cold was it, she wondered. How do the clothes work? I avoided saying anything about the inflatable Stormy Seas jacket. How was Ted? She put some stake in my knowing him, as if the fact of him, through her personal equation, connected me to a recognizable safety. She didn't know him, and never could have known him. For the seven years I came to know him myself, she met him only once, for an afternoon lunch in California, five years after I'd gone fishing the first time. By saying that she never could have known him, I mean that even I, as her daughter, could not have brought her together with him. There were so few forces involved in even my knowing Ted. There was no context, no face on it that we could recognize. We strained to know something, whatever we could, of each other, yet had nothing but our wills working in our favor.

Crab fishing is not a sport. The objective is merely to shift, with speed and accuracy, the pinchered creatures from space to space. The fisherman's job is to find the crab, coax them off the seafloor, into a webbed box, and then, once on deck, out again by turning the pots nearly upside down and shaking the odd, clattering mass onto a metal sorting table or into knee-high plastic totes. Bob and I were always the ones to plunge into the frenzied activity of sorting. The rejects, anything female, anything illegal because it was too small, anything of an out-of-season species, we threw into a plastic tote, which we dragged across the deck and dumped overboard through a chute under the rail of the boat at midship. The keepers we stuffed into another tote, which we dragged to the middle of the deck, where a lid to a hole in the tank, manhole-sized, was pushed aside. We poured, pushed, and stuffed the crab into that tank. Pumped-in seawater kept them alive until we delivered them to the canneries of Dutch Harbor or the Pribilof Islands of Saint George and Saint Paul.

A boat that is fishing well, pulling the gear, and resetting it right away because it's "on the crab," is a fantastic orchestra of human and mechanical energy. It's full of the geometry of heavy gear, the movement of massive loads of crab, and a precision of timing that doesn't leave a second to think or even to look around and consider it. A full pot of crab makes a sound like a shattering when it tumbles on the metal table; the dark surface of water in the tank snaps when a crab hits it; pots and lines and human efforts move at the pace of the wind and waves that the *Obsession* dug through. At certain sharp moments I did feel a part of a game.

Mark Trilling was an all-star third baseman in Oregon before he dropped out of college and started fishing. Bob might have been the resident grandma of the crew, the only person on deck I really trusted, but Mark was the one I aspired to work alongside. He ripped into me a couple of times for standing too close to a stack of lines attached to a pot just dumped in the water, lines feeding overboard in a blur, but he didn't spend much extra effort baiting me, like Steve did.

Mark's job on deck was to throw a grappling hook attached to a delicate white line out to the buoy setup when we drove up beside it. Even when the boat was bucking into abrupt waves, Mark had a loose stance. He also had a smooth, low way of talking to himself, as if he were standing on the bow of a drift boat on a calm river: "Come 'ere, com on 'ere, come on in…" He sounded like he was talking to a small, invisible bird he was trying to bring to a nest. Ted, up in the wheelhouse, idled the engine. The boat slowed and ground downward in the water. Mark waited until we were as close as we would get, about thirty-five feet, to the buoy, swung the hook and line like a lasso, and then let it go.

To miss it was to fail. To miss it was to blunder. To miss it was to incite the harassment of Steve and Bill, neither man any more skilled at throwing the hook than Mark. Both of Mark's arms would shoot up and the white line followed the hook out across the water like a ribbon, even if the buoys rose overhead on a swell. Mark paused a moment to let the hook sink, jerked back on it, and then, hands a blur, he hauled in the hook and the line attached to the buoys. Once they were at his feet, he fixed the line into a crevice in a hydraulic block that dangled right above the rail of the boat. Steve hit the switch. Line began coiling blindingly through the block and then into the mechanical coiler, where it built into a circular pile. A few yards down the rail, Bob and I stood poised on either side of the pot launch, waiting to see what broke the surface in the pot.

That afternoon were on the crab. The pots, four-hundred-fifty pounds when empty, were breaking the surface bulging, crab legs poking through the webbing, almost a thousand pounds full. Leverage and balance are the keys to landing a pot on a heavy launch. Each pot landed with a thick clap, metal to metal. As soon as we could unhook the rubber door ties and flip back the door, we cleaned the crab out in a mad blur, wildly chucking the refuse overboard, rebaiting the pots, and dropping them back in away. The boat engine idled when we pulled the pots, surged while we sorted, slowed again as we neared the next and Mark gathered the hook for his toss.

Bill, in a lethargic stealth, ran the crane from a stool near the forepeak. Steve and Mark handled the coiler and the heavy shots of line. I was on bait chore and, with Bob, the sorting. While the boat barreled forward from string to string, we huddled under the shelter deck, stuffing down Milky Way bars and Cokes. Was this an eight-hour shift? A gray storm moved in. Gulls drifted and called above the frenzied deck.

Everything moved in succession, almost temperance; as it extended, it eased; as it passed meditation, it leached sympathy: Dump the keepers in the tank hole. Jog back to the crane well corner under the shelter deck. Lean on old coils of rope and watch Mark look for "the bag" across dark water until our sodium lights caught it, toppling in a crest, gleaming red. Was it a ten-hour shift? Twelve? I didn't know what time it was, but I wasn't unsteady or even truly cold. Jog to the coiler while the line winds in. Jump to keep blood in my toes. Laugh obligingly at Steve's crab penis joke. Move an arm back to clear the knot in my shoulder, move the sorting table forward, even as Steve and Mark clean out the pot, rebait it, launch it. We're on the crab. We're on the crab. Swing the tote around, fill it with keepers. Pitch them in the tank. Start over.

Drawn, maybe to the point of obsession, at least to the point of compulsion, to Ted's unconventional, hard-working, dangerous, distant life, I followed resolutely behind him. I convinced him and the others through my quickness finding a rhythm on deck, through never hesitating, through proceeding quietly, my Grundens snapped and belted, out the wheelhouse door behind the boys and out across stacked pots or an open deck shining in ice, seawater, or sodium lights. I scrambled to gear up for work when we were nearing a string. Bob and I traded off on the cooking chore, and I jogged into the galley to scramble eggs as shifts neared their end. I staggered from my bunk to the wheelhouse for my driving duty after the man closing his watch before me woke me up. I radioed the cannery when our tanks were full and we were heading for land.

When we turned back out to sea after delivering, heading into the towering mountain ranges of the gray Bering Sea, Ted, at the helm, would sometimes say "I like this image, the bow of the boat iced up, moving forward in the night." I began to know what he was saying. I fell into a partnership of work with him that felt remote from my first rubbery journey across the pots, distant from my other lives, from the calendar, from the movements of other people I'd known.

One night on deck I was bent over, clearing keepers into the live tank, when a wave the size of a Sealand container cleared the railing and hit me full against my backside with the force of a frozen concrete wall. I went down on one knee. My other foot lost the surface, went plunging forward into the tank hole. Suddenly I was flat on my stomach on deck, up to my hip in the tank. Water was filling my boot. I could feel the rubble of crab shells through rubber. I didn't say Shit. I didn't say Fucking shit. I coughed for air. Another wave caught on the rigging, shattering across the forepeak, the deck, me, my back, left the deck awash, its own small sea. Thirty feet above us, even the windows of the wheelhouse were dripping and shining.

I didn't know what had happened, but I did know a flash of terror, peril that could finish me—something I hadn't felt in weeks, even years. I'd just lost my balance. One hit of sea. One submerged limb in a tank full of king crab. I pulled my leg out, my sock dense with freezing seawater, my bones and brain vibrating. I ran back to the shelter deck, hoping the boys hadn't noticed how long I'd been down. All the data I could take was legible in that hit. Buried in all the wool and rubber gear, I shook a fear that carried into my eyes. The skin on my hip was raw against my sweats. No one said anything. They barely looked to my eyes.

A few minutes later, Ted got on the hailer and said, "I can't see shit out here and I'm lost. Let's finish up in the morning."

Once inside the wheelhouse, the boys went down below to mow through hot dogs, pizza, and Mountain Dew. I sat up in the dark pilot room, looking out at the replays of that wave. They rose, rose some more, overbalanced, and smashed across deck boards. Another trough, another rise. A shower on deck. Categorical. From up here, silent, a movie screen on mute. I pulled salt and herring scraps out of my hair, rubbed my swollen hands. Ted methodically reset the electric plotter and changed our course. At the top of the Loran screen, the numbers read 55.23.21 N, 167.10.27 W. The radar screen lit up snow squalls as blue blurs. He saw that wave, I thought. He pulled the weather map off the fax machine. When he spoke, it was gently, as if to himself. "You don't have to stay out here. You know, working this fishing job."

I looked at his face, oddly aglow by the neon of the dials. The fax machine continued to tick and print. All our weather came to us from Japan, so I'd somehow started imagining that the weather maps did too. Or that we were actually near Japan. When I looked up from work some afternoons on deck I saw the red sun breaking the shale-colored clouds and then slipping silently below the horizon, right into Asia. I didn't say anything to Ted, even if, for a second or two, I thought I had a response. "There are a lot better jobs out there than this one," he said.

"I know that." I had the funny sensation of both: Ted's detachment from me, and his investment in me. Reliable in will; unfamiliar in form: I was both. Closely attached to my fear, a kind of pride from bumping back up on deck, for the endorsement the boys' silence granted me. I said nothing, and Ted and I never broached the subject that directly again. After that, events made decisions for us.

Two weeks later, tired and very hungry after an afternoon of work that ran until midnight, I balanced an overflowing plate of spare ribs and potatoes and a glass of milk to the galley table, but I couldn't put my plate down, because the table was covered in Playboy magazines. "Can't we please just get the Playboys off the galley table so we can just eat?" I half-mumbled it, pushing a few back with my glass. Steve immediately hit the roof, stacked up three dog-eared magazines, and slapped them down on the Formica table right in front of my plate. Unwisely, I persisted, by, doubly unwisely, baiting his expertise: "Those are all just silicone breasts in those pictures anyway," I said, trying for a ring of authority. Deconstruction did not suit the boys. Was I sorely mistaken? I was sorely mistaken, because Steve himself knew exactly what a silicone breast felt like, he had felt plenty. But so had Mark and Bob and Bill, and what ensued, as I peeled a gummy paste from the ribs and stared passively at the breasts on the cover blonde, was a long and heated discussion about, yes, which of the men had felt more silicone breasts.

Lies, lies, lies. I'd told my mother enough to comprise an entire parallel life, a fiction as intricate as a ton of webbed crab legs. The fact of lies, in fact, seemed part of the fabric of our knowing one another. Somehow, sometimes, I guessed that enactments of dramatic physical freedom were the best ways to pull against her. Mother wrote me long letters, front, and back sides of the page, which I picked up at the cannery in Dutch when we made it into town. Her long reports, her insistence on close presence, wore me down with a kind of dim exasperation. I was free. I was free. I could hear myself, see myself. But when I got her letters, spoke to her, it felt like a surrogate truth.

If I could have explained crab fishing to myself, I'd have explained it to her. But how could I justify something that seemed, at bottom, really about extending a question? I thought my attachment to Ted was the tie I needed, but, looking back on it, it really—couldn't really be—the thing keeping me there. The costs, potential and actual, of the freedom of crabbing are too high for many people. For me though, at that time, the ultimate freedom of the enterprise appeared to be the drawing card, the real lure, but it was actually the cost that compelled me. How far would I go to realize a self that no one had articulated, that I had found merely by guts? I didn't and couldn't know how much the cost was, how far I was willing to go, how much I could cash out in pursuit of this most private force. That overwhelming unknown was more compelling to me than the freedom, the love affair, the stories, the money in my half-share pocket. Selfishly, I sent Mom postcards. Selfishly, I told her the crabbing was excellent, that we never worked at night, that Ted and I were good working friends. The men on the crew are protective and kind. The weather's been unseasonably mild. I'd almost made enough money to justify the worry. I'd be home in the summer to look for real work in a real place.

The more weeks and months passed, the faster they seemed to fly. Time had a cryptic way of simplifying, of depicting the advantages of fishing. The work, while tough, was made easy by its attainability. There was one job to do, one objective. The day could be met in a day. I could often awaken to these actions—actions that had formerly appeared insignificant, even crass—and see them as clear, the propulsion of the matter and importance. Chopping herring, mending webbing, painting 54374, the Fish and Game number, on buoys. Dangers and securities became weirdly blurred. The more necessary I felt and became, the more old fears slipped swiftly behind.

When on the crab, we baited the pots and threw them right back over. A string like any other: I left Bob to finish sorting at the table, turned, raced to grab a bait setup, and came back to the launch. We were in forty-foot swells, but it wasn't difficult anymore. Mark hauled the shots out of the coiler and tossed a couple of them on top of the pot that sat hip-high on the launch. With the door of the pot open, I sat backward into it, as if I were leaning, my head low, back into my bunk. Once inside the pot, with one hand grasping the top iron bar of the doorframe, I leaned even farther back, the other arm reaching with the dangling bait setup that would fasten to the middle of the pot. It was like lying almost flat on my back and, with an arm extended overhead, lifting a twenty-five-pound weight off the floor—all in a flash. My feet stuck out the front of the pot and came up off the deck as my torso, arms, stomach, and neck all reached back. No pausing here. For a second, I was deep in the pot. I saw all the sky and sea between the diamonds of webbing. Mark and Steve were coiling lines. Bob was stuffing bait jars. Ted was up in the wheelhouse, driving. I was sitting, even momentarily, in the most dangerous spot onboard, inside a crab pot that was moments from tipping seaward.

The dangers were these: One, if Bill hit the launch switch, the bars that the pot sat on would lift my legs farther from the deck, and I'd fall to the waves, a ballerina in a music box. Two, if I thought about this, I wouldn't be able to keep up, or even to keep working. The muscles of my stomach ringing from the reach, I snapped the bait string in place in the matter of a second and swung forward, my head low to clear the upper bar of the pot, and then out. One step to the side, and Bob and I pulled the door over and down with a yank, stretched and fastened the rubber door ties, and stepped back. Steve hit the switch.

Of all the distinctive sounds from the crab fishing world—the whine of the coiler, the hiss of the hydraulic block, crab refuse cracking between rubber boot soles and deck boards—there is no more impressive sound than that of a crab pot falling into the sea. A crash and a seethe all at once, a mass of foam, a percolation, it falls. The water gathers in it. The water gathers it in. Mark bent to gather a shot of line and tossed it, then another, then a third, in after the pot. Then he stepped out of the way and I moved to his spot by the railing, a buoy in each hand. They went, just as suddenly, first awkwardly skyward. Then they slapped down and bumped behind us— resolute beacons on this passing segment of sea.

A run into Dutch, in the middle of my second season, and I dashed to the cannery to check for the *Obsession*'s mail and messages. In the pile was a pink note for me, telling me to call home as soon as I could. When I did, I was impatient, more possessively sealed into the world of the boat than ever. I was competent, accepted; more of Ted's equal, less of his project. I'd passed muster with the boys, understanding their odd camaraderie. Tired, intrepid, important, I'd adopted their gaits, their cadences, the safe and predictable way we behaved as a unit of orphans, righteously, faithfully severed from the world outside.

Mom answered the phone in Virginia, and quickly, excitedly, got down to business. Someone from an office in Denver had called her, looking for me. They wanted me to fill in on a crew that was leaving to work in Antarctica in a month. I was shocked, and had to work to remember that I had excitedly applied for that job, ostensibly driving forklifts as part of a cargo crew at the South Pole station, over two years ago.

"You'll consider it, won't you?" Mom was trying to be diplomatic here, trying not to plead, but I could hear the pull in her voice. Through the window of the cannery office I saw the mountains of Dutch smudged and muddy, the *Obsession* motoring wearily across the harbor toward the fuel dock, snow ripping sideways between it and me. One tether bound me taunt to Ted, the *Obsession*, and the crew. One tether, however, me to her. When would one of them snap from the strain? When would both snap? When did Antarctica become a better place for a daughter?

"Yes. Okay, Ma." I suddenly wanted to move, to say "I'll call the guy. I promise." I had to run to meet the boys, but as I did, I saw them ahead of me already different, as if my perception of them were out of my control, and had shifted even as I resisted its shift. Were they dirtier? Less united? Less hopeful? I'd tried to commit my every cell to them, and now the events were rendering me a traitor, someone they'd suspected me of being all along, someone with a few too many options.

We pulled out of town by midnight, late. On that trip, I learned about momentum on an afternoon when we were stacking empty pots on deck. What had once appeared impossible came to be, with a few tricks, manageable, energizing. A small series of moves could create a staggering geometry, geometry in motion: Wait for the right rolling wave under the boat. Use it for the gravity it lends. Grab the crossbar, chest-high, of an empty pot and push it, high on its end, away from the launch and across the slick deck to the corner below the wheelhouse. Keep a wad of pot-ties in the belt of your gear and use them to tie it off, the bars of the pot to the bars of the railing. Get another pot, do it again, securing the second pot to the first. Build an entire layer. Build another as the crane raises, dangles, and sets pots before you. Stack them cleanly, as if they were books on a shelf. Build a third, climbing and balancing stories above the sea. That afternoon that became that night, the five of us were working in a speed and rhythm of baiting, sorting, and stacking that was a pure addiction. I didn't tell the boys I was leaving or even thinking of leaving.

Toward the end of that trip we worked almost incessantly against the closing date of the crab season, and almost always in the vicinity of the 168th parallel. Some nights, in a half-sleep, finishing a watch, or starting one, I could, without arranging it, think of Ted, and the thought would inadvertently begin, "Years from now…" as if I could already look back and hear its imminent silence. Something authentic had come of something fabricated, but my hold on its matter, my hold on comprehension of it, seemed to slide away as certainly as the season, with a will, a sense of timing, and a pace that matched even my own.

In the end, at the end, many stretches of work seemed to meld one tale that I repeated and repeated, long after I'd left for Antarctica, returned, fished again, quit, taken up life with other people, in other places, sometimes with Ted, ultimately without him. In the tale, it's night when we start working, or else we've been working and night fell and I didn't see it fall. A night like any other, our orange raingear blurred against the crab and equipment, an ice-railed stage. Snowflakes fling stupidly down across the deck, the pots, the rim of the bait box. I look up. I can't see anywhere, anywhere outside the sodium lights, can't make out a single feature of night. It's like I'm in space. It must be like space. It's the only thing I can think of. I see the wheelhouse, its windows black, knowing Ted is inside, driving, setting the plotter, watching us. A roller, high as that wheelhouse, shines at a crease of foam on the peak. It's much bigger than the wheelhouse, but nothing is crashing. We're just rolling, up to take the crest, and back down. I'm on a tiny deck, so minute. I don't feel a fear like I'm going to die here, but I feel I could so easily die—I could so easily be extinguished and there would be nothing to account for it at all. We pause at the base of the mountain, iridescent as always, foolishly new. Infinite smallness is what I separate out, only a piece of this unscrupulous voyage. ⚓

MARTHA SUTRO fished tanner crab in the Bering Sea for two seasons while on sabbatical as a high school teacher. She has an MFA in creative writing from the University of Montana. She currently teaches creative writing and literature in Schenectady, New York, where she lives with her husband and son.

PIECES OF THE WIND

WENDY ERD, who has setnetted for salmon in Bristol Bay, near Pilot Point, calls up the wind, evoking the land, the native culture, the work on the water she is forced to leave after twelve years.

FOR FIVE DAYS a southeaster's been blowing twenty-five or thirty knots out of the mouth of the river. In Bristol Bay, everything vertical is an instrument for the wind. The hinges on our outhouse door creak, the abandoned truck at the airstrip clatters its open door, even the bent blades of grass sing. A gray ceiling's clamped down and I can barely see the middle sand-bar that's emerged beyond our moored skiffs. This wind works with the outgoing tide, smoothing down the chop. On the flood the real face of the storm will show, when the incoming current will stack waves against wind. We need westerlies to push salmon into the nets on our side of the Ugashik River.

Last year, my husband, Peter, and I spun our index fingers counterclockwise in the air the way Esther had taught us. A Yu-pik Eskimo from Manokotak, she knows the native traditions for imploring the weather.

"Turn the wind," she'd said.

Whenever we remembered we'd implore the weather, and in a few days' time a screamer set of onshore waves and driving horizontal rain set in and seemed to last for weeks. Way more than we'd bargained for.

Esther passed us heading down to her beach site on her four-wheeler. Her four children, bundled in raingear, clung on behind her.

"Esther," Peter said, "it doesn't seem to work. He showed her his own method, the slow downward strokes of his fingers he'd used to calm the storm.

"No," she said. "That's rain."

Five guys cluster around the two-horse outboard. The tiny cowling, no bigger than a lunch box, lies on the ground, and from the net-mending rack, I hear them grappling with a mechanical problem, manpower heavily outweighing the horse-power. I start humming the song I sing to myself: "Men, men, men, men, how does it work, let's make it work." Nut-and-bolt thought. I rarely have it. When we got a new truck I was happy it was red.

I spend my summers in a sixteen- by twenty-foot cabin with five men, a cap-sule of testosterone. We're here to luck out our living commercial fishing. I straggle out in the middle of the night in long johns and eat oatmeal with the crew. I let my appearance go. We stare bleary-eyed out into the slanting rain before we slump off into the darkness to check our nets. I tuck my hair into a blue cap, smear Bag Balm on my hands, and stride off lugging a five-gallon can of gas. We drag our rubber raft through the calf-deep mud and then jump in on the edge of the tide. I pull-start the recently tuned two-horse motor and lump over the waves to dock alongside our moored skiff in the roaring, six-knot current. I'm exhilarated. I've stepped into a man's world and for a moment I'm at the helm.

Two miles downriver from our fishcamp, the Ugashik sweeps by a few dozen sand-etched houses clustered on a bluff. Below the village of Pilot Point, on the beach, Pete Hansen's hunkered over his up-ended four-wheeler, protected from the blowing sand by his plywood shack and his shop full of enough junk to cobble anything together. He squats between broken trucks, a wringer washer, and an old wooden salting tierce from the abandoned cannery. His eyes are narrowed with sev-enty years of squinting into the sun and wind. He's rigging a screwdriver for a pull-cord handle. Our dog, Bob, wag-tails his way in close. "I hate dogs, hello, Bob." Pete, gruff as far in as you could dig a pocketknife in old ironwood.

"What the hell are you doing on my barge? Someone's always screwing with my stuff," he'd yelled at us our first morning in Pilot Point twelve years ago when he found our tent pitched on his abandoned scow in Dago Creek. We'd sought refuge there, hoping we'd sleep above a brown bear's reach. Then each morning af-terward, he'd arrive in the fog in his yellow Helly Hansen raingear and invite us to ride in his four-wheeler's trailer five miles back to his shack for rotgut coffee and warmth.

He pushes his wheeler upright. "Now, got to go get the Tyune going." He looks past us to his old Bristol Bay boat, beached as a whale on cribbing in the sand. He'll patch her together for just one more season.

At night, there are ghosts in the abandoned cannery, Chinamen rising up from their laundry chores at China Lake, fishermen wisping in on the fog. At the base of the green bluff below the village, throwing shadows across Pete Hansen's shack, history sprawls in a huge complex of corrugated red tin: warehouses, crew quarters, canning rooms, net lofts, and the mess hall with its MUG UP sign over a boarded-up door. We creep into the sprawling catacombs of memory by inching our way through a broken six-pane window. The crunch of glass underfoot echoes up two stories to the tall ceiling beams; fir 2x12s fifty feet long that Alaska Packers shipped in by schooner in the 1890s when the river still ran deep by the dock out front, before the mud filled in and shut the whole place down. We're trespassing on both property and time.

Upstairs, wire-mesh lockers sag open, cages that once over-wintered fishermen's old cotton web, soggy life rings, rusted Coleman stoves. In one corner wooden corks are scattered like tiny torpedoes in the dust. The stories of the fishermen hang in the air like moonlight through dusted glass. The wind lifts a loose piece of roof tin and bangs it over and over with just the same rhythm as the river; water and wind relentless, silting over men and history and fortunes made and lost again.

Peter and I love to be the first to fly in by bush plane to fishcamp early in June before our neighbors arrive. They roar and buzz and bang their setnet camps into readiness. In the pre-season stillness we can hear the birds. Loons on the pocket lakes, sandhill cranes gargling over, and ptarmigan on the tundra ridges behind our cabin who call, "come 'ere, come 'ere, come 'ere;" then sing out, "go back, go back, go back," if we walk too near.

Yesterday we heard an orphaned baby seal crying in Alex's old cannery retort, a huge metal barrel he uses to stabilize his bank against the ever-changing course of the river. The seal had squirmed its way to the top of the beach and found shelter inside, where its sorry sound was amplified. "Mom," it sounded like to me.

Johnny Ball had dragged the seal by its hind flippers down to the mud edge of the river, trying to save it, but it wiggled high up on the sand again until its small dark body was powdered and dry. You could see where the four-wheeler tracks had slowed and spun circles around it. As usual, none of us had the heart to shoot it, though that would have been the kindest act.

Nefutti was born in Ugashik, the next village upriver, an hour's skiff ride on a calm day. Once, as a young boy, he went on a hunting trip with his uncle. While they were gone, the flu epidemic of 1918 swallowed his village of Ugashik whole, like the gulp of some dark and foreign leviathan.

Our first year's fishing, before he grew ill, he'd putt up the beach from the village on his four-wheeler and come in our cabin for tea. No cookies. He'd shake his head. "No teeth."

We'd bring our first king salmon of the season to Nefutti and his wife, Figli. They couldn't wade the low-tide mud to check their subsistence nets. Eighty years had worn and bent them like wind-stunted alders on the tundra.

"Hey, Nefutti, we brought you a king we found in our net."

"Mmmm."

"Nefutti, looks like you hurt your leg, are you okay?"

"Fell off my four-wheeler." He laughs.

"You need any help? It must be hard to get around."

"Nope."

"Boy, it's sure been windy on the beach. Chewing away at the mud. Maybe it won't be so deep this year. Bugs aren't out yet, though. Not much showing up in our nets. You think the fish will come again this year?"

"Yep."

"Well, take care, we've got to go haul some water and get to the post office before Jan shuts it. Hope you enjoy the king. We'll stop by again when we get a chance."

"Okay."

Catie came by to challenge our setnet camp against hers in a speed knot-tying contest. On a piece of soft lay line we were to tie one double keg knot, then a clove hitch finished with a bowline. I tied the first set by habit, but then I couldn't tie a bowline upside down; that part of my mind temporarily seized up. Sometimes, I can't conceptualize the physical world that is so crucial out here.

This year for the first time in eleven years I'm not fishing with Peter. We split our crew into old, young, and rookies and Peter and I each run a boat at our own sites.

A few days ago I couldn't judge when to tell my bowman to throw the anchor so I could run the skiff for the bank without catching and snarling the line in the prop. I'm desperate then to see clearly.

"Now," I shout, and know it's wrong even though I'm captain.

The anchor line pays out starboard into the current. My deckhand watches as we drift close but too far off the bank for him to leap out.

"Sorry," I say for the third time, humble. "Pull it in."

On the fifth try, it is perfect. I ram the bank, my deckhand jumps out and sets a stern anchor. This year I will learn from my own mistakes, I study the indicators of wind and tide and set my bearings on a course of self-confidence.

It's Sunday, so Esther says we have to say a prayer before we pick the herbs. She kneels on the damp tundra moss and asks forgiveness in a quiet voice. The fish haven't come. It's July 14 and the river's surface is still unbroken. No jumpers. No silver splash to announce their tremendous push. Remembering her grandmother's wisdom, Esther stopped by our cabin.

"Eeee," she says, "We must burn Labrador tea leaves and scatter the ash on the tidelines. Then they will come."

Both her inherited knowledge and the cycle of returning salmon that we pray for are ancient. She laughs a lot and I hold on to her waist and ride behind her as she bumps her four-wheeler across the rolling tundra. Esther says we have to dry the herbs quickly, so we use a propane torch. Later, at my cabin, I scorch a coffeepot of gathered herbs. The smell is mentholated and of the rich wet earth. In midsummer's twilight I walk along the tide line and throw the scant ash. The next morning the river sings and squirms with salmon.

For years, I refused to run a skiff. My husband charged the brown swirling water, paying out the net, shouting directions. I worked the bow, pulling in buoys and lines, anchors and chain until my forearms bulged. Peter coaxed me to try the physically easier but more critical job as captain, steering one of our twenty-four-foot open boats, but at a demanding moment, I'd lose all awareness of left from right and walk away, begging him to take the tiller handle back.

"Motor panic," he'd say, shaking his head.

Today salmon swarm the river. From the few hundred I see jumping, I know a great silver wall battles the dropping tide. The murky water is thick with finning fish. One bumps into my rubber boots. A million spawners have pushed up the Ugashik on peak days like this, days we've earned a third of our year's income. I can't afford to make mistakes. I watch Peter head upriver with his crew. "You'll do great." He waves and disappears into the glint of sun on water.

"Five minutes," my crewman in the bow counts down until we can officially set our net, wound and stacked in the stern beside me. All along the riverbank, six-hundred-feet apart, other setnetters rev their motors, waiting. Something steadies me then, the years I've watched Peter, the times I've practiced, the faith I see in this young guy's eyes.

"How much time?"

"One minute." The river ticks past.

"Now!"

I gun the motor and net pours out of the boat, white corks popping over the stern in perfect punctuation, yes, yes, yes. In less than a minute, the last line whips out, chasing the web. "Throw out the anchor!" I holler. "Snap on the buoy!"

We make a perfect set; three-hundred-feet of webbed fence stretch from shore and strain the river. Spray explodes in a frenzy where fish battle the mesh. The hard foam corks tug under water with the immediate weight of our catch. I wheel the skiff around like a rodeo girl into the incoming tide and steer for the net.

"Ride 'em!" shouts my crew.

With an economy of motion we work the next feverish hours, pulling in web, untangling gilled fish, sending the emptied net over. Pull and pick, grunt, pull and pick. Not talking. Intent. As fast as the cleaned net hits the water it thrashes with freshly tangled fish.

I leave my crewman picking into a small holding boat and deliver the first wallowing five-thousand-pound load by myself. The conditions are perfect for this turn of confidence, the water muddy silk as I pull alongside our tender a mile upstream. I idle in, leap across six brailed bags of shining fish, and throw the bowline to the tender man on deck.

"You all right?" he asks.

"Sure." My smile cracks the salt, fish blood, and scales dried on my cheeks. I am better than I can remember.

I unload and pull away empty, letting the current turn the boat's bow downstream. I feel the pride men must often feel, my hand on the tiller, the late sun catching the outboard's spray, converting the dark river to diamonds.

Below their surfaces, life in Point Pilot and the river pass with the same murkiness, falling away as they replenish. When we come back to the village each June, we brace ourselves to ask who age, alcohol, or the river itself has taken.

I saw Desee at the airstrip filling up her four-wheeler with gas. She wore a Russian Orthodox pin on her down jacket, and I asked her why their cross has a crooked lower stave and an extra cross above the Christian bar.

"The upper cross is for his crown, you know, 'King of Kings,'" she said. "The lower tilted bar, well, that's what Christ's feet were nailed to, and when he died, his weight shifted and it tilted to the right."

"Grim," I said.

"Yeah, but it reminds us of his sacrifice."

On the way home to our cabin up the beach, hauling a fifty-gallon drum of water in the four-wheeler trailer, I drove past the church's cemetery high on the hill in the village. The wooden orthodox crosses lean north, as though listening, the white paint

sand-etched off the wood. Now, after many summers, I know three buried here: Old
Nefutti; young Loren, who fell drunk off a fishing boat on his twenty-first birthday;
and Anna Tracy, who told us she watched Japanese bombs fall on Unalaska.

As much as I tug, my hand will not fold to fit through the stiff neoprene tube
I wear to support my aching wrist. I've pulled thousands of fish from our nets, and
now, left alone, my swollen fingers curl around an invisible salmon. Salt and fish scales
sparkle to the floor in the Coleman light. It is 2 a.m., nearly slack tide, and time to
check our nets. Silent shadows, each of us bends automatically into damp waders, life
jackets, and cold boots. The intensity of the season has pulled us into itself. We cannot
remember in the dim hours of dawn and dusk whether we are beginning or ending
another day. We will wake, though, when we walk out into the night and face the river
and the wind again.

When the *kinnikinnick* turns scarlet and the first few silvers thrash in our nets, the
women and children from the village drive their pickups and four-wheelers down the
back ridge and spend all day picking the coarse black berry they will mix with Crisco
and sugar and call *agooduk*. The red salmon push is over; half the setnet cabins are shuttered. Between the Ugashik River and distant Mount Pulik, the women's parkas are
bright circles of color on the endless tundra.

No one in the village knows this is our last season in Pilot Point, except old Johnny Ball. We haven't the heart to say so. After twelve years of frenzied fish picking, two
bones in Peter's right thumb are worn flat and grind at each other. Fishing in Bristol
Bay has become more competitive, more contentious. We've had to fish apart at times.
Peter takes one skiff and goes to fish the outside beach where the ocean breaks, while I
stay with my net inside the river. I watch the swells build at night, the dark roll in, peering out the window until I finally see the halo of his halogen light growing brighter
on the horizon of the emptying river. He is slow, pushing the current, coming home.

The night before our plane comes, we ride into the village to say good-bye. Johnny's father-in-law, Alex, only a few years older than Johnny, lets us in, barely. He opens
the door just a crack and peers out, "Yes?" John Ball behind him hollers out, "Come
in, come in," over the yammering of their three poodles and both TVs.

We are unlikely friends and the best of friends. At seventy-five, Johnny is a Seventh Day Adventist who'd love to convert us and doesn't. Peter and I are children of
the sixties, not a reverent bone between us.

"One last game of crib?" he asks Peter. "Be there," he hollers at his cards. He
shakes his head at a bad cut. "First your money, then your clothes," he says.

After twelve years I hear these quips in my sleep. We've brought back the scrimshawed cribbage board he loaned us years ago so he could skunk Peter at our cabin when he wasn't tending his net that stretched next to mine. We don't talk about the future. Just move the pegs around. But when we get up to leave he shakes our hands a long time. Thick-throated, I bundle up quickly and push out his door. Clamped behind Peter on the Honda, we roar down the hill past the church's silhouette and skirt the shuttered cannery.

The wind lifts the sand and my eyes tear until my face is wet. Even with my eyes closed, I can see the river darkening and feel the chill of August creeping in. ⚓

WENDY ERD divides her time between Hanoi, Vietnam and Homer, Alaska, where she helps communities tell stories in print, exhibits, and video documentaries. She has received local and statewide grants for both her poetry and nonfiction. Her most recent work appears on highway signs in Alaska's Copper River Basin as part of an innovative project called "poetry in place," where verse written about Alaska landscapes are displayed artistically for the enjoyment of travelers.

NIGHTS OF ICE

SPIKE WALKER relates the tale of the *Tidings*, returning to home port Kodiak after crabbing in one of the coldest winters on record. When their vessel suddenly rolls, the skipper is trapped inside and the three crewmen, without survival suits in frigid waters, face impossible odds.

FOR JOE HARLAN, captain of the fifty-three-foot crab boat *Tidings*, and his crew, the 1989 Kodiak Island tanner crab season had been an exceptionally tough one.

From the opening gun, they'd ignored the weather, fishing hard through the merciless cold of an arctic storm. They were working the waters down in the Sitkalidak Island area on the southeast side of Kodiak Island, some eighty nautical miles from the fishing port of Kodiak. But Harlan and his men had been pleased at their luck.

They'd been pulling gear in the biting cold of the short winter hours of light, grinding through a total of some one-hundred crab pots. Harlan had agreed to pay his men a ten percent per-man crew share that season. In just two weeks they'd boated more than forty-thousand pounds of tanner crab. Crew shares had already topped $10,000—per man.

But they had been pounded night and day by wild northwest winds packing chill-factor temperatures of minus fifty degrees and williwaw gusts that made fishing that 1989 season one of the most perilous ever. One crab boat had gone down not far from Harlan and his men, near Chirikof Island. All four of the crewmen had died. So far, only one body had been recovered.

On another crab boat, one deckhand had lost three toes to frostbite when he ignored the water sloshing about in his boots while working on deck. As a fellow crewmate recalls it, "Before he knew it was happening, it had already happened."

On the very first day of the season, Joe Harlan had lost one of his own men to frostbite. He had rushed the man into the ancient Aleut village of Old Harbor on the south end of Kodiak Island and hired a bush plane to fly the man to the hospital in Kodiak for treatment. The man had broken no hard-and-fast rules of the sea; he had merely tried to sort crab wearing only cotton glove liners. And he had developed large blisters on the fingertips of both hands, which would keep him out of commission for the rest of the month-long season.

Less than two weeks later, the tanner crab catch fell off dramatically. And skipper Joe Harlan turned to his crew, hoping to cut his losses and call it a season. "Well, you know what you've made so far," he began. "And the way the crabbing has been going these last few days, you know what you can expect to make. The way I see it, we have two choices. We can stay out here and scratch away on a five-or-ten-crab-per-pot average until the Alaska Fish and Game Department tells us to quit. Or we can quit burning up our fuel, store our gear away back in Kodiak, and get out of this cold son-of-a-bitchin' weather."

After weeks spent working in the single-worst extended cold spell ever recorded in the Kodiak weather books, the crew of the *Tidings* did not hesitate. They'd been "successful enough" for one season.

Built in 1964 in the shipyards of Seattle, the fishing vessel *Tidings* had a wheelhouse that was mounted forward on the bow. She was considered one of the nicest boats around at the time because she had a toilet, something that was considered rather extravagant in those earlier, "hang it over the side" days.

Packing the recommended load of some thirteen crab pots on her back deck, the *Tidings* was closing fast on Chiniak Bay of the port of Kodiak, cruising through moderate seas, paralleling the coast of Kodiak Island about one and a half miles offshore, when, late on that frigid night, "all hell broke loose." Joe Harlan had been looking forward to slipping into the close and comfortable shelter of the Kodiak port, and with the exception of ice forming on the wheelhouse and railings of the *Tidings*, their journey north along the full length of the island had gone as planned.

But at Narrow Cape, they ran into some bad tide rips. Spray began exploding over the length of the ship, and they began making ice heavily.

Joe Harlan soon rousted his crew from their bunks.

"Guys, we've got to get this ice off of us," he said as he woke the men. With his crew gathered in the wheelhouse, Harlan pointed at the windows surrounding them. They were encased in ice. Only a clear space the size of a quarter in one window remained.

"Knock the windows clear, and then be sure and get the ice that's stuck to our railings," directed the skipper. "But don't let yourself get frostbitten. As soon as you get cold, come on in!" he insisted.

In an amazingly short time, a thick layer of ice had formed on the *Tidings*. Ice covered the boat—except, that is, for the crab pots themselves. Harlan and his crew had wrapped the commonly ice-drawing forms of steel and webbing in a layer of slick plastic, one that drained quickly before the spray from the ocean had time to harden.

The crew of the *Tidings* made good work of the ice-breaking task. But they longed to get back inside, out of the murderous cold. There they would flop down on the floor and warm themselves in front of the heater in the galley.

Back inside, skipper Joe Harlan was making a routine check of his engine room when he spotted seawater rising fast in the ship's bilge. Seconds later, the *Tidings* began to list to the port side.

Either the crab tank's circulation-pump pipe had ruptured inside the engine room or the steel bulkhead separating the engine room from the crab tank had split a seam. Nobody would ever know for sure. The moment Harlan spotted the water, he rushed to the back door and yelled to deck boss Bruce Hinman, "Grab your survival suits! And then start kicking the pots over the side!"

Harlan was standing in the wheelhouse when he felt the *Tidings* roll. Instinctively, he knew the ship would not be able to right herself. Yet he couldn't believe it. He found he was unable to accept what was happening to the vessel he had come to trust and even admire. Then a ridiculous thought shot momentarily through his mind: He had an unspoken impulse to order his crew to "run back there, hop overboard, and push the thirty-ton vessel back upright."

With the *Tidings* sinking fast, Harlan knew she would finish her roll and sink completely in about the time it would take him to utter a single sentence. Turning to his VHP and CB radios, he made a snap decision.

In the past, he'd listened to many Mayday calls to the U.S. Coast Guard in Kodiak. As glad as he was to have them standing by for his fellow fishermen, Harlan also knew that the Coast Guard usually wanted to know "who your mother's sister was, the color of your boat," your date of birth, your last checkup, proper spelling, and the like. So rather than shoot off a Mayday to the Coast Guard, Harlan decided to take a gamble.

For much of the night, he'd been listening on VHP channel 6 to the friendly chatter of the boats traveling ahead of him up the line. He grabbed the CB mike then and yelled, "Mayday! Mayday! Mayday! This is the *Tidings*. We're off Cape Chiniak and we're going down!"

As he spoke, the *Tidings* fell completely over on her starboard side. Below him, Harlan could see batteries breaking loose and flying across the engine room. He felt his heart freefall into his belly. Before he could unkey his mike, he "lost all power. Everything went dead."

Harlan heard a tremendous crash, and it seemed that all at once everything inside the boat—pots, pans, toasters, even rifles—came flying loose. Then the large hulk of the refrigerator came tumbling from its mounts. Harlan was thrown across the width of the wheelhouse. He struggled to regain his footing, but instead he tumbled backward down into the fo'c's'le.

Then, like a whale sounding, in one continuous motion the stern kicked high, and the *Tidings* sank bow first, straight for the bottom. She slid toward the ocean floor in one steady motion, burying herself full length in the night sea. And there she paused, floating with only a few feet of her stern showing above the surface, with Joe Harlan still trapped inside.

As Bruce Hinman recalls it, shortly before the *Tidings* foundered and rolled over, his skipper had slowed the vessel to allow all six-foot-three and two-hundred-ninety pounds of Hinman's huge frame, as well as his fellow crewmates Chris Rosenthal and George Timpke, time to get dressed and make their way outside. A ten-inch-thick layer of sea ice had already formed on the *Tidings'* superstructure, and was growing fast. Clad only in their work clothes, they hurried outside to do battle.

Hinman, Rosenthal, and Timpke attacked the ice with baseball bats. They broke ice and tossed the chunks overboard as fast as they could move. And as they did, they squinted against the sharp, eye-watering gusts of arctic wind, and winced at the biting cold. They worked in drenching conditions in a chill-factor reading of some minus fifty-five degrees Fahrenheit, the coldest ever recorded in the area. And they swung at the growing layers of ice now encasing the bow railings and bulwarks surrounding the wheelhouse, certain in the knowledge that their very lives hung in the balance.

Suddenly, the crab boat began to list sharply. The growing list soon tilted past forty-five degrees. Seawater rose over the portside railing. Hinman was removing his survival suit from its bag when a tall wave broke over the twisting slope of the deck. And just as suddenly, he and the others found themselves dodging a deadly shuffle of fifteen-thousand pounds of crab pots sliding forward toward them down the steep slope of the deck. As the bow of the *Tidings* nosed farther forward into the icy sea, the seven-ton stack of crab pots accelerated its slide, further distorting the already-untenable balance of the sinking ship.

Accelerating as it came, the tall and deadly stack of sliding crab pots closed on the terrified crewmen like a moving mountain. The square-fronted stack of steel and webbing plowed into the back door of the ship's wheelhouse like a runaway freight car. It slammed against the rear of the wheelhouse with the effect of a door closing on a bank vault, leaving their skipper trapped inside.

With the shifting weight accelerating the angle of the plunging bow, the *Tidings* rolled with an astonishing velocity, pitching the four crewmen scrambling across her back deck bodily through the air and overboard. The suddenness of the portside motion had caught everyone off guard. It was as if an all-powerful force had suddenly gripped the *Tidings* and flipped her—as if her fifty-three feet and forty tons were no more substantial than a bathtub toy in a child's hands.

Bruce Hinman felt the sudden shift, and he found himself hurtling through space; several of the crab pots followed. His right arm became entangled in the webbing of one of the pots—and just as suddenly, the six-hundred-pound crab pot began to sink like a rock toward the bottom, dragging Hinman, kicking and struggling, along with it.

It all happened so quickly. Hinman had been knocked senseless by the sudden shock of the Kodiak waters, ensnared by one of his own crab pots, and was now being dragged along on an unforeseen journey into deepest darkness toward an ocean floor more than a thousand feet below.

He knew instinctively that if he allowed panic to rule him, he would be lost. And he fought to choke back the rising tide of unreasoning fear within himself.

As he descended through the darkness, Hinman gained a measure of composure. He would fight against the building fear by taking action. He was perhaps seventy feet beneath the ocean surface when he managed to jerk his ensnared right arm free.

Then he placed both of his stocking feet against the webbing of the crab pot and pushed away violently. The fast-sinking crab pot disappeared quickly, tumbling off into the black body of sea below him.

When Hinman looked up, he was awestruck by what he saw, for a blinding orb of radiant light hovered above him. There was something beautiful, even angelic about the vision before him. Brilliant in splendor, it bathed him in spirit-lifting columns of golden light that seemed to beckon him home. He ascended feverishly then, stroking overhead toward the comforting swath of inexplicable light like a man with a building hope, a hope tempered by the fear that at any moment another toppling crab pot might very well descend upon him and carry him back down again.

At that moment, Bruce Hinman's past life flashed before his eyes. Launched instantaneously through time, he watched the events of his life play out before him, as he recalled later, with "the speed of thought." The prevailing feeling was of being cast adrift on a wondrous journey, unhindered by earthly impediments of time, matter, or communication.

Hinman recalled feeling "lost in time without an anchor." And the look and feel of special moments long past came back to him now with complete clarity. They flashed and froze there in his consciousness, in a kind of nostalgic collage of all that had once mattered in his life.

He saw his two little boys; his former wife, Carol; his two adopted foster daughters; and both of his parents, as well. Then Hinman was back under fire in Vietnam, just as it had all happened, with soldier-buddies dropping all around him. A millisecond later, he was a boy again, scrambling along the banks of Lake Shasta in northern California. And he was swept back into the very moment when he had come so close, as a child to drowning. It all scrolled past him now, and each memory carried with it the exact same heart-tugging emotion he had felt at that time.

Bruce Hinman exploded through the surface, leaving the visions behind. He rose bodily into the bitter night, then wrenched hard and began inhaling deep lungfuls of the precious air.

When he regained himself, he spotted the stern of the *Tidings* drifting nearby. She was hanging straight down in the water. Adrift now, without a survival suit, lost in a whiteout of silvery gray ice fog, Hinman knew the odds of outliving his predicament were slim. He dog-paddled, fighting to catch his breath.

When he could, he yelled for his crewmates, "Hey, Chris! Where is everybody?" A voice sounded out of the darkness perhaps fifty feet away, "Hinman!" He recognized the voice of his good friend and crewmate, Chris Rosenthal.

"Harlan's in the boat! He's down inside the boat!" Chris shouted.

George Timpke, their third crewmate, soon acknowledged him as well. He was clinging to a piece of flotsam off in the darkness approximately one- hundred feet away.

Short of diving equipment, Hinman knew he had no way of reaching his trapped skipper. Swearing aloud, he soberly acknowledged to himself that his good friend Joe Harlan was a goner. And a single thought shot across his mind. What am I going to say to his wife, Mary Ellen?

Now Hinman felt the almost caustic effects of the bitter wind and numbing ocean against the flesh of his face. He also knew there would be no way to climb back aboard the sinking vessel, no way for him or his other shipmates to climb clear of the life-sucking cold of the Gulf of Alaska water, and he felt at once helpless and angry.

"Now what?" he shouted into the arctic night.

Harlan had been roughed up considerably when the *Tidings* had rolled over. In fact, he had come close to breaking his right arm. He scrambled to gather himself and climb out. Ordinarily, the ladder leading from the engine room to the sleeping quarters stood upright and led down into the engine room. But now the vertical leg of the ladder posed a serious obstacle. With the *Tidings* tilted straight down as she was, the ladder now lay unevenly across the inverted space before him, sloping as it stretched between cabins. Scaling it would be a little like trying to climb the underside of a stairway. With his battered right arm, it would be a difficult gymnastic feat.

Now the startled skipper found himself "all the way forward" in the darkest inner reaches of the ship's bow, some fifty feet below the surface of the sea. As the boat continued to leap and roll, he could hear the ongoing crash and clutter of stored parts falling and scattering overhead.

Suddenly, in the gray-black light, a roaring blast of seawater broke through the door to the engine room. The tumultuous white water broke heavily over Harlan, lifting him bodily and washing him out of the fo'c's'le. He gasped for air as the icy flood cascaded over him. As he was carried along through the inverted space of the ship's galley, Harlan reached out and snagged the handle to the wheelhouse door. He tugged frantically, but with the water pressure sealing it shut, he found it immovable.

As the small galley continued to flood, Harlan found himself struggling to remain afloat in the narrowing confines. The galley sink and faucet were now suspended on end below him while beside him, in the claustrophobic space, floated the gyrating hulk of their refrigerator.

Harlan gulped air and dived. He knew he had to think of a way out. He swam down through the watery cubicle of the galley to the sink, grabbed the faucet with both hands, and kicked viciously at the starboard side window behind it. But the leaden cold of the water seemed to drain the power from his blows. This is hopeless, he thought as he swam back toward the pocket of air above.

The moment his head emerged, he was greeted by a terrifying roar. The flood of gushing seawater into the room seemed to be accelerating. The sound of it echoing in the small sliver of space was deafening. The water sloshed back and forth between walls that rolled and dipped in a dizzying motion around him. Again, the refrigerator drifted into him. And he fought against a building sense of horror.

Treading water, Harlan tilted his head back in the narrow space next to the ceiling and tried to inhale the precious air. But the shocking cold of the seawater continued to make breathing difficult, and his breath came in shallow huffs.

Well, this is it, he thought. This must have been how Jim Miller died on the *George W.*

Harlan considered praying, but it occurred to him that doing so would be an admission that he was going to die. He also made up his mind not to snivel. He would not pray, and he would not blubber. He would face the outcome, whatever that might be.

Joe Harlan weighed the chances of escaping through the galley door and out onto the back deck. But with the *Tidings* standing directly on end as she was, he knew the entire fifteen-thousand-pound stack of crab pots would be pressing down against the door at that very moment. And, with the refrigerator floating in front of it, he conceded the escape route had been lost.

Yet, even at the time, in the midst of all the terror and commotion, Joe Harlan realized that there was something strange about his ongoing ordeal—he could see virtually everything. With his adrenaline flowing, his senses had somehow become heightened—and now a whole new world seemed to open up before him. When he dived again, he saw, through the blue-green tint of the water, the forms of the faucet and the window behind it, while the blocky brown figure of the refrigerator bobbed above him, suspended in the water overhead.

Harlan knew there were no lights burning on the boat. Everything had gone dead. There was "zero power." Perhaps it was moon-bright up top. But then he recalled that there had been no sign of the moon on such an inclement night. Yet, submerged as he was, Harlan could see clearly through the seawater inside the boat, as well as out into the light green sea space on the other side of the window.

Adrift in the ocean current, the hull of the *Tidings* bounced now in the lumpy winter seas like a floating berg of ice, with barely ten percent of her whole self still showing above the surface.

Entombed inside the sinking hull of the *Tidings*, Joe Harlan was also feeling the weight of his impossible predicament closing in on him, and his emotions built toward a breaking point.

He thought of his lovely young wife, Mary Ellen. She had soft brown hair and beautiful blue eyes. They had met four years before in Kodiak; Harlan had hired her to do the cooking for the boat during a herring season. They had married soon after that, and now they were the proud parents of a beautiful one-year-old daughter, Chelsea.

In the hard-working and yet contented years since then, Joe Harlan and his wife had built a fine house together outside of Kodiak in the Bells Flats area along Sergeant Creek. Harlan could see the ocean from the balcony. During the salmon-spawning season in the lush and beautiful summer months on the island, he often had to put up with Kodiak bears that wandered onto his backyard property and competed for those same spawning salmon. He had one of the best silver-salmon fishing holes.

Harlan loved his family. Besides, he had mortgage payments to make and a lot of living to do. The whole damned thing just wasn't fair. He couldn't bear to accept it! He couldn't just give up!

The injustice of the moment sent Harlan into an emotional spiral that carried him over the edge. And he erupted into a blind rage. Wild with anger and determination, he sucked in another brief pull of air and dived again for the sink. He would make another attempt to break out the window. But this time, he would try another method. He swam to the sink, then grabbed the faucet tightly again with both hands and began repeatedly ramming his head into the glass.

Suddenly, the window exploded from its mounts. Harland watched as it tumbled out into the pale green void and fell into the watery oblivion below.

All of a sudden, Harlan felt outside of himself. Imagining himself to be a sea otter, he swam nimbly ahead through the small opening as if it were the most natural thing, arched his back, and headed directly for the surface.

In the strange and unexplained illumination that still remained, Harlan was able to see the hull of the *Tidings* as he swam upward. Man, I can't be that far from the surface, he thought as he stroked "up and up and up." The moment he broke through the surface, he felt himself return to his old self. It was like breaking into a completely different world again!

Harlan gasped wildly for air.

Bruce Hinman was drifting next to the bobbing stern of the *Tidings* when a man's head exploded through the surface, popping up right alongside him.

Choking, thrashing against the water, the man coughed heavily and spun in his direction.

"Hinman! You ugly son of a bitch!" he yelled.

It was none other than his skipper, Joe Harlan.

"Joe! Damn, I thought you were dead!" shot back Hinman, elated to see him.

Hinman's levity at seeing Harlan was quickly tempered, however, by the hopeless realization that there was no way to survive the present predicament. The canister containing the life raft had apparently failed to release when the *Tidings* rolled over, or perhaps it had released, only to get tangled up in the rigging or the crab pots. It didn't matter. Without that life raft, they knew they were all as good as dead.

"What are we going to do?" Hinman shouted.

"Did we get off a Mayday call?"

Harlan had tried but he didn't know if anyone heard it.

There was nothing the men could do now but tread water and wait. With the wind blowing offshore, there would be no way to try to swim to shore. The deadly effects of hypothermia commonly paralyzed and drowned most men adrift in such seas in a few minutes, at least those wearing only work clothes. Some began to sink the moment they hit the water. Even if Harlan and Hinman and the others could remain afloat, the wind and waves would eventually carry their bodies out to sea, where they would be lost forever.

When one crewman realized how grim things looked, he announced that he might just as well swim back down into the wheelhouse of the *Tidings*, get his pistol, and shoot himself.

Suddenly, a huge object exploded out of the water between Hinman and his skipper. It was the fiberglass canister that housed the *Tidings* life raft. The canister was about the size and shape of a fifty-five-gallon oil drum.

"Grab that SOB!" yelled Hinman.

The four crewmen converged on it. "Pull the cord!" yelled Joe Harlan.

While his crewmates treaded water nearby, Hinman began to peel off the line as fast as his numbed arms could move. He pulled and pulled, and after what seemed like several hundred feet of line later, he aired what everyone was thinking.

"God Almighty! This must be some kind of joke! We've got nothing but a coil of line here!"

"Pull! Pull faster!" yelled a terrified crewman.

"Damn, man! I'm pulling as fast as I can," shot back Hinman.

Moments later, Hinman was forced to stop. The frightening cold was beginning to press in on him, and he'd run out of breath.

Joe Harlan soon rejoined Hinman in the effort. He pulled what seemed to be literally hundreds of feet of line from what they had supposed to be the life-raft canister. It was beginning to look like a fisherman's prank—an unbelievably cruel prank—had been played on them. What if the white fiberglass canister floating in front of them, the canister designed to house the ship's life raft, was filled with nothing but a large, unending, useless coil of line?

Minutes dragged by as Hinman continued to extract the line. As hundreds of feet of useless and entangling line played out in the water all around the floundering crew, their worst fears began to take on the feel of reality. When they came to the end of the line, a winded Bruce Hinman wrapped the line around his numb, pain-racked hands and gave a final tug.

Nothing happened.

The crew treading water around him let out groans filled with disbelief and a mounting panic.

Harlan's mind raced. I just can't believe this is happening, he thought. After all we've been through, to come up short like this.

Joe Harlan moved in to help. He leaned back in the water, placed both feet on either side of the end of the canister, and wrapped the rope around both of his clumsy, cold-ravaged hands. He reached down all the way then and pulled with everything he had.

The stubborn knot on the other end of the line gave way suddenly. Then came the pop and hiss of the CO_2 cartridges discharging. In the next instant, the bright orange canister exploded open and the raft began to inflate. But it inflated upside down.

As longtime fishermen, two-hundred-ninety-pound Bruce Hinman and two-hundred-pound Joe Harlan continued to work together. They quickly assessed the situation and, without comment, approached the task at hand as if driven by the logic of a single working mind.

Inflated and upright, these rafts are fluorescent orange in color and round in form, with a diameter of eight feet. Floating, they look like giant inner tubes, or perhaps like those inflatable backyard pools that small children use, but with a dome tent mounted on top.

Swimming to one side of the raft, they crawled atop it. Then, planting their feet (and combined weight of five-hundred pounds) on the downwind side of the overturned raft, they reached across, grabbed its upwind edge, and lifted it in unison. When the twenty-five-knot wind caught the exposed upwind edge of the raft, it flipped it upright, scooping more than a foot of icy seawater along with it as it did.

"All right!" yelled one shivering crewman as he breast-stroked nearby.

Drifting in the murderous cold of the ocean currents, the entire crew was thoroughly chilled, their movements sluggish with the steadily advancing effects of hypothermia. Hinman and Harlan decided to drift alongside the raft in the painfully cold seawater and help their crewmates crawl aboard through the narrow doorway of the raft.

Being by far the huskiest of any man in the *Tidings* crew (or in the entire Kodiak crab boat fleet, for that matter), Hinman insisted on going last. It was a wise decision, for when all had been helped aboard, so numbed was he, and so completely had his strength been sucked from his body, that it took not only all of his own failing strength but also the body-wrenching efforts of the entire crew to haul him aboard.

Never in more than a century of brutal Alaskan winters had a storm front this cold struck the Kodiak Island area. A minus twenty-five-degree reading in Alaska's

dry interior country near Anchorage or Fairbanks was considered cold, even dangerous, although not unusual. But it was unheard of in the moist marine waters of the
Gulf of Alaska.

The storm winds howled incessantly. The unrelenting gusts turned the raft's
doorway into a virtual wind tunnel. Caught without a single survival suit among the
four of them, and constantly awash with more than a foot of icy Gulf of Alaska seawater crashing about inside their raft (and with more seawater washing inside all the
time), the crew of the *Tidings* knew their lives were still in serious jeopardy.

In truth, the record cold front threatened to freeze them where they sat. Packed
tightly inside the cramped and drenching confines of the dome-covered raft, the
cold-ravaged crew of the fishing vessel *Tidings* huddled together, shivering violently
as panting columns of steamy breath jetted from their mouths.

Bruce Hinman rubbed his hands together furiously. He crossed his forearms,
folded his hands under his armpits, and turned numbly to his skipper.

As if the record cold and unconfirmed mayday hadn't been enough to worry the
crew of the *Tidings*, they now discovered another unsettling fact: Their painter, leading out from the life raft, was still tethered to the sinking hull of the *Tidings*. In theory,
the raft was attached this way to keep the crew members in the close vicinity of the
boat as long as possible. But the status of the inverted *Tidings* was tenuous at best, and
they knew she could be heading for the bottom at any moment. If she did, the life raft
and all its occupants would likely be pulled down along with her.

The bridle cord attaching the raft to the painter was designed so that it was
tethered directly in front of the raft's entrance hole. In any windy conditions, this
meant that as long as the raft remained tied to her mother ship, the gaping hole of the
doorway would always end up facing directly into the prevailing wind.

That wind now drove close-cropped ocean waves against the stationary side of
the raft. And icy walls of sea spray began exploding in through the front door and over
those inside. Short of cutting the cord and casting themselves off into the mercy of
the night, there was nothing to be done.

In minutes, the blunt force of the record cold, the knifing edge of the arctic wind,
and the drenching blasts of icy sea spray had rendered the men almost unconscious.
They prayed then, and waited. And as the murderous cold bore down on them, a
heavy silence fell on the crew.

Like the rest of the men, skipper Joe Harlan could no longer feel his fingers. But
when he sensed the growing sense of hopelessness in the raft, he turned to his men.

"Look, guys, we're going to make it. Try not to worry about it. We're in the raft.
That's the important thing." He paused.

"We've just got to keep fighting it," he added. And he set about to keep the men busy. "Now is the time to get things done. And the first thing we need to do is to get that door flap tied shut'"

Those nearest the door opening soon discovered that the flap ties were frozen fast to the walls of the domelike ceiling of the raft. The going was slow and painful. No one in the entire crew seemed able to carry out the simple task; their numbed fingers had lost all dexterity. Yet, if the crew was going to survive, it was imperative that someone tie the thin strips of nylon fabric to the bonnet of the raft itself and shut out the deadly chill of wind and sea. Harlan encouraged them to keep trying.

With the rest of the crew now on task, Hinman and Harlan worked frantically to open the survival kit. Perhaps there was a knife inside that would allow them to cut themselves free of their mother ship. They soon came upon a small package containing the essential lifesaving equipment such as flares, water, and food. But whoever had packed the raft had wrapped the package in layer upon layer of silver duct tape. Joe Harlan discovered that his fingers were no longer taking messages from his brain. His fingers had given out, and so Harlan began attacking the wide silver-gray tape, ripping at it with his teeth.

One crewman started praying again. "Dear God, help us! Dear God, help us!" Over and over he repeated it.

At first, Harlan appreciated the prayer; then it began to wear on him. With the icy weight of the Alaskan cold front bearing down heavily upon them, the freezing crewmen were starting to fade. Finally, Harlan spoke to the crewman. "You know, you need to shut up now," he said steadily. "This is not good for our morale." The young crewman fell silent.

"Guys, we're going to make it. We're going to make it. So let's just keep thinking that way," Harlan added.

Joe Harlan was proud to see how his crew worked together. In a situation where fatalism might not have been out of line, they were doing all they could to save themselves. There isn't a coward in the bunch, he thought.

When they finally got the survival package open, Hinman and Harlan found no knife; they did manage to locate a small flashlight, yet its batteries had lost most of their charge. And they were forced to squint hard in the dim and intermittent flashes of light to read the flare instructions and figure out how to work them.

Harlan held out one of the flares and turned to Hinman. "Bruce, how do you work one of these damned things?"

Hinman looked at the oddly constructed flare. It had foreign instructions printed on it. He handed it back to Harlan.

"The goddamned instructions are in French!" shouted Hinman. And he cursed a streak.

Unable to read the instructions, and fearing they might accidentally launch the flare into the face of someone inside the raft, Joe Harlan decided that for the time being he would not attempt to launch one at all. Joe Harlan now felt himself slowing down dramatically. And each time the cord line leading from the raft to the *Tidings* pulled tight, the life raft would once again contort wildly beneath it, and the severely hypothermic men inside would be drenched in yet another icy blast of seawater. It soon grew so cold inside the raft that the men agreed that they'd felt warmer while immersed in the sea itself.

Finally, after herculean efforts, they managed to get the flap tied shut. But even then, it only partially blocked the painful, drenching blasts of exploding sea.

Adrift in the cold and utter darkness, they remained tethered to the bouncing, drifting hull, blown back and forth across the rugged face of the sea by a knifing twenty-five-knot wind and battered by an unforgiving sea. With nearly a thousand pounds of men sprawled on the floor inside, Harlan felt certain that the constant jerking of the waves would soon tear the raft in two.

Harlan knew what he had to do. He searched for his own knife. He felt a lump inside one of his pockets, reached in, and pulled out a stray shotgun shell. Finally, he managed to locate his knife. But when he ordered his hands to open, they refused. Then, holding the knife in the palms of his stiff hands, he bent forward, took the edge of the steel blade in his teeth, and pried it open. Leaning outside through the doorway of the raft, he slowly and deliberately sawed on the line.

The line parted, and suddenly they were adrift. The violent, neck-snapping action of the raft vanished abruptly. Now as they rode up and over the rolling seas, they could hear the roar of the wind and the breaking of unseen waves off in the darkness all around.

Then a thought came to Harlan: Hypothermia isn't a bad way to die. After the initial cold goes away and you go numb, you just start slowing down. Pretty soon, you get lethargic, and you just feel like going to sleep.

He fought against the seductive nature of such thoughts by admonishing himself. "Don't you give up! Don't you go to sleep!"

Bruce Hinman furiously rubbed his hands together. He crossed his forearms and folded his hands under his armpits. Then he pulled the door flap a few inches to one side and scanned the late-night seascape all around.

The sinking of the fishing vessel *Tidings* brought with it an especially insistent message. This was the second ship to sink out from under Hinman in the last month. Both had sunk off that very same point of Kodiak Island coastline—Cape Chiniak.

The U.S. Coast Guard squad, flying out of the Kodiak Island base, had been kept hopping all season long. The rescue of Hinman from the sinking *Cape Clear* several weeks before had been performed in huge seas in yet another blinding snowstorm. The Coast Guard helicopter pilot had descended bravely out of the night and hovered down over the sinking vessel. But the helicopter's rotor blades had struck the ship's mast, very nearly killing Hinman as well as the eight men on board the chopper. Adrift then in the tall seas, Hinman had fought hard to keep from drowning as the torn and flooded suit he wore threatened to sink him. He was completely played out by the time they finally managed to hoist him aboard the Coast Guard chopper.

And now he and his crewmates were waiting to be rescued from yet another crab boat. Hinman was staring out through a silver moonlit haze of ice fog swirling across the lonely black face of the sea when he spotted a set of approaching mast lights.

"Hey!" he yelled aloud. "Here comes a boat!"

The fifty-eight-foot fishing vessel *Polar Star* had been under way several miles off Cape Chiniak when the *Tidings* called for help. The skipper and owner of the *Polar Star*, Pat Pikus, was wrestling with poor visibility at the time. He had been standing alone at the helm, moving ahead through a steamy, boiling cloud of ice fog, when the call for help suddenly leapt from his CB radio: "Mayday! Mayday! This is the *Tidings*! We're off Cape Chiniak and we're going down!" Then, just as suddenly, the frantic voice fell silent.

Pikus quickly awakened his crew. "Everyone get up right away!" he yelled. "We've got a problem!"

He paused while his crew scrambled to life. Knifing, thirty-knot winds, with a bladelike edge of 26°F, were driving across the face of the sea. More important, Pikus knew there were no charts that could adequately describe the chill factor—nor the utter aloneness a drenched and drifting crew would know on such a night. When crewmen Shannon McCorkle, George Pikus, Gene LeDoux, and William De Hill Jr., had gathered in the wheelhouse, he turned to them.

"Boys," he said, "we've got a boat in real trouble nearby us here. And cold as it is outside, I'm still going to need one of you men to go climb up on the flying bridge and keep a watch out from there."

The wind was blowing offshore at the time, and Pikus began his search by making passes back and forth across the brackish water between the shoreline of Kodiak

Island and an imaginary point several miles offshore. He had no sooner begun his effort when another skipper's voice jumped from the radio.

The skipper claimed that the last time he'd seen the *Tidings* she'd been cruising several miles offshore. Still another skipper added that he believed he'd seen a tiny blip on his radar screen in the very area where the *Polar Star* was now cruising. But his radar had only fastened upon it once; then it had disappeared, and had never shown again.

After completing several grid-line sweeps, Pikus was about to head back into shore for yet another pass when, squinting through the boiling fog, he thought he saw something dead ahead. It turned out to be the silver flash of a small piece of reflector tape and it was stuck to the side of the dome of a life raft.

Slowing his approach, Pikus and his crew soon spotted the stunning figure of the *Tidings'* stern bouncing slowly and rhythmically through the choppy black seas. The *Tidings* had somehow managed to remain afloat, standing on end, with almost her full length buried beneath the sea. Only the last few feet of her stern and rudder now showed above the surface.

As he watched, the exposed stern of the wave-slickened hull performed an eerie ballet. What remained to be seen of her rose and fell through a jet-black world of swirling fog and howling wind, a void as cold and oppressive as a journey into the unlit bowels of a walk-in freezer.

Pikus was afraid that in the strong winds his vessel would drift right over the top of the life raft. So he swung in downwind of it, then maneuvered in close.

"Hello! Hello! Is anyone there?" Pat Pikus yelled out his side wheelhouse door.

A muffled cry came back. Then the door flap on the side of the raft's dome flipped out and someone yelled, "Yah, we're here!" The raft was caught in the bleak glare of his sodium lights.

When he pulled alongside, Pikus looked right down into the raft. He had never seen a more pathetic sight. "No one wore survival suits," he recalls. "A couple of them were without shoes. There was a lot of water slopping around in the raft." The entire crew looked as weak and hypothermic as humans can get and still remain alive. "They wouldn't have made it another ten or fifteen minutes," he recalls.

By the time the *Polar Star* came abreast of their raft, Bruce Hinman was barely conscious and completely unable to stand. The crew of the *Polar Star* climbed overboard and literally dragged him from the raft, up and over the side, and aboard their ship. Hinman remembers landing on his back and the icy crackle of his sopping-wet clothing freezing instantly to the deck.

Joe Harlan reached up and tried as best he could to grab hold of the railing. When they saw that he, too, was unable to be of much help to himself, the rugged young crewmen aboard the *Polar Star* reached down and, in one motion, hoisted him up and over the side. They tossed him onto the deck and out of the way in order to make room for the rest of the survivors.

Lying on the deck where he landed, Harlan spotted the door leading into the heated space of the *Polar Star's* galley. Unable to walk and unwilling to wait, he rolled over onto his stomach and began crawling toward the door. Pausing en route, Harlan gathered himself, and, rising up on one elbow, took one last glimpse at what remained of the *Tidings.* Waves were exploding off the few final feet of her stern.

"Good-bye, girl," he said aloud. Then he collapsed back down onto the deck and began crawling again toward the warmth of the ship's heated interior.

So intent were they on rescuing the other survivors that no one among the ship's crew noticed Harlan go. He managed to crawl in through the galley, down the hallway, and into one of the staterooms, where he pulled himself up into somebody's bunk and lay there shivering violently.

"Don't let them go to sleep! Keep them awake," the Coast Guard ordered repeatedly over the radio.

When the crew of the *Polar Star* found him, Harlan peered up at them with dark, sunken eyes from the soft, warm bunk in which he lay.

"Look," he said, "I want you to know that I'm married. And I've got a kid. And I don't want you to think I'm a homosexual or anything. But I need someone to take off all his clothes and climb in bed with me here. Because if you don't, I think I'm going to die."

It was *Polar Star* deckhand Shannon McCorkle, son of well-known Kodiak harbormaster Corkie McCorkle, who did the honors.

"He was the one who brought me back to life," recalls Harlan gratefully. "The heroes of this thing were the crewmen of the fishing vessel *Polar Star.* There's no doubt in my mind. If we'd been out there even another fifteen minutes, we would have died. We were that close to buying it."

By the time the *Polar Star* men managed to lift aboard the nearly frozen crew of the *Tidings,* nearly a foot of ice had accumulated on the decks and superstructure of the *Polar Star.* The instant the last man arrived on board, they left the raft to drift, and immediately struck out for Kodiak.

When the *Polar Star* arrived back in town, there was an ambulance waiting, but Harlan wanted nothing to do with the hospital. "Look," he told the EMTs, "I want you guys to take my crew to the hospital. Have them checked out and make sure they're okay. But I'm going home to see my wife and my daughter."

Throughout the entire ordeal, Harlan knew that it was the love of his wife and daughter and home that had kept him going. Now barefoot, his wet hair still matted against his head, Joe Harlan was clad in nothing more than a wool blanket when a friend drove him home. His wife came out to greet him. It was a tearful reunion.

That winter, during the bitter cold of the crab season, Joe Harlan had grown a beard. Now even his one-year-old daughter did not recognize him. When he approached and picked her up, she asked him, "Are you Santa Claus?"

Once inside, Harlan took a long, hot bath, devoured hot platefuls of food, and spent time relaxing with his wife and daughter. At 8 a.m. the very next morning, Joe Harlan called a ship broker in Seattle. It was time to start shopping for a new crab boat. ⚓

SPIKE WALKER fished the Bering Sea during the king crab boom years of the 1970s and '80s, then turned author with his best-selling *Working on the Edge: Working in Alaska's Most Dangerous Professions*. Since then he has written *Nights of Ice; Coming Back Alive;* and *On the Edge of Survival: A Shipwreck, a Raging Storm, and the Harrowing Alaskan Rescue that Became a Legend* is his latest work. He lives in the Pacific Northwest.

PRIBILOVIA

**SHANNON
ZELLERHOFF**

passes through
the Pribilovia Islands
on a crab boat,
musing on the
sharp, enigmatic
presence of the
islands, both
dangerous and
alluring.

COMING INTO THE PRIBILOF Islands is always tricky. There are no natural harbors. At Saint
George, there is a narrow cut usually occupied with a pot dock
and a processor barge chained to the rock. As we ride in on
rolling swells, we try to take a straight line in to avoid rocks left
and right. One of us is on the stern, the other is in the crow's
nest. Our captain adjusts our course. After five days of fishing,
the crab-processing barge is a welcome sight. To anyone else, it
would be an emergency landing.

We tie up outside the outflow pipe. In the waste and gurry
float crab carapaces and ground crab shells, paper cups, hairnets, a
rubber glove. An open hatch exposes the guts of the factory. Like
an incision into the body, it isn't pretty, just interesting.

The engineer stands by the opening, smoking, one foot on
the rail, his coffee mug resting on his knee. He stares like a frozen
gull. It begins to snow into the wind, great big fluffy, wet flakes.

Inside there are hundreds of men and women working desperately to make enough money to change their lives. Some are
from as far away as Africa, some from Honduras; most are young

white kids from Seattle. It's an adventure, a way to pay bills, rescue a family, and land a job on a fishing boat.

We know our way to the galley by heart. Weaving through the labyrinth of gauges, plumbing, stairwells, machinery, pumps, boxes, safety bulletins, fire hydrants and extinguishers, we arrive on the top deck. But we do not simply blend into the crowd of crab-processors waiting for their midnight meal. We are guests: the crew of the boat that brought the crab. People want to talk to us, as if we were celebrities. They want to compliment us on the beautiful crab we caught--their white bellies, their hard shells, their strong claws.

"You don't have any dead loss," they say, remarking on the arrival of two-hundred-fifty-thousand pounds of opilio stuffed in a jostling live tank. "They seem to all have their legs," which makes us proud.

It's a delicate balance getting the crab from the pot to the sorting table to the live tank. Speed and grace. Crab with missing legs are not very desirable, and some processors refuse boats with bad reputations regarding this. We are like folk heroes to some, for we have seen dozens of ports along the Northwest Coast, and our boat, tiny by comparison, represents a certain freedom to them. With a crew of five, we will leave the stinky, steamy steel sarcophagus for the silent threat of the oily sea. On our heels will spin the water boiling from our prop and by our temples flow the wings of great flocks of gulls. We will work for days on end inhaling nothing but cigarettes and caffeine. At any given chance, we will dash inside to change our socks and devour an entire box of cereal each. There will be cat naps where we, still dressed in our oilskins, will crash out on coils of line. A buoy for a pillow. The hiss of the sea a lullaby. "Uh, five minutes," broadcasts from the loud-hailer. Our skipper telling us to wake up. There'll be a pot to haul in less than three.

But for now we stand in the galley of the processing barge without bracing ourselves, thankful for what we are about to receive. Ham, steak, potatoes, steamed frozen veggies, fruit cocktail, stuffing, gravy, chocolate pudding, dessert, and piping hot coffee. We will eat seconds and thirds.

The harbor at Saint Paul is a whole different story. You have to make sure you can fit. The breakwater looms like the unnatural hulk of a sea monster. It has claimed a vessel or two for its lair. The seas do not stop here; they heave themselves upon the breakwater, tearing huge pieces off on the sharp volcanic rock. The white foam hangs in the air, suspended in the wind, and freezes to the icebound wall.

The VHS squawks. The *Amber Dawn* is heading out. We wait for her to pass us on the outside, excited by her dramatic diving and rising over the tireless swells of three long, storm-wrought weeks. On deck there is ice. We have been beating at it with baseball bats and rubber sledgehammers since Saint George, thirty miles to the south. Clad in our orange PVC Grundens and Helly Hansens, an armor of slush has encrusted us. Our bodies are steam engines. We pass the neck of the breakwater. In seconds, we are tied up alongside the processor *Unisea*.

The engine is killed, the alarms ring. We look around again to make sure we are safe, and go inside the cabin to change into our dry clothes. Coveralls, fox hat, freezer gloves. The walk to the village is short. We pass a new cannery and the harbormaster's office. From the other side of the breakwater, the Bering Sea roars. Arctic fox hide and seek. There is the city maintenance shop, the post office, the King Eider Inn, and the only store.

It is sleeting and dark at four o'clock. The sea will be a mess tomorrow—after all, she can't make up her mind. I find solace in a pay phone booth. With a calling card, I dial home. In the store, we each search out our cravings. Fig Newtons, candy bars, favorite cereals, fresh smokes, clean socks. The children laugh and smile, the elders are suspicious, our peers are more curious, like the fox. I spy a newspaper but its headlines are meaningless. All my friends are still afloat.

The history of these islands is not pleasant. Slavery, fur seals, whaling, cod, and now crab, the natives have always been a people of incredible character and resiliency. Even though they never chose to live on these islands, they have not moved away. Like the few caribou and fox that have been introduced, they subsist because they must.

The guys have gone to the bar. I walk back to the boat, kicking pumice stones into the snow. I go up the ramp to the processor and thread myself through its maze like a meadow stream—empty, emotionless steel—down several catwalks to our boat, snugged to the other side. The cradle of our lives. I swing one leg over the rail, then the other. For a while I'll be alone. The sky is askew with tormented colors, gulls, and clouds.

Dark light fumbles with all of the eerie sodium vapors of the industry. Icy blues, steely grays, Exxon black. A flash of red paint. On deck, there is a warm yellow orb of light. The snow falling is still. The winds have died down. A raven wants our garbage. I light a smoke and put one foot up on the seaward rail. The harbor starts to freeze. ⚓

SHANNON ZELLERHOFF was born in Cambridge, Massachusetts, where she was adopted at seven months. Raised in New England by a nurse and a minister, she was exposed at an early age not only to salt air and boats, but to neighbors mending lobster traps and to famous sea-farers such as the late Captain Irving Johnson. She tried working on farms and in canneries in Maine, but finally turned to the Alaska fishing industry where—as a local lobsterman suggested—"it ain't so much about family businesses up there. They might even hire women." Starting in Homer, she longlined her way out west via the Pribilofs to Unalaska Island. Over eight years she fished for opilio, bairdi, king crab, halibut, cod, salmon, herring, and tuna. Shannon left the fishing industry in 1998 to work

LET THE KID RUN THE BOAT

SIG HANSEN
recalls his first real
season running
the *Northwestern,*
his family's infamous
crab boat, and
his trials and
misadventures
as a greenhorn
captain.

O UR PLAN WAS to get to Alaska early, before the
fall crab season, and go out west to Adak Island
for brown crab. In July we all got onboard in Ballard, passed
through the locks, and motored north. Mark Peterson took
that trip off, so the rest of the crew was Pete Evanson, Brad
Parker, Steiner Mannes, and Edgar, who was eighteen and
just starting working on deck. The oldest men on board were
Evanson and Parker, who we called "the old man." They
weren't even thirty. I was twenty-three.

Aris, the greenhorn, was sick for the whole seven days
motoring across the gulf. He just lay in his bunk puking. At
one point he thought some Rolaids might help his stomach,
but that just made him puke foam. He felt horrible. I'd been
there before. You just stare at other people eating and wonder
how they can possibly do it. You're hungry, but the last thing
you can do is eat. It's the hangover that never ends.

I had been relief captain on the *Northwestern* for a few
trips here and there, but this was my first season as full-time
captain. I'd been given my first shot the previous year when

Tormod had taken a break. Tormod had been grumbling about teaching me the ropes of being skipper, and I don't blame him. "Why should I teach him all my tricks when he's just going to take my job?" he muttered to a deckhand. Meanwhile, Mangor Ferkingstad, my old mentor, was the deck boss, and he was looking to become skipper. He was blunt about it. He went to my dad.

"Either you let me take it," Mangor said, "or you let the kid run the boat."

It was the farthest thing from the Old Man's mind, but once Mangor mentioned it, I guess my dad liked the idea. At the time I was home on a break, sick with the flu. Dad came into my room and was mumbling about something.

"What's wrong?" I said.

"You want to take the boat?"

I didn't really realize what he was asking me.

"Yeah, yeah, whatever."

"You're going to take the boat."

So then I flew up there, thinking he was going to take me out and show me what to do. The last thing I expected was to become captain. It was opilio season. My dad had always thought of opilios as trash, a tiny inedible bug that had to be thrown back when they happened into your traps because they took up the valuable space needed for king crab. He ran for miles to get out of them. To fish them on purpose was degrading work. As an old-school king crabber, he thought opilios were beneath him.

Dad flew up to Dutch after me and met up with Magne Nes. By this time, these guys were all considered old-timers. I was getting ready for the trip, not quite sure what to do. And then Magne told Dad, "Just leave the guy alone, Sverre! Let him do his own thing."

Then it hit me. My Old Man was seriously expecting me to go out as captain without him.

It was May. The weather was nice. One of dad's friends, Walt Christensen, jumped on the boat docked next to me. He gave me a blank bearing book—to record my fishing positions—and said this is how I do it. I followed Walt out to the grounds. When we got close to the rest of the fleet, he radioed and said, "You're on your own."

I had been watching Tormod and my dad, so I had a good idea of how to navigate and set gear. Now I just had to figure out where to set it. I had a radio. Channel 12 was the squarehead channel. The Norwegians always had their own channel. When we were doing watch at three in the morning, we could always find some other squarehead to talk to. "Anybody on there?" He'd be on another boat, some Norwegian guy, a crew member. We were always communicating.

The fleet understood it was my first time, so they hazed me. By then, Mangor had been hired as skipper of the *Western Viking*, where he did very well. I had to radio him and ask him how to punch in waypoints on the Loran—Long Range Aid to Navigation, which is what we use to find our pots once we've set them. The others knew I was having a hard time finding the crab. There was a learning curve for me, and the crew had to suffer through it. My strings of pots were a mess. They were incorrectly spaced, jumbled on one another. I got tangled in my own gear or ran over the buoys with the propeller. I also seemed to come down with dyslexia. I'd miswrite the number of a pot, so after wasting time searching for number 89, I'd find 98 instead.

When I did get on a really decent pile of crab, the crew could right away hear it in my voice on the radio. They knew I was on the crab, and they were all laughing. "Sounds like you found a pile!" Oddvar said on the radio. I was so proud to hear this praise from him, someone I'd looked up to for a decade. I was happy. I was having a blast. But I still didn't feel like a real skipper. I felt more like a dumb kid sitting in a chair pulling pots. At the time, I was twenty-two and may have been the youngest skipper on the fleet.

Most of the skippers were old-timers. If a boat is less than two-hundred gross tons, the captain doesn't need a license. The only thing determining whether I could be captain of a vessel the size of the *Northwestern* was if the insurance company would agree to insure me. It was very subjective. If the pool managers thought you were good enough, they would let you in. Otherwise they'd blackball you. Many years later I learned that some of the pool managers didn't think I had what it took. In fact, one guy in the company had made a bet that I was going to mess up and hurt someone. Years later he revealed this secret to me and admitted that he'd actually lost money betting on me because I'd survived those early years without an accident.

Eventually I created my own way of doing things. I got to know my boat and crew to where they were like an extension of me. I was obsessed with numbers. The crew called me Captain Casio, because I was always plugging numbers into my calculator. If we could pull X amount of crab in Y minutes, then we were earning Z dollars per hour. One time, a skipper in the fleet announced that he was taking the day off to go to port to watch the Super Bowl. I was stunned. My crew was looking at me, wondering if we should do the same. I whipped out my calculator. So, four hours to watch a game?

"Well, four hours of crab, that's ten grand," I said. "You want to miss that kind of money? That's the way it works."

Pulling a full pot is the best feeling in the world. But being a psycho, I always get depressed because I know the next time it won't be as full. That thought bothers me. I should be happy, but I always want more. I never looked at fishing primarily as fun. It's work. I tried sport-fishing for marlin in Mexico once when I was a kid, but I didn't like it. Some damn dentist caught the thing instead of me.

Anyway, there we were in the summer of 1988, motoring north, for my first full season as captain. We were all relieved when we reached Akutan. We called Charlie McGlashan on the radio and he came down to the docks to welcome us. Charlie Chan from Akutan was his nickname. He was one of my father's best friends, like family. We cooked up a platter of kumla, Norwegian-style potato balls—his favorite. It's a poor man's tradition that goes back generations. We mix the potatoes with rye and boil them for an hour, then add salted lamb, carrots, and rutabaga, then pour melted butter over it. It's hearty and bulky. The old people say if you eat it, don't go swimming—you'll sink. We learned to cook it from our parents when we were kids. We took the food up to Charlie's house. It was always good to see a familiar face. After dinner, he took us up to the Roadhouse for a beer. His aunt owned the place.

Akutan hasn't changed much since my dad's first trips there in the early sixties. Trident Seafoods replaced the old floating processing ship with a new cannery, which employs up to eight-hundred workers in peak season. Those workers live on the west end of the harbor. The village on the east end is relatively untouched by modernity; still only about seventy-five people living there year-round. Over the years, the Aleuts intermarried with the Scots and Russians. The natives moved into the village, and eventually formed a corporation that owns much of the land and business.

Akutan makes Dutch Harbor look like a big sophisticated city. Because the terrain is so steep, there is no airstrip, and the only way in beside boat is the Grumman Goose, an eight-seat amphibious airplane that flies from Dutch Harbor when the weather is good. My brothers and I prefer fishing out of Akutan because there's really nothing to do but fish, and we can stay focused. I like working as much as I can, with no one telling me when to stop. Dutch Harbor has the bars and people and all sorts of distractions. Since Akutan has traditionally been my family's hub of operations, we don't go to Dutch as often, so it's easy to avoid the bars. When we finally do get out in Dutch, we tend to go overboard.

The night we had dinner with Charlie in Akutan, we had just missed the big excitement. The night before, two cannery workers had fought in the bar. One pulled a knife and stabbed the other. Killed him. As Charlie told us the story, Aris the greenhorn looked at me. I know he was thinking, what am I getting myself into? Looking back now, the murder was probably an omen of bad luck to come.

From Akutan we steamed for Adak, about four-hundred miles west. It's way out there. Some seasons have been closed in Adak, and not too many fishermen of the new generation have been out there.

We had Aris filling bait jugs. As a greenhorn he didn't get a crew share; we paid him a flat $100 a day. Of course we hazed the greenhorn, because that's how it goes.

"Hurry up! Get over there! Come over here!" One time I went down to the galley while the crew was taking a five-minute break. Aris was slumped at the table, face in his hands.

"What do you think of crab fishing, Aris?" I said.

"It's a living hell."

I laughed. "Okay, five minutes is up."

Almost as soon as it started, the Adak trip was a disaster. Instead of the single pot fishing that we normally do, we were experimenting with longlining, in which all the pots were attached to a single line and hoisted in by a much larger power block. Out west near Adak, in the eastern part of the Bering Sea where the seafloor is flat, you're fishing above underwater volcanic cliffs. As we were dropping the lines of pots, the fathometer was reading one-hundred-twenty fathoms. The problem was, I was getting a double-echo off the bottom: the water was actually four-hundred fathoms deep—twenty-four-hundred In other words, I had dropped two strings of twenty pots nearly a half-mile underwater, and had no way to retrieve them. I didn't know what the hell to do. It was as if I'd thrown them off a cliff. My stomach clenched. I felt like I'd been kicked. This was more than $50,000 worth of pots stranded on the bottom of the ocean. I was screwed. I went down and told the crew what I'd done. They glared at me. No one knew how to get the pots back. They weren't pleased to be working for a rookie captain.

You have to remember that I'd been working all my life to get where I was at that moment. I was finally skipper of the *Northwestern*. I had stepped out from Dad's shadow, proving I had what it takes to run a crab boat. The next thing you know, I'd made such a mess of things that I had to swallow my pride and call for advice from the very last person I wanted to talk to: the Old Man. On a clear night our single sideband radio would connect directly to his house in Seattle.

"You did vhat?" My dad understood English perfectly, even on a radiophone. He had this habit, though: if you told him that you screwed up, he'd make you repeat it, as if he didn't understand. He just liked to see a guy squirm.

"I dropped the pots at four-hundred fathoms."

"Four-hundred fathoms?"

"Yeah."

"How many fathoms?"

"Four. Zero. Zero."

"You can't fish four-hundred fathoms, you dummy!" he said jokingly. As he had gotten older, Dad had adopted dummy as one of his favorite words. I think he picked it up from watching Sanford and Son.

"I know that, Dad."

"There's no crab at four-hundred fathoms. And you'll never get the pots back."

"Yeah, Dad."

"You can fish fifty fathoms. You can maybe fish one-hundred fathoms, but you can never fish four-hundred fathoms!"

I stared at the radiophone. No fucking shit, Dad.

We ended up dropping a drag line from the block. At the end of the line we attached a big metal hook. We knew approximately where the string was, and dragged the hook back and forth over the ocean floor, hoping to snag the longline. We did this for hours. I was pissed. Everyone on deck was pissed. We could just feel the money pouring out of our pockets, not catching a damn crab.

Finally the guys let out a yell. The nylon line tightened like a cable. We'd snagged it. We started to reel in the line. Unfortunately we'd hooked it more or less in the middle, so once it surfaced, it was a jumbled mess with pots hanging off either side, as if you'd picked up a railroad train in the middle. After nine hours of hauling and hassling, we salvaged most of the twenty pots, but not all. We had to cut a few loose and let them sink. So already we were in the hole. We owed money to the boat—that is, to my Old Man – which would be subtracted from our crew shares.

We started fishing. We were dropping gear two islands to the west of Adak, off Tanaga Island. The seas were calm, but the fog was thick and there were just a few boats fishing. It was hard to see what we were doing. When the string was dropped, hundreds of feet of line were floating beside the boat. I called out on the intercom, "All right, am I clear to go ahead?" They gave me the signal, and I hit the throttle, but when the propeller started spinning it sucked the line into its blades in a big tangle. The main engine died. I knew right away that we were screwed: The nylon line was wrapped around the prop, heated up, and melted into a solid ball.

So there we were in the middle of nowhere, with no engine and no way to get the prop untangled. There was just a handful of other boats spread over the many miles of islands. I got on the radio and pretty soon another vessel came over and towed us into Tanaga Bay. There was nobody to help us—no towns, no mechanics, no people—but at least we could drop anchor in a protected bay until we figured out what to do next. We sat there for a couple of days. The greenhorn Chris Aris celebrated his twenty-first birthday moored in Tanaga Bay. Finally I was forced to call Dad—again.

"You did vhat?"

"Got a line wrapped in the propeller."

"You dummy!" he laughed. "That will kill the main engine."

"I know that, Dad."

"Why did you run over the line?"

Yeah, yeah, yeah. I hung up and rolled my eyes.

Finally the crew and I came up with a plan—if you could call it that. A nearby boat delivered a scuba tank and a wetsuit. None of us knew how to dive, but Brad Parker volunteered to go first. The water was freezing, and the old wetsuit didn't look thick enough to keep him warm. So we had a brilliant idea that we'd seen in the movie *Escape from Alcatraz*. Parker stripped down to his shorts, we smeared him with butter, and then wrapped him in plastic wrap straight from the kitchen drawer. We were laughing hysterically. It was like wrapping up an appetizer to put in the fridge. Then he put on a layer of long underwear over the plastic wrap and the wetsuit over that. He heaved the tank on his back and strapped a knife to his waist. The tank of oxygen was supposed to last forty-five minutes, which seemed long enough to get the job done. We hoisted him on the crane, swung him out, and lowered him into the water.

None of us knew how a wetsuit worked: It uses your body heat to warm the thin layer of water between your skin and the rubber. As it turned out, the plastic wrap trapped the body heat in Parker's body, so it couldn't warm the water. When he let go of the line and took a couple of strokes toward the stern he freaked out. The ice-cold water shocked his system, and he got claustrophobic in the suit of butter and plastic wrap. He dog-paddled back to the crane and we hauled him up. We stripped him out of the wet gear and wrapped him in dry clothes.

"That sucked," he said. We started thinking up Plan B.

An hour later someone took a look at the scuba tank. In the chaos, the valve must have been left open. All the oxygen was gone. Another day passed. No oxygen. No diving. No motor. No crab. No money. Then we had an idea—the diver could breathe from the air compressor hose in the engine room. I called the guy who had lent us the tank and asked what he thought.

"Ah, that's not really good air," he said. "And besides, it's not pure oxygen, it's just air."

We didn't see any other option. I put on the wetsuit—without butter or plastic wrap. We unrolled a hundred feet of rubber tape from the air compressor, inserted it into the scuba mask, and duct taped the whole assembly to my head. They lowered me off the crane into the skiff, and then I plopped in the water. Fuck it was cold. But I didn't have time to think about it. I dove underwater and swam toward the prop. The line was just a mess, a hundred fathoms or more of it, snagged up there like a bird's nest. I started hacking away with the knife. The air in my mask tasted like oil. It was nasty air from the machinery. I was hanging onto the propeller underneath the boat, and it felt like the boat was jumping up and down twenty feet. But the water was actually flat calm. Then I realized I was getting high from the fumes I was breathing!

I collected myself, and then I started hacking away at the melted ball of line with the knife. It took a long time but I got it free. I rushed up to the surface. I got on the crane and they hoisted me up. I was shivering and cold and my hands were blue, but I was happy to be on deck.

"Give me a smoke," I said. We started the engine and motored back to sea.

On that trip we also learned that just because we could fish didn't mean we could catch. We were pulling blanks. It was horrible. Longlining crab pots is a cluster fuck. These days, fishermen have perfected efficient ways of doing it, but back then we were experimenting. As we pulled these twenty pots up, we had to coil the line that connects them, and we ended up with stacks of line everywhere on deck. When it was time to drop the string, some of those coils were just sitting there unattached, while others were "live" – that is, attached to the string and extremely dangerous once those pots went overboard. It was confusing and frustrating, especially when the pots came up empty.

We were hauling around the clock. During a short break for breakfast we were just exhausted. We had a smoke and coffee and just sat around the table for a quick break. I leaned my head on the table for a little rest, and passed out right there. The rest of the crew also fell asleep and then, waking, crawled under the table and crept off to their bunks for a nap. I woke up six hours later, alone at the table, with my face in a plate of scrambled eggs.

That night we were working under the sodium lights, pushing it as fast as we could to make up for all the time we'd lost. Steiner Mannes was one of the deckhands. He was only eighteen at the time, but definitely not a greenhorn. Steiner came from a fishing family. His dad was Borge, another of my dad's good friends, and his brother Johan, who I'd fished with for years. Steiner had been fishing in the summers when he was in school. He was a good fisherman and made a full manshare. He knew what he was doing.

As we dropped the pots, Steiner nudged one of the coils with his boot to get it out of the way, thinking it wasn't live; but it was. The line tightened around his boot. There was a moment—a split second—where he looked down and realized what he'd done, but before he could react, the line cinched and knocked him off his feet. The string of pots was sinking behind the boat, and it yanked him toward the stern, like he was tied to a bumper and getting dragged behind a car. He was sliding on his back, yanked by the leg; the only thing between him and death was the three-foot-rail that kept him onboard. The deck was clear of pots, which meant he had about one-hundred feet to get dragged before he went overboard—and just a few seconds to figure something out.

Brad Parker chased him down the deck, hacking at the shot with a knife. He was sawing at the point where the cord was bound over the rail, but he couldn't cut all the way through. As Steiner approached the rail on the stern, there were only a few seconds before the inevitable. He would slam against the rail, maybe break his legs as he pushed against the line, and then get hauled overboard.

He came bouncing toward the rail, and with his last bit of strength braced his boots against the steel wall. The shot tightened and cinched down on his boot, but by some miracle, his foot wiggled free. The shot pulled his rubber boot to sea, but Steiner was left on deck, barefoot and breathless, stunned that he was still alive. Parker's knife was rubbed to a nub.

Steiner was incredibly lucky. It was the closest we've ever come to losing a man on the *Northwestern*. I learned that the mistake I had made was trying to set the gear too quickly. What could have been a tragedy was, instead, just the worst crab-fishing trip we'd ever had. "I remember I didn't want to remember it," says Edgar, "because it was probably one of the most god-awful seasons I've ever been through in my life."

By the time we unloaded our meager catch of brown crab, we had lost so much gear, soaked so much bait, and burned so much diesel, that we owed money to the boat, instead of the other way around. When the woman from Fish and Game inspected our logbook while we were unloading, she couldn't believe that we'd pulled thousands of pots – and had so little to show for it. She simply didn't believe me.

Of all the men on board that trip, the person who earned the most money was the one guy who'd been guaranteed a wage. The greenhorn Chris Aris walked away with $100 per day, while the rest of us dummies got zilch. ⚓

SIG HANSON is the captain of the *Northwestern*, one of the boats documented on the television show "The Deadliest Catch." Hansen grew up in a prominent commercial fishing family and began his own career as a boat captain in the 1980s, steering the *Northwestern* at the age of twenty-three. "Let the Kid Run the Boat" is excerpted from his memoir *North by Northwestern: A Seafaring Family on Deadly Alaskan Waters*.

WOMAN'S WORK

MARY JACOBS, who has been working on boats with men for years, seeks out an all-woman crew to help her run the Invader for a summer of salmon fishing.

HALFWAY THROUGH SALMON SEASON John Finley fired me, replacing me with a better-looking, more exciting woman. At that point I made a vow to some day skipper my own boat with an all-women crew.

A few weeks later, John called, pleading for my return. "I haven't been able to catch a fish since you got off the boat," he said. I returned to the *Invader* and put my resolve on hold. I worked on becoming indispensable, waking at the first peep of the alarm clock, making sure the tea pot was boiling and the oatmeal was started before I nudged the shoulders of my sleeping skipper. I inventoried and uniquely organized the galley and parts locker while memorizing the tide tables and tidal corrections for each bay. I quietly studied John's technique and kept a logbook of diagrams of fishing methods and sets.

At the end of the fishing season, John flew to Seattle to retrieve his baby boy. My boat duties expanded to unpaid baby-sitter as I cooked meals and changed diapers for John's son, Locke. The three of us lived and fished on the small boat until we saved enough to buy a small crabber. When I became pregnant with Balika in 1975 we settled into an isolated cabin in Mush Bay, on the west side of Kodiak Island.

Four years later, on a spring morning, I gazed at the twenty-nine-foot fishing boat sitting like a stranded whale in the tidal area near our gardens. The *Invader's* bow nestled against the cottonwood posts that held up a fence made from old nylon net and antique floats. I watched the golden beach grass sweep across the black and white raven eye that was painted on the *Invader's* port bow. It seemed to wink at me.

"I miss salmon fishing," I said to John. The whistling pot beckoned me to the propane stove. Pouring the hot water into the pot, the tea leaves swirled hypnotically.

"I don't. The competition is too stressful," John said. "I'm looking forward to gardening and welding another thirty crab pots before king crab season this fall."

I handed John a cup of tea and sat across the table from him, inhaling the blend of sweet peppermint and medicinal comfrey. "What would you think of me going without you?"

"Go," he said without looking up from his book. "I'll watch the kids."

"Could Mary Relyea and Viki leave their kids here?"

"I guess, as long as it isn't for the whole summer."

Locke, eight years old, burst through the front door followed by three-year-old Balika. Locke grinned as he held a basket of petite bantam and brown Rhode Island Red eggs. "We got ten this morning!" He said.

I looked at my children, excited about April's simple gifts. I wondered if they would forgive me if I abandoned them for the summer.

John scrambled eggs while I walked out the front door and down the beach. Climbing on the *Invader*, I thought about all the work that had to be done, the summer away from my family, and the tiny cabin that four of us would have to live in from June through September. I wondered what kind of leader I'd be. I'd seen other first year skippers act obstinate and intractable. When the net snagged or tangled, a petulant skipper would rebuke his crew. I wondered if I had the knowledge and experience to take the boat out without John. Sitting on the flying bridge, I looked into the open fish hold half full of ice and rotting leaves. In the stern, a power block hung from a question-mark-shaped davit.

The *Invader* had been built in 1938 as a dory for a fishery where crews rowed nets off the beach from a sand spit outside of the Karluk River on the south end of Kodiak Island. When John bought the *Invader* in 1963, it still had oarlocks. He had raised the rails and turned it into a competitive sixties-era seiner. To fish the *Invader* this year, we would need to replace the gas engine with a diesel.

After daydreaming I returned to the house to resume home-school teaching. I knew I had to get Locke started before he wandered out on the beach and I had to remind him, as I did most days, that school-work had to be done before playing. He groaned but opened his math book. Balika pulled up a chair beside him and pretended to read his books. As soon as Locke started solving problems, I wrote my friends, single mothers, in Kodiak and asked them to crew for me.

'A month later, the *Hak-Sie* anchored up in front of our cabin and two tow-headed eight-year-old boys tumbled into a skiff, followed by Viki, in hip boots and a ball cap. Mary ferried bags from the cabin of her ex-husband's boat and passed them to Viki while ten-year-old Cherise admonished the boys for struggling to start the outboard. Soon, the wooden skiff, bow-heavy with its load of blonds perched on sea bags, and piloted by a grizzly bearded Chuck, idled into the beach. Balika and Locke waded out, oblivious of the skiff's wake overflowing their rubber boots.

A few days later, Jane hitched a ride on a crab boat out to Mush Bay. I pulled up to the anchored boat to greet Jane, the tall athlete, barely out of her teens, who looked like she could be a California surfer. She was already garbed for fishing in her drab green Helly Hanson rain gear; her sun-kissed hair curled around the edges of a pink bandanna. I had hired her, sight unseen, after I read her letter stating that she loved the fishing life-style but had been miserable with her brother and his testosterone-driven crew.

That afternoon we set to work cutting worn web from cork and lead-line of an old net. For the next ten days, we rehung and patched web as we had learned from our mentors. The mass of web dwarfed the shoulder-high beach-grass next to the boat and, as the high tide lapped at the base of the hillock of web, we started the groaning diesel. Jane, Mary, and I stacked the net into the *Invader's* seine pit while Viki pulled sticks, roots, and rocks out of the web as the power block yanked the net off the beach.

From the beach, John and one of his fishing buddies watched us load the seine. John's friend shook his head in disbelief when John declared that he was giving up salmon fishing. "Why?" he asked.

John drawled, "Argh, its women's work."

The boat readied for the following day's noon opening, three-year-old Balika crawled into my lap with an armload of books. We read and laughed. Then she hugged me and said, "Mom, I'll never leave you." At that point tried I to remember why I wanted to skipper my own boat.

At first summer light, the kids still asleep, the four of us women left five children with John, determined to succeed.

Viki was the toughest. She volunteered to sleep on the half bunk, a shelf that ended eighteen inches above the oil stove. When her sock-covered feet hung over the stove they perfumed the cabin with foot odor and fish slime. A model in Vancouver, Viki had started doing drugs to keep skinny. After becoming pregnant, she fled the city. In 1971, shortly after my arrival in Kodiak, Viki disembarked from the ferry *Tustumena* wearing a tight tank top, a baby boy slung on her hip; wispy strands of lemon zest hair framed her high forehead. Her buggy blue eyes focused on her boyfriend walking down the gangplank a few steps ahead.

During her first couple of years in Kodiak, Viki skiff-fished with the father of her son. When they broke up she claimed the skiff and chainsaw and moved herself and her son, Tony into an abandoned cabin on Woody Island, a short boat ride from Kodiak. In a bar, Viki would smoke Camel Straights and slug down full glasses of brandy flavored with orange juice. In the early morning, men around her slid off their stools while she challenged them to another round. When we were in town, she would stagger to the boat at the start of the work day. Viki would bark orders and reprimand us for touching her skiff. "Who left the outboard down?" she'd demand. Any explanation would be ignored as she began to complain that we had mended the net in her absence and hadn't left her a hole in the web to patch. I would fire her in the spring, but during the summer I would miss her competence in the skiff and her ability to get by on two hours of sleep. I'd always hire her back.

Mary Relyea's honey blond hair was usually pulled back from her angular features into a thick braid. When she and Chuck arrived in Kodiak in 1970, John hired Chuck to work on the *Invader* and Mary began dancing topless at Tony's Bar. During the day, Mary, a graduate in art from UC Berkeley, researched Alaskan native designs and painted the *Invader* to look like a Tlingit war canoe. A killer whale adorned the flying bridge, raven eyes illuminated the bow, and black tail feathers embroidered the gray hull.

A gale blew during our first opening so we ducked into a sheltered cove. A waterfall cascaded over the cliff where the gusts transformed the stream into mist. The *Invader* shivered in the buffeting williwaws. Nervous, I shivered too, but in anticipation. While holding hook for the traditional half hour, an exhaust leak caused the cabin to fill up with smoke. After checking for fire we pulled an empty net and slunk home for repairs.

A week later, our exhaust rebuilt, the becalmed ocean tempted me to motor under the full moon to the capes that jut into the strait between Kodiak and the Alaska Peninsula. During the three-hour run Viki and I drank peppermint tea, shelled peanuts, and smiled at wind-milling puffins and bow-crossing porpoises.

The next morning I forgot the significance of river-like currents corresponding with the tide cycle; I set the quarter-mile-long net between two anchored gill nets. I attempted to hold my end of the net in position, as did Viki, but fifteen minutes into the set we had drifted close enough to clearly read the name Floyd on the setnet marking buoys. I gave the order to pull the net back, fast. As we pulled, the ripping current shoved boat and net, and hopelessly tangled them into Floyd's net and anchors. We pulled harder and the hydraulic lines to the hauler broke, spraying slippery oil over us and the boat. We strapped off the net and for the next six hours, till the tide changed and pushed us away from the gillnet, we took turns at the helm, towing gently to prevent further entanglement. Meanwhile, I hack-sawed the broken stainless steel hydraulic lines, their braided stainless steel coated with rubber, and pounded new fittings into the high pressure lines. At one point Floyd came out in his skiff to check his net; he saw us, shook his head as if to say, dumb chicks, and returned to his cabin.

After that, we fished every opening and seldom returned to the homestead. My style as a skipper developed—I was a bitch. At the tender, I'd survey the crew's grocery list and complain about buying meat and coffee. "We can eat fish," I said. "Herb tea is better for us."

"You can go without if you want; I can't," Mary responded, her blue eyes glinting in defiance and her chin set in determination. "No job is worth going without coffee for. And I like fish as much as the next guy but I can't eat it every day. Your canned venison notwithstanding, I need, in order to work twenty-hour days, greasy fried chicken, or a succulent steak at least once a week."

Between sets I nagged Mary to hurry. "Do you have to chop vegetables so perfectly?" The next day, I bitched about Jane's repetitive grilled cheese sandwiches.

"Scoutchie the net!" I'd yell at Mary, "The fish are running. We've got to get it back in the water. Do you have to make perfect diamonds?"

Mary would scowl at me and remind me that she had patched web faster than a half dozen experienced net-menders.

During closures I would search for better fishing during the day. At night I made the crew do all-night wheel-watches to bays throughout a salmon district that extended around the circumference of Kodiak Island and, on the Alaska Peninsula, from Cape Douglas, at the mouth of Cook Inlet, one-hundred-fifty miles south past Wide Bay. Creeping at five knots, the underpowered wakeless boat, from a distance, looked more like a rock than a seiner.

Our searching paid off; when fishing reopened, we were surrounded by schools of salmon. Several times a day, three of us would squat at the edge of the rail and scoop a brailer-full of salmon from the puckered end of the net. Heaving in unison, we would spill the writhing salmon against our rain-gear clad legs and into the boat. As the boat filled up, wiggling salmon would tickle our thighs.

Most days the crew took turns pulling the anchor, and I generally steered from the open flying bridge in the 4 a.m. dusky light. Then the crew would go back to sleep while I drove to the fishing grounds. We had no auto pilot so I was unable to leave the helm. One morning, the crew asleep and me hungry, I dug around under my seat looking for an apple. I found a bag of butterscotch candies and not wanting to be tempted to eat them, I tossed them overboard. I'd seen skippers throw every dish on the boat overboard in a fit of rage because the dinner dishes weren't done. I didn't think at the time that getting rid of the candy was a big deal. Later that day Jane scrounged under my seat for the same butterscotch candies, her forehead knitted with concern.

"I threw them overboard." I said. Jane looked at me in disbelief, an impending squall visible in her eyes.

"They're my favorite," she sobbed. "My mom sent them." Then she distanced herself from me as much as a person can on a twenty-nine foot boat. She collapsed, shivering like a landed halibut on the seine pile.

I felt like shit, and my shouted apology sounded like the squawking of the nearby seagulls. I requested that candy be kept in the crews' bunks, and that I was to be kept ignorant of its existence.

We all missed our kids. But when we returned to the homestead, the imagined idyllic scene of kids skipping rocks and picking strawberries dissipated. Four, not five children stood at the water's edge, anticipating our arrival.

"Where's Tony?" Viki asked, starting the skiff to take us to the beach.

The skiff slid onto the gravel. Mary R and I disembarked to hugs and everyone talking at once. Viki leaped from the boat and ran inside the cabin where John was preparing a dinner of fresh-picked cauliflower, zucchini, and brown rice.

"I couldn't get a hold of you so I contacted Tony's dad and he took him down to your mother's in Vancouver," he explained, Viki's glare backing him into the counter. "The boys," he continued, "peed in a soda bottle and tried to get Balika to drink it. Tony was the instigator."

"How do you know that?" Viki hurled at him. "Locke is the troublemaker."

The incident caused discord for the rest of the summer among us three mothers. Viki would rail against John, Locke, and Danny. Mary R would defend Danny and I, like a proper skipper, would concentrate on fishing and refused to discuss the situation.

I continued to try to be an aggressive and fearless fisherman. I'd seen John or other fishermen set their nets a bit before the scheduled opening, and when one net went out, all others followed. At Packer Spit I set out five minutes before the season opened; other fishermen sneered and pointedly waited till it was legal to put out their nets. I felt like a thief in a convenience store in front of the security cameras. Luckily, Alaska Department of Fish and Game did not fly over and ticket me but, in spite of never again setting more than fifteen seconds before an opening, I would never live down a reputation for breaking rules.

We all prided ourselves in our efficiency. Working in quiet harmony contrasted with our previous experiences of tyrannical skippers harassing their crews. I remembered the pain of John calling me "cunt" during the stress of pulling in the net as fast as possible, his cruel and angry attempts to urge me to hurry. When John called me names, I may have momentarily hurried, but the discouragement I felt was, in the end, demoralizing.

For the most part, I was oblivious of what the other fishermen thought of us. Few spoke to us. I didn't know then that some referred to us as the "crack crew." Nor were we aware that, when we peed off the side of the boat, binoculars were trained on our asses, and surrounding mariners were guessing whose derriere was exposed.

At times, crews on nearby boats would display curiosity or infatuation for us, but mostly for Jane. One sunny morning Jane and I sat together on the flying bridge while we were under tow by the *Eskimo Princess,* in calm water between islands. Our engine silenced, we listened to water whooshing against our bow while Mary slept and Viki prepared whole-wheat fried bread on the diesel stove. Sharing a plate of apple slices, taking turns dipping each slice into an open jar of peanut butter, Jane and I inhaled the yeasty bread smell. A crewman stood on the stern of the *Eskimo Princess* and signaled Jane that he wanted to visit. She smiled and shrugged, knowing the difficulty of slowing the tow so that he could pull us in to climb aboard. Not to be discouraged, he grabbed the towline and swung off the stern of the steel seventy-foot vessel. For the next ten minutes Jane and I watched the surreal scene of him approaching our boat, hand over hand, one-hundred-fifty feet down the inch-thick tow line. The *Eskimo Princess's* wake bubbled under his buff shirtless form and the *Invader's* bow charged into the water below his bare feet.

One mid-summer weekend I decided that we should socialize and relax a bit in the cannery town of Larsen Bay. Twenty-five boats were tied up six deep for the length of the dock. Crews patched nets and changed engine oil. Sleeping bags and mattresses aired out on decks. Six packs of cheap beer hung in net-bags chilling in the fifty degree bay water. Another skipper came by, bottle of PA vodka in hand. I supplied the Tang as mixer and we toasted my success at catching as many fish as most of the men. Both of us tipsy, we careened from boat to boat as he introduced me to the other skippers. I felt important belonging to the society of salmon skippers. Yet it was humiliating to meet a skipper whom I had screeched at for setting his net too close to mine. He seemed unfazed by my foolishness.

My new friend and I climbed from boat to boat, Tang and dwindling vodka in hand. It was flat calm but the boats seemed to pitch as if in high seas. I remember slipping off the dock and someone pulling me out. I don't remember how I got back to the *Invader,* but when I woke up, my head throbbed. I was alone, feeling less like a colleague than a novelty, my clothes in a soggy pile on the floor.

After our social weekend I returned to searching for fish during closures. For the most part, my crew put up with my determination and intensity. At times both Viki and

Mary reminded me that I needed to "lighten up," prompting me to reflect about the advantages of fishing with women friends.

Most days, Viki adeptly towed her end of the net, and when her skiff was alongside the *Invader* she skillfully handed the tag-line to Mary. Viki still teases me about the time when, with her perfect teeth set in a proud grin as the skiff brushed up against our port side, she signaled that she had seen jumpers in our net. I ordered her to stop smiling. Maybe I remembered John's fears of celebrating caught fish before they are loaded aboard; or maybe I thought other fishermen would notice her beaming and rush to our hot fishing spot. Or maybe I thought that to catch fish we had to be seriously engaged in our work, that satisfaction should be delayed until the settlement checks were cashed and we returned to our families.

Throughout that year, and in trips to come, I would figure out that it is possible, in fact preferable, to have the company of friends on the boat and to actually enjoy our summers catching fish. My bitchiness, as my crew can confirm, didn't disappear with maturity. But those moments of working in harmony, and the raise in our settlement checks, certainly cooled my strong, smoldering will. ⚓

MARY JACOBS studied Anthropology at the University of California at Berkeley; in 1970, she quit college to seek adventure and fortune in Alaska. After a year of working in canneries she began crewing on fishing boats. In 1979, Mary began running the *Invader* with an all-women crew. Over the next twenty-five years she had a successful career fishing for herring, salmon, and halibut. Over the years, she bought larger vessels and hired quite a few men, but her most memorable seasons involved a crew of independent women working in harmony. Jacobs studied creative writing at Kodiak College and the University of Alaska Southeast. She has won Kodiak's Showcase of Excellence award for her writing, and had articles published in the city of Kodiak newsletter and in *Pacific Fishing*. She continues to explore the genre of creative non-fiction in writing several stories every year. For several years she read stories at Astoria, Oregon's Fisher Poets Gathering. She is retired from fishing and often returns to Kodiak to visit friends, children, and grandchildren.

GREENHORN

MICHAEL CROWLEY
makes the lucky
break from working
on the docks to
working on the
deck of a wooden
halibut schooner—
but the rewards for
a greenhorn are
tenuous.

THE SNOUT OF THE HALIBUT schooner *Attu* slammed through the spume-creased roller, hung there a moment, and then dropped into the trough. Propelled by one-hundred-twenty tons of fir planking spiked to heavy oak frames, a diesel that straddled her keel, and ice and bait packed in her hold, the sixty-five-foot schooner would have buried herself in the back side of the frigid Alaska sea, but as the hull cut into the water, her shoulders caught her, stopped the descent, and exploded the water out from the hull.

I hung over the rail, my vomit mixed with the roller's dark froth as the sea hurried on to its inevitable collision with the Alaska mainland. Below, in the dark waters, the *Attu's* big four-bladed bronze prop grabbed hold of the ocean and sent the schooner plowing onward—toward the next rearing wave.

In the fo'c's'le, Greg and Kenny were wedged into their bunks, anticipating and bracing for each drop into the void and the climb back up. Pinky and Russ were huddled over the galley table, engaged in an intense never-ending cribbage game, with bragging rights more than money at stake. Up in the wheelhouse, the stub of the skipper's cigarette burned the night, falling and rising in time with the boat's motion. This weather didn't bother them a lick. No matter how much or how quickly the old wooden hull rolled or plunged, not one of them even burped. At dinner, Dick the cook, had slung spaghetti on plates, then heaved a big pot of sauce on the galley table.

"Kid," Dick said, "you need food if you're goin' be any good on this slab. Course, if it don't settle just right in your gut, just take a piece of that bacon there," and he pointed to the shelf over the stove where a package of bacon lay ready for the frying pan, "tie it on a string, soak it in this here grease," and he tilted the pot to me so I could see the inch or two of grease and oil on top of the sauce, "and then work it up and down your throat and..."

I never heard the end. I'd been looking out the companionway at the masts weaving crazily across the stars and moon; my stomach was starting to follow the motions of the wheelhouse as it swung from one group of stars to another. One look at the spaghetti sauce grease, and I was leaping for the ladder and then stumbling to the rail before painting the ocean with what little remained of the food I had in me.

It wasn't fair. There I was, damned near worthless for deck work, yet the first time I had seen this crew, most of them could hardly stand. That was in the Pioneer Bar in Seward, Alaska.

For almost six weeks, I'd been driving a forklift at Seward Fisheries, hauling carts of halibut to be weighed after they'd been dumped out of the unloading net to have their heads sliced off by a stainless steel guillotine. After one long day, a bunch of us dock workers headed to town. At the bar, the plant foreman was looking at three guys in the corner. "God, we'll never get them unloaded in the morning," he said. It was half the crew of the *Attu*. Two of them were leaning against each other, struggling to keep from falling down while trying to hoist the third guy to his feet. He wasn't just drunk—he was passed-out-pissed-in-the-corner drunk, and before long, all three were stacked in a heap on the floor.

The next morning, the *Attu* only had about thirty-five-thousand pounds of halibut to unload, but it took as long to get the fish out of the hold as it would a boat with one-hundred-thousand pounds. Two of the crew from the previous night were in the hold, pulling halibut into the unloading net. Every time a net load of fish was hoisted out of the hold and up to the dock, both of them flopped back into the slime, fish, and ice, asleep until a hail or an empty net was dropped on them. And when a load of fish was hauled to the scales, the skipper had to be awakened to verify the weights.

Despite their condition—obviously hard-case fishermen—I wondered what it would be like to be out on a boat like the *Attu* for weeks at a time. I wanted to find out, but then I hadn't the foggiest idea how to go about it.

I was a refugee from the Lower 48, escaping San Francisco, the university, and the chaos and turmoil of the late sixties. Somewhere I still had an overcoat with buckshot holes in the back, courtesy of the Oakland County Sheriffs' Department after they'd swung, like a ragged Roman phalanx, around a corner, their mouths open, gulping for air, their eyes full of blood, anger, and adrenaline. They had leveled shotguns down the street, at the backs of fleeing students. Later in the day, I'd watched one of the sheriffs swing his shotgun up to a rooftop along Berkeley's Telegraph Avenue and blast the life out of a kid who had maybe—and maybe not—hurled a rock at the street below.

I had seen too many figures slide through the alleys and back streets, one stumble ahead of a beating or a bad drug deal. Side stepped too many piles of dog shit on the sidewalks. Pushed through too many panhandlers' outstretched hands. Finally I did what others have done for generations when they didn't fit in—fled to the wilderness for strength and rejuvenation.

There was no more wilderness in the West, so it was north to Alaska. In the late spring of 1968, I stood in a line at the San Francisco airport, a backpack and suitcase at my feet, a ticket in my hand, less than $100 in my pocket, working hard to ignore the airport signs that read:

DO NOT GO TO ALASKA EXPECTING
TO FIND WORK. THERE ISN'T ANY.

Once I got there, despite the airport signs, I was lucky. Petersburg Fisheries had chosen that spring to pump a lot of money into Seward Fisheries to draw boats to its docks that would otherwise have gone to Kodiak or Prince Rupert to unload. Within a couple of days I had a job, and soon I started asking every skipper who unloaded fish if there wasn't a chance aboard his boat. "Sorry, kid. Won't take any greenhorns," was the response again and again.

One skipper did say: "Kid. Maybe you'd make the good man, but forget it. Save your money. Someday go on one of those nice cruise ships. Then you can say you've been on the sea."

That same week, halibut schooners came in to unload after the first trip of the season. After that, no other type of boat interested me. With a long, lean hull, two masts and a small wheelhouse aft, the halibut schooner still had the lines of the old sailing boats. In fact, none were built after 1927, and most came from yards around

Ballard, Washington. They were shaped with adzes, slicks, steam-powered ship saws, and the brute force and ingenuity of squarehead ship carpenters and designers.

At one time, my brother and I had pitched sleeping bags and backpacks onto the floor of a Southern Pacific boxcar as it was hauling out of the Oakland freight yard. We had rattled north to Vancouver, British Columbia, and then east across the foot of Canada to Halifax and Lunenburg, Nova Scotia, in search of old sailing codfishermen, from the time of the *Bluenose* and the *Gertrude Theabaud*.

Standing there on the Seward docks, I knew this was the closest I'd ever get to the old sailing schooners. These halibut schooners felt like kin—distant kin to be sure, with modern diesels bolted down over the keel and sails long gone from the masts— but kin nevertheless.

One afternoon, some of the gang from the docks pulled up at the house and cried out: "Hey, Crowley, the *Attu* can't find its cook. They'll take you if you want to go!" I didn't hesitate a second. For the first time I'll see the sea from somewhere other than a distance, I thought, my pulse racing. I didn't have the proper clothes or gear for fishing—no foul-weather gear, no thick-soled boots, no "wristers" that protected your shirtsleeves forearms, no wool pants or long underwear, which I knew were worn even in the summer. But some of the crew pitched in and gave me wristers; a guy at the cannery gave me his stream leaders and a set of rainwear that was good for an afternoon of lake fly-fishing. It wasn't much, but I would have worn anything.

It wasn't long before that dream seemed short-lived. Steaming out of Resurrection Bay, Donny, who was one of the most easy-going skippers you'd ever meet, had a rush of guilt at leaving the cook behind. A short discussion took place in the pilothouse, then the wheel spun hard over, the throttle pegged, and the *Attu* headed back to find its cook. And my fate now was—hell, I didn't know what.

The *Attu* tied up and the crew piled into two beat-up cabs and headed into town. The bars were the first place to check. Then inquiries were made of several select women, and finally Dick was found in a restaurant, unconcerned—as if it wasn't the first time—over the possibility that he'd almost missed a fishing trip. Once more the *Attu* headed out of Resurrection Bay. And I was still aboard. After Dick's retrieval, Donny was obviously uncomfortable having a greenhorn aboard, but he told me, "It wouldn't be fair not to take you. You can go. And if you're worth it, you'll get a quarter-share this trip. After that we'll see how you do," he said, noncommittal. I knew that to mean that the crew would vote on the size of my share based on how I did. A quarter-share was generous, I felt. Some greenhorns only got oilskins and boots on their first trip. But hell, I would have gone for nothing, even had I known I'd be hanging over the railing half the way across the Gulf of Alaska.

Not far out in the gulf, Donny pointed the bow on a course to take her outside of Kodiak Island, where we would start fishing. Locked inside the schooner's hull for the next three weeks were five fishermen and me, along with $700 worth of groceries, and 6,000 gallons of fuel to feed the *Attu's* big Caterpillar diesel. Beneath the main deck's hatch were ten and a half tons of flake ice and 8,500 pounds of frozen bait: 3,500 pounds of salmon, 2,000 pounds of octopus, 2,000 pounds of cod, and 1,000 pounds of herring.

The wind was picking up and stood right on her snout as the schooner cut through the chop. On the foredeck, spray whipped past our faces as we stared off to westward.

"You keep an eye open," Russ said solemnly. "Soon as you see the first halibut come to the surface, holler out."

I nodded.

"See, when halibut start swimming to the top, well, then you know you're in a good spot to set your gear," Dick added.

They stood and watched with me for a minute, then went below.

I had only been up there about five minutes when I heard the laughter roll out of the fo'c's'cle. I realized that I'd been had. Halibut are bottom feeders, as I soon learned, and they spend their life on the ocean floor, not swimming about on the surface. Sheepishly I went below to get my deserved ribbing.

About one that morning, Greg woke me.

"It's time to bait up."

"Now it starts," muttered Pinky, one of the few things I'd heard him say that wasn't laced with four-letter words and references to female anatomy.

"Sixty skates," Donny called out from the wheelhouse. That was a lot of gear in the water. A skate is a single nylon line usually about three-hundred fathoms, with a hook attached every twenty feet or so. From out of the hold came salmon, octopus, and herring, enough to bait more than six-thousand hooks. My job was chopping bait—the very bottom rung of the ladder that leads up to a full share. Russ showed me how to cut up the bait without chopping off my hand or fingers. The frozen octopus goes on a big round block of wood that sits on the hatch. Then, using a meat cleaver, the octopus is cut into chunks about three inches by an inch and a half. What makes chopping bait potentially treacherous, especially for a new guy, is the continual pitching and rolling of the deck. Bring the cleaver down just as the bow slams into a wave, and fingers are part of the bait.

To get ahead, Russ was also chopping bait, while the rest of the crew started baiting the skates. The crew wouldn't let me bait—not until near the end of the trip.

It would be a long time before I would bait a skate. As Pinky would periodically remind me, "The only time greenhorns don't screw things up is when they're asleep. And since we don't get much of that, we're just trying to protect you from yourself."

Six or seven hours later, the last of the skates were tied up. The flagpoles and buoy lines were all in place; the anchors were rigged, and the bags ready to go over the side.

"As soon as we eat, we're setting the gear," says Donny.

The cook's got a breakfast of eggs, sausage, pancakes, juice, potatoes, and coffee. This is the first complete meal I've been able to put down since we left Seward three days ago.

It took three hours to set the gear. We put six strings of ten skates each in sixty-fathom water. The strings were set over a small ridge, parallel to each other with a three-minute birth between them. Six hours after we set, we started picking up the first string.

Donny swung the *Attu's* bow into the wind to pick up the flagpole while Greg filed the end of the gaff hook to a sharp point. Coming alongside the flagpole, Russ and Greg heaved it aboard and wound the buoy line around the gurdy's sheave (The gurdy, a stand-up affair, with a horizontal sheave, is the winch that hauls the ground-line aboard.)

Once the buoy line came aboard, Russ sat down on an old metal tractor seat at the far edge of the hatch, placed a skate bottom on the deck, and began to coil the groundline. When he finished one skate, he carried it aft and rebaited it while someone else coiled down the next skate.

Greg worked the roller, a small aluminum drum that acts as a lead to the gurdy and over which the groundline passes. The roller man's job is the most demanding and important job on deck. He has to gaff the fish and bring them aboard and make sure the line doesn't part on the bottom. At the same time, he has to watch out for flying hooks. A few years ago, a hook caught up in a plank, then snapped free and lodged in Donny's eye, robbing him of half his sight.

"Hey! Hey!" Greg cried. "Fish coming! Fish coming!"

As the *Attu* rolled down to the water, Greg snapped off the gurdy and in the same motion struck at the ocean with his gaff. There was a flurry of water.

"Gimme a hand," Greg cried, his body pumping up and down, then left and right as the fish struggled to escape the gaff and hook. Russ jumped next to him, swinging his own gaff. They both pulled hard, each with a foot braced against the gunnel, backs straining, until they heaved a dark, wide shape above the rail. One final effort and the fish came over the side.

"It's about one-fifty, I'd say," Greg offered as he slipped the hook from the halibut's mouth. Russ swung a heavy wooden club, stunning the fish. It flapped its massive tail once before Russ slung it onto the hatch. He slipped his knife inside the belly flap, and in two or three quick motions, he cut the gills free, sliced open the belly, and removed the stomach and guts. Last, the sweet meat and blood line were scraped out, and the fish was dropped into the hold, ready to be iced.

While all this was happening, I was still chopping bait, wondering when—or if—I'd be able to go to the roller and bring in fish like that. It seemed so strange that this crew, which could barely function when I first saw them, now worked so smoothly together at sea, each knowing exactly what was expected of them. Now, I was the odd man out, the one viewed with skepticism and suspicion. I knew it would be a long time before that changed.

All the while, the *Attu* moved smoothly over the long, easy swells of a distant storm.

At 6 a.m., twenty-nine hours later, the original sixty skates had been hauled and Donny called a halt. In between strings, we reset all but a few skates. We'd start hauling again in three hours—it was our first break. I didn't even take the time to dip into the hot chocolate Dick made. After washing away the salt caking my face and eyes, I stripped out of my oilskins and boots and rolled into the bunk. Thank God it was the bottom bunk, because I didn't think I had the energy to climb into a top bunk. I'd heard of some fishermen who don't even bother to shed their oilskins when they sleep, so they're ready to go as soon as someone wakes them.

That's how it went for three weeks; for every eighteen to thirty hours of work, we got three or four hours of sleep. Hook after skate after skate after hook, night and day until I lost track of how many days we had been out. I became an expert at quick catnaps. Standing up, sitting down, I could doze for thirty seconds or two minutes and wake up and feel refreshed, at least for a short period of time. I was continually wet and cold. The sport-fishing boots I was wearing leaked through a multitude of tiny hook punctures and knife holes. The oilskins were equally porous. My daydreaming was no longer of cars, women, parties, or even the end of this trip, but owning a stout pair of rubber boots with felt liners and real honest-to-God fisherman's oilskins.

The only thing that kept us going was food, and there was plenty of that. Every meal was a several-course affair, but there were only ten to fifteen minutes to wolf the food down and follow it up with coffee before you were back on deck.

There was occasional relief from the long hours on deck when we made a run to another fishing spot or when a big enough storm moved in. One long run meant nearly eight hours in the bunk. Another time it blew seventy to eighty miles per hour and we did nothing but jog to a flagpole for the day and a half it took the storm to blow through.

That was my first storm, and when I went for my wheel-watch they told me only to "keep 'er into the wind" and to hand-steer her because the iron mike couldn't keep up with the boat's motions. It was a rain-blown dark night that had turned the Gulf of Alaska into a swirling, tumbling wasteland with marauding seas slamming against the hull and filling the deck. For the first time in my life, I knew real fear as I felt the *Attu* sink and then rise, trying to shake herself free of boarding seas. I wanted someone with me up in the wheelhouse who knew what the hell they were doing, but I stuck it out alone, spraddle-legged behind the wheel, fighting my own anxieties and the heaving vessel, gripping the spokes of the wooden wheel probably as hard as they'd ever been gripped.

After that introduction to Alaska weather, I found a quiet kind of reassurance in standing behind the big wheel and checking the course on the binnacle compass, armed on each side with painted cast-iron spheres. Well, here I am, I thought. For the rest of my life I'll be able to say I went longlining on a halibut schooner in the Gulf of Alaska. I knew not many would be able to say that.

When it came time to wake the next man for his wheel turn, I'd take a quick look around the horizon to locate any boats, climb the three steps out of the wheelhouse, and scurry across the main deck to the fo'c's'le and galley, timing the run to make sure I didn't get doused by a wave in the process, then push open the companionway doors and drop into the fo'c's'le—a wedge-shaped cavernous space lit by a small light bulb.

Farther forward were two sets of bunks, seven feet by shoulder width, about right for a coffin. On the port side were two more bunks. Some of the bunks were strung with curtains smudged with dirt and fish blood. Behind those curtains was the only privacy a crewman had for three to four weeks at a time. For most it was a room away from home. For others, like an old Norwegian halibut fisherman who told me, "Kid, a woman's place is ashore. A man's place is on the boat," it was home itself.

One morning after breakfast, just before we started to haul in the skates, Donny climbed out of the fo'c's'le and announced in a loud voice, "We're going to shake the gear as it comes aboard." Everyone sighed with relief. We were going to take the old bait off the hooks, tie up the skates, and go in.

Once all the skates were stacked on the stern and we started washing down the boat, the *Attu* headed up Shelikof Straits, then went through Ouzinkie Narrows and across Monashka Bay on its way to Kodiak. Up in the fo'c's'le, the crew took turns at the porcelain sink that drained into a bucket. They poured hot water into the bowl to wash up and shave, then splashed on cologne to mask the stench of three weeks of sweat, halibut slime, and blood. Going into Ouzinkie Narrows, I threw the same underwear I'd worn for three weeks over the stern: the mark of a completed halibut trip.

Once ashore, I took the several hundred bucks I got for my quarter share and bought myself a good pair of rubber boots, oilskins, wool pants, and a wool shirt. I wasn't a fisherman yet, but at least I could dress like one.

After a couple of days' lay-up, we headed out on back-to-back trips, stocked up with bait, fuel, and food. This time, I was determined to move up to half share, but I knew I had to do more than chop bait and dress fish, which I had started to do the previous trip. After about a week, Donny took me aside and said, "Okay, Mike, why don't you try coiling a skate?"

It didn't look that hard; he even slowed the gurdy down to make it easier, but I was nothing but thumbs. Everyone else aboard laid the groundline down in neat coils about eighteen inches in diameter, with the hooks laid out on the coiled line. Day after day I tried to coil like the rest of the crew, but all I accomplished was to cover most of the foredeck with a snarl of line and hooks. Russ said it was danger-ous to even be near me when I was coiling. "Get caught up in that eagle's nest, and you'll never get out," he said. Finally I started to doubt myself. The fear of failure raised its snout, and all the self-assurance I'd started to gain slid away. The romantic image of being able to earn my way at sea, to be accepted at full share, had come up against reality and reality was winning. For the first time I started to think of myself as clumsy, uncoordinated, and ignorant.

Every waking and sleeping moment I thought about coiling, going over it in my mind, trying to visualize how to hold the line, how to reach for the hook, and all the while afraid I'd never get it down. At the end of the trip, I knew Donny would say: "Sorry, Mike, it's just not working out." Or maybe they wouldn't even wait till we got to shore. I'd heard about the greenhorn that turned out to be such a misfit that the crew put him in the fish hold for a few hours and then sent him to his bunk for the last two weeks of the trip. He was allowed out only to use the head and could only eat when everyone else was in their bunks for their three or four hours of sleep.

My coiling and snarls stalked me relentlessly. In one dream, the groundline and hooks were coming through the hatch and into my bunk. I began to coil it, but no matter how hard I tried, it was only creating a bigger snarl. In the midst of my tor-ment, I was woken up by Russ: "Hey, Mike. What the hell?"

I came out of my slumber and both Russ and Pinky were staring at me, shaking their heads, and laughing. I had been coiling the electrical wire mat that ran over my bunk to the reading light. I'd ripped it off the wall and was trying to coil it down over my chest.

By the time we'd finished the trip, I had gotten the hang of coiling. It wasn't pretty, but it was passable. At least the crew didn't leave what it was doing and gather around the hatch and comment about my abilities.

I'd also been given a half share, though in terms of money, it didn't mean that much. Fishing had been lousy. We'd been out forty-five days and hadn't made expenses. My half share entitled me to pay $14 back to the boat for the last trip's pod. But I wasn't worried about money. Until we went fishing again, it didn't cost anything to sleep on the boat, and there was plenty of grub in the lockers. ⚓

MICHAEL CROWLEY lives in Maine and writes about commercial fishing for the *National Fisherman*, serving as the boats & gear editor. He is also a contributing writer for *Work Boat* magazine. He wrote the text for *Down the Shore: The Faces of Maine's Coastal Fisheries*. Previous to coming to Maine, Crowley spent several years on halibut schooners out of Seattle. Between halibut trips in Kodiak, suffering from a hangover, he saw a for-sale ad in the *National Fisherman* for a scaled-down replica of the Canadian schooner *Bluenose* based in Camden, Maine. She was built by William Lawrence Allen, first mate on the original *Bluenose*. Always a sucker for a nice-looking boat with a romantic pedigree, Crowley bought the schooner. Because Maine is a long commute from the halibut grounds in Alaska, he quit baiting halibut hooks and began a writing career.

"For they plant the wind, and shall reap the whirlwind ..." —Hosea 8:7

ONE SKIFF, TWO WOMEN: A CONSTANT HARVEST

LESLIE LEYLAND FIELDS and her twenty-two-year-old daughter reluctantly work together in a skiff off Kodiak Island, planning a last season of commercial fishing together.

IT'S A SLOW NIGHT on the water. I'm thankful. But it's a jellyfish night, or rather, a jellyfish week. The ocean is thick with them, like mucus, these aurelia aurita, moon jellyfish, the clear kind that look like ocean water plus Knox gelatin, with a little hyphenated cross as its entrails. It doesn't stop the work. Naphtali, twenty-one, motors the skiff forward along the net as a steady stream of jellies slop through the bow roller into the skiff. The floor of the skiff is now just a mass of congealed water and little broken crosses I have to stand on and in.

I don't mind these. They feel somewhat antiseptic, and even holy, with a holy-ghost body. But other jellyfish come with them, these giant glops of oranges, pinks, rusts, as large as sinks, even bathtubs at times, their stinging strings like snot trailing behind. They're bagged in the net and as we move forward, they'll travel the length of the twenty-six-foot skiff. We lift our hands as they pass, narrow our eyes to protect our faces and skin from errant splashes of acid until each one disappears off the stern with a slurp. Some leave their entrails at my feet.

Every minute or so I release the spring in my neck and look around. We're on the backside of our island, Harvester Island, a four-hundred-acre teardrop that rises up to a single peak at nine-hundred feet. "Ours" sounds proprietary, but we are, in fact, the only inhabitants of the island. We pick berries and wild flowers from its grasses, but our real catch is here, in these waters. We're on the Shelikof Strait, a forty- by three-hundred-mile length of water, fenced by mountain ranges on both sides, Kodiak Island on the one side, the Alaska Peninsula range on the other, as toothed and lofty as any mountains I've seen in the world. They are one of the few fixtures in this world that remains in place. The water is always moving, carrying us the ten miles from one net to the other, one island to another, delivering the salmon we depend on to our nets. But the ocean currents are generous and indiscriminate, delivering far more than fish.

"Are you picking the kelp?' I ask, my voice an attempt at neutral. My views on the futility of kelp-picking are known. I'll haul out the bull kelp, the massive heads, and twenty-foot long tubal bodies that throng and choke the net. I'll untangle the twigs and branches that get forked in the mesh along with the kelp; I'll extract the sculpins knotted at the bottom of the leadline— but the grass and finger kelp and rockweed—when the tide turns, the current will pull most of it out.

"Yes, we're picking everything. There's not many fish, so at least we can keep the net clean," she says, snapping her large green eyes at me. It's her father's fault she's so precise. When I fished with him in the early days, no matter the state of exhaustion, the darkness, or how many thousands of fish had been picked already that day, every finger of kelp had to be extracted. I worked in dumb silence beside him, my protests abandoned.

She's throwing the grasses and kelp in the skiff, behind her and beside her, where it joins the jellyfish on the bottom.

"The tide's already begun to turn," I say with an attempt to sound casual.

"Are you sure we have to keep the kelp? If we throw it in front of us, the current will take it away. "

"It's not going anywhere for another hour, at least. I don't want to have to pick it out of the nets again."

I know the rules. Whoever is running the outboard, is the skipper. Never mind that she is my daughter, thirty years younger. But whatever comes into the skiff has to come out. And it's my job to get it out. Already I'm ankle deep. Soon we'll have a load of everything from the ocean but fish. I squat just inches from the slop and begin bailing it over, slowly, so it doesn't splash into my eyes. It's our doing. We set our nets and tend them as though we've picketed a backyard plot. But this is Alaska. And our plot covers ten miles of open, stormy ocean. Why do we think we can weed and tend the ocean?

. . . .

I get frustrated when I fish with my mother. Today, as the jellyfish slide over the roller and plop down onto the floor into a Jell-O-like pile of clear, pink, orange, and red goop, she reacts like a girl, scrunching her nose in disgust and turning her face away from the invading army.

In the skiff and in life, I've learned to play opposites. Since she is cringing, I stoically speed up, whipping forward through the net, empty but for these glooping aliens. When we finish, she pulls a pole out of the bow to release the net back into the water. I reverse with the motor and we ease away, the tangled mesh, corkline, and leads all sliding over the bow and into the ocean to sink once more into an invisible underwater wall. Mom looks back at me with a grimace and gestures to the ankle-deep soup of jellies.

"I guess it's jelly week, huh?" she says.

"More like jelly month," I respond, impatient to continue on. She looks at our fish, maybe five or six for our efforts, and makes another veteran comment.

"This is so pathetic."

"Yep," I reply.

She looks at me for a second as if she had something to add, but seeing my face steeled into the mask I wear for serious driving, she stops herself. She looks around the plastic totes for the bailer and starts scooping up big pieces of mangled jellyfish and dumping them over the side. She does it half-heartedly, and we get to the next net before the skiff is close to clean.

"She gets dizzy when she bails," I think to myself, and try to muster a better attitude. But the sun is shining today, and the jellyfish smell like a sickly-sweet medicine gone rotten. If she doesn't keep the skiff clean, it's going to stink this afternoon

. . . .

The tide is twenty-one feet today, which means the lines and nets in the water are all as taut as wires. "Sway's coming up!" Naphtali shouts at me over the sound of the outboard. I wasn't watching, though that's my job as bowman. I'm not as attentive as I should be in the skiff. Sometimes I'm sorting through decades of summer and work here, every fish that noses over the bow and into the skiff comes laden with history, generations of fish before it. In my early years out here, in the late 1970s, I worked in the skiff with Duncan, my husband, her father, until the year I said no more. Naphtali will never really know all I've done and all that happened in the skiff before she was born. I don't intend this constant harvest. It's a heavy load sometimes. I want new memories. And I want to better remember the good that has happened on these waters as well.

The sway buoy rises before me now. I clamber up to the bow shelf as best I can in my full raingear and leaden boots. I lean over into the water to lift the sway buoy and the line of the net over the bow. I seize it, but the line is so taut, it can snap my arm in two. I cannot budge it. But we can't finish this net unless I lift the line over the bow.

I hang there, one arm anchored to the immovable line, the other holding the rest of me from going overboard. I keep trying, using two hands now, though I risk slipping on the wet aluminum or falling overboard entirely. I do not feel powerless. I am strong, I think. I have built houses, run long miles, hiked mountains all over the world, but I am not young. I cannot bulldog my way through even this first hard task.

This is my idea. We're going to fish together an entire season next year, just Naphtali and I in the skiff. It will be my last season in the skiff, a final hurrah. Who better to spend it with than my only daughter? This is our trial run, right now, in the last week of this season, before Naphtali returns to college, before I return to Kodiak with my sons for school. The thought of returning to the skiff next year excites me—and scares me. I don't know if I can do it, for so many reasons. Right now, this unliftable line is one of them.

"Can't get it!" I call back, finally signaling my retreat. I don't look back at her.

"Let it down," she announces flatly. I know she's disappointed in me. I pull the pole out of the bow, let the net snake back into the water, and we reverse out of the net. We'll pick it up in another place, returning to this spot from the other direction.

She's not crazy about the plan for next year. She didn't even want me to come out with her tonight. What about a whole season?

. . . .

She can't get the sway over the roller. I can see her straining in the bow, using all her weight as leverage against the tight line, but I can't keep the sternness from my face. Uncle Wallace and his crew are on this net, too. Putting it down and starting again is an admission of weakness, acknowledging some difference between this feminine crew and the normal male configuration, and unlike my mother, I can't do that yet.

I go up to the bow to try and help her, but she was right, the line is too tight to lift. As I back away so we can re-approach the net, she smiles in triumph as if to say, "See? That wasn't so hard."

What she hasn't thought about is what's coming next, a hard landing on a net that we now have to pull in by hand without the motor's help. We've avoided one problem, but pulling up to the leads in this new approach is going to be worse.

She comes to the stern after we land so we can get the leads up to my picking pole. Both of us stretch out splayed, claw-like fingers and grab the mesh. We arch our spines and lean backwards, pulling with the strength where we have it—in our butts and thighs. We breathe and pull in tandem, watching the heavy, weighted leads slowly emerge from the water and inch towards us. When they are within armshot, I reach for them, hugging them to my chest and leaning my torso back into the skiff. Mom has a pole ready and we snap it in place. After five minutes of pulling, we can now proceed to the first of five sections of the net.

We do two sections this way, pulling in the slow, steady agony of draft horses and then proceeding down a line that has no fish for our efforts. Uncle Wallace, who has finished his portion in the time it takes us to do less than half of ours, drives up and offers to get the rest. I'm exhausted from pulling, and mom has never supported stubbornness when help is offered. I swallow my pride and nod. They jump on, and we drive to an easier net.

. . . .

I came to commercial fishing in Alaska thirty-two years ago the old way, by marriage—a way that younger women scorn as weak, following a man. I hear it in the narrow voices of twenty-something women who have interviewed me. They make assumptions, that leaving all you know and joining another life five-thousand miles away is dependent. Believing that staying these decades through work-obsession and profound isolation is weakness.

I've fished through the years as I could—in between six pregnancies and nursing six babies, between writing books and prepping to teach college classes, cooking massive meals, carrying water in buckets, washing clothes in an old wringer washer. I was afraid if I stepped out of fishing entirely, if I lost the kind of endurance and fearlessness required on the water, that I would never go back. I would get weak. And I would start getting old.

My daughter's story is different. She was born into commercial salmon fishing. As a baby, on calm days, we would dress her in tiny raingear and bring her out into the skiff sitting upright in an aluminum laundry tub. I remember one night out on the water when she was three. We found a herring in the net and handed it to her. A fish just her size! Her hands joyfully circled its small body. She held the herring the entire time we were out, then near the end, as we motored to the delivery boat, the tender, she set it down in the bin with the salmon, and petted him good nap. At the tender, as we sorted and tossed the salmon into the brailers, I turned beyond her eyes and slipped her herring, splashless, into the water. In just a few years, she will do this herself, I thought. She'll know instantly what to pull into the skiff, what has value, and what to throw back.

By the time she was nine, she was fishing every day. At twelve, she was full-time in the skiff. At sixteen she ran her own skiff, training and running crewmen five to ten years older than she. I know her story; I gave her a huge part of her story. But I don't know, really, what she thinks of it. We don't talk about this. I don't know how she tells it to others.

We fish from a setnet site that perches on the edge of the Shelikof Strait. In the summer, our islands are as green as jewels, snugly surrounded by the blue sea. It is the most beautiful place in the world.

My grandfather came here to fish for salmon in the sixties, bringing his wife and three sons to a wilderness cabin on Bear Island. Its previous occupant had been an alcoholic who, as he descended into madness, swore that people were coming and cutting steaks off his cows as they grazed. My grandfather passed fishing on to my uncles and father, who taught me to take pride in my work on the sea, our strength as a family, our enduring legacy. I was told we were the biggest setnetting operation in Alaska, that we worked on some of the roughest water for setnetters, that our season was one of the longest.

I believed all of these things because I could not imagine another family having the audacity to fish in waves so big you couldn't see over them to the other skiffs, wind so hard it whipped williwaws into our stiff backs as we kept working. I believed what I was told—and I've learned since that those facts are not the whole story.

We have four nets still to go now. We're on the Seal now, a long net that extends one-hundred-fifty fathoms, six-hundred feet, out into the bay. The nets are full of jellyfish and random kelp on this side of the island too. As we begin the slow pull of jellyfish over the bow, and occasional weeding of grass, we talk. We talk about life after college, applying for a Fulbright, living in South America. We talk about the books we're reading. I'm reading Uwen Akpan's Say You're One of Them. She's reading Kingsolver's The Poisonwood Bible. I tell her about the essay I'm working on; she describes a theatre piece she's starting.

We're soaked in ocean water, standing in an organic soup, fish blood streaks our raingear, bent over nets that never end. I can almost say I hate this work right now—but these words, these words about words. These words with the one whose name means "she speaks beautiful words." The skiff is brimming and buoyant with these words. I want more of them. Next year, Naphtali will have just graduated college. She won't need fishing money for tuition anymore.

When she was seventeen, she stood before me in her raingear, soberly pulling on her gloves before the afternoon pick. The summer had just begun. "I can't face another season." She looked at me, numb. A stone fell into my pocket. I had no words to cheer her for the three months ahead. She knew what was coming, how every day would play out, but we needed her. She needed the money for college. She couldn't quit or leave. Every summer I think is her last.

Naphtali motors the skiff now past the sway buoy and comes in for the landing. This is my part. I throw myself over the side and try to snag the corkline with my arm as we approach it, but she's going too fast and she doesn't come in close enough. I miss.

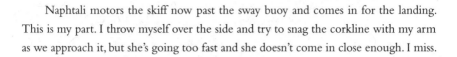

Mom's standing in the bow as I maneuver the skiff towards the shore sway. She's too busy planning our season to notice the upcoming corkline and I have to tell her to pick it up before we miss it altogether. The first time we try to land she misses it and looks back towards me with a slight frown,

"Slow down, Naphtali. I don't have six-foot-long arms."

"Exactly," I think to myself as I reposition the skiff for a softer landing, "that's why this project is a bad idea."

As we pull up toward the lead line together she is still talking about her idea of fishing and writing together. I don't want to dampen her enthusiasm, but I'm not convinced.

"What's in it for me?" I ask. "I understand the interest for you, returning to fishing after twenty years, but what do I write about? Fishing's all I've done. It's normal; I don't write about normal."

She shoots me one of her looks. "But writing gives you the chance to see things in a way you've never seen them. It gives you permission to take notice of what you ignore in your routine."

I stare down at the muscled humpy writhing in my hand. I look at its perfect pattern of scales, the marbled blue and green of its head. "I already see," I think mutinously.

She'll keep her place in the stern, and I'll stay in the bow most of the time. This means my daughter is my skipper; I am her crewman—all summer. I don't know if I can. I get sick in heaving seas. The work in the bow is the heaviest. My back, shoulder, and hips are getting testy. I am not what she wants. I am smaller than her, not larger. Not a twenty-one-year-old but a fifty-two-year-old and not a guy but a woman and not just a woman but her mother.

Could anything be worse for her? I doubt it. But she has lived so much of her life in an aluminum boat. I've missed too much of it. It's simply floated by. I can't get it back.

I was seventeen the year I started driving full time. Driving terrified me, I had been a bowman since I was nine, perfecting the art of leaning over the side of the skiff with my hip-booted feet vertical in the air, pressing my hipbones against the side to keep myself from falling into the water. I worked with my dad at first, then my brother and I got our own skiff and now, finally, I was alone and in charge, skipper of my own vessel, number fourteen.

Growing up, I was petrified of failure, especially in fishing. Suddenly there I was, standing at the stern of my own skiff, skipper, accountable for so much more than just grabbing the net and picking fish. Anything that went wrong was my fault. In the bow I had freedom; I would dance around as we drove from net to net. I felt lithe and powerful as I threw kelp out of the boat and lifted the sway buoy over the roller. Standing in the bow was quiet, away from the persistent grumble of the sixty-horsepower motor. I got to lean my head close to the waves, knife in hand, and cut strands of bull kelp off the net while the skipper stood and waited.

Now, trapped in the stern, I would be forced to watch new crewmen agonize with nets and lines and kelp, knowing I could do the job better. I would be responsible for keeping my bowman on task, making sure my skiff was keeping up with the others, landing on beaches without scraping my prop against a rock.

Driving propelled me to the status of the crewmembers I had always idolized. Now there was no distinction between our respective work. I, like them, was expected to demonstrate a clear head in all situations. The autonomy scared me. When I screwed up, as I inevitably would, there would be no one with more experience to point to. My father's intensity in the skiff was legendary—and now it would be directed at me.

I was a great bowman. I wanted to stay there.

· ·

Between nets, as we motor from one to the other, I bail, returning what isn't ours back to the ocean. I hold the rail tightly but my arm is loose, my knees stay soft, my legs absorb the bucking motion of the boat. I scoop carefully as we go, releasing the water, jellyfish, and sludge in a controlled dump, taking note of the prevailing wind, so we're not bathed any further in it. It's a constant exchange. We sieve from the water the salmon fish—eager and egg-bent for their river, the river of their birth, to spill their seed and milt. So many thousands the riverbeds are choked and the system is overspent. We collect them, then, these extras we call ours, who would further overwhelm a tired ecosystem. And between our gatherings, we give back what we don't want and can't use.

Sometimes the ocean takes from us as well. My husband and sons have nearly sunk their skiffs under crushing waves more times than I know. Naphtali, at fifteen, out in a forty-five-knot blow, was snatched from the skiff by the hand of a wave. She went under, then came up gasping, the ocean heaving her up again. My first years in the skiff, one of my jobs was to nurse the net as it uncoiled, sizzling, pulled into the ocean at full speed by the motor. If my boot caught, I would go overboard with it. I almost went over more than once. I dreamt of the ocean pulling me in and under, my own orange rain-geared body uncoiling underwater, an ungraceful orange blossom.

Later, we deliver our fish to the tender, mostly silent now in the near dark, the day's work declared done. The salmon we caught were mostly today's fish, not thirty-year-old fish, I note. And all the conversation. I am filled to overflowing. It's possible to do this, I think. I look over at Naphtali, scrupulously cleaning her skiff. Her face still hasn't softened.

. . . .

I'm not sure I want to do this next year. When she lifts up a line, I worry about her back; when she bails, I want to do it for her. She brings out the same protective instincts that I scorn from the men around me. She's impatient with my worry, as well. I'm not used to being the strong one in the skiff, the last resort if a line won't snap neatly over the bow or the leads refuse to rise out of the water. Now, I cringe when she strains against a line while I maneuver with the motor, doing little to help her. I don't really want to do this.

I wonder if this transition to watchful worry will only continue, if fishing is a foreshadowing of our relationship to come, and I don't want to think about it. Maybe that's why I'm reluctant to work with her on the water.

I'm not ready to take care of my mother.

. . . .

I wonder, what will be our harvest for a season together? I don't want all of it. I want the words, the net of words we'll weave around it all. Our lives rejoined, stitched together again. But I don't want the grasses, the jellyfish, the old memories, the kelp; I don't want the eight-foot seas in a storm; the missed lines, the blood, the arguments.

If I could, I would throw some of this back, but it all comes together in a massive knot, like the nets themselves after a storm, when the threads wind into a foot-thick chord we then must heave from the water and untangle, mesh by mesh.

I know now what I am hoping: that we are strong enough to haul it in; and that some of those times, we are strong enough to let it go. ⚓

LESLIE LEYLAND FIELDS lives in Kodiak during the winters; summers she works in commercial salmon fishing with her family on a remote island on the edge of the Shelikof Strait. The last season before publication of this book was her thirty-fourth. Fields is author of seven other books, including *Surviving the Island of Grace: A Life on the Wild Edge of America; The Entangling Net: Alaska's Commercial Fishing Women Tell Their Lives,* and her most recent, *The Spirit of Food: 34 Writers on Feasting and Fasting toward God.* She travels frequently nationwide to speak at conferences, retreats, and universities.

A DAY IN THE LIFE

I WAKE BEFORE THE ALARM, as I always do on fishing mornings. Nights before fishing, I'm never really asleep but only waiting, monitoring the wind and water. For hours already, I've listened to the creek trickle and the songbirds warble. Now I sit up and look outside. The skiff—which I always check first—is still on the mooring, slack on its line and milk-cow tame. In the northeast sky, behind layers of low clouds, the sun glows with an oyster-shell light. The water lies as flat and dull as a pewter plate, its edge solid against the shore. It's my kind of fishing day. It might also be a very good one. We're in the third week of July, and the sockeye run should be close to its peak.

Ken stirs. "Wicked surf," he teases. He knows I've worried all night that the weather might change. He's never in his life worried about something he couldn't affect, and he prides himself on his ability to fall asleep the second he puts his head down and to sleep through the most raging of storm.

I get up and dress, then make myself a bowl of instant oatmeal. I learned a long time ago that if I didn't eat before

NANCY LORD,
who has setnet for salmon in Cook Inlet, Alaska, for twenty-four seasons, depicts a day in the skiff.

going out to fish, something would happen that would keep me from eating until way past the point of low-blood-sugar grouchiness. It's one of the laws of fishing, like another I generally obey: take raingear or it'll be sure to rain. Ken, however, doesn't need to eat. He waits until the last minute to get out of bed and throw on his clothes.

Chest waders, flotation vest, raingear, hat, glasses, gloves, lunch box. I run down my mental checklist. Make sure Ken has his knife. We go out the door.

The tide is still coming in, an easy tide to set on. It's a day of tides, all in all—large enough to move fish but not large enough that the water will suck out as we watch, or leave our low-water sets in rock piles. We carry our nets to the water's edge; then we carry the rowboat down, and Ken rows for the skiff.

Ken motors in and we load the nets. He does leads and I corks, piling them into the center and port bins so they'll set neatly over the stern, in order. We work quickly and silently, except when I ask, "This one?" before grabbing a new end and Ken grunts in response. Most inlet setnetters divide their allowed gear into three thirty-five-fathom nets—indeed, that's the norm for most areas—but we fish more nets of shorter lengths, as short as ten fathoms. Throughout the day we move, switch, replace, and tie these together, depending on location, stage of tide, height of tide, wind, waves, current, time in the season, and how things are going. Ken's the master at devising these fishing plans, and I'm the crew that follows directions and just sometimes suggests we move a net sooner or let one soak a little longer.

No fishing day is the same as any other, and we always think we can be a little smarter about how we fish, work harder, and catch more salmon.

Ken ties one end of the corkline to the setline at the high-tide mark and climbs back into the boat; I pull us out along the setline; Ken lowers and starts the motor, and at exactly 7 a.m. we set our first net. Leads and corks tumble out over the stern as I watch for snarls, and then, when we reach the end of the net, I wrap a bight around the setline and tie the net off.

We both turn expectantly to see what's happening behind us—whether fish are hitting the net, whether this will be a fishy day. I continue to watch behind us for splashes as we speed to the next set, but the corkline lies in a perfect gentle crescent against the current.

Our first sets go like clockwork, right down the beach. I love when it's like this— the smooth, voiceless teamwork, the echoing clank of orderly corks over the stern, the practiced feel in my hands. I don't think so much as I am. The body knows; is in my fingers, my shoulders, the knees that brace me. My physical self knows the grip of line, the quick tightening, the double hitch pulled over itself. If I stopped to think about what I do, I would surely fumble.

The nets are out, and I stoop to scrape seaweed and sand from the bare boat bottom. I'm sweating inside Neoprene; the sun, breaking through the clouds, has lit the fireweed and monkey flowers on the hillside into a blaze. The red salmon come when the fireweed blooms. So they say; so the old-timers said about the sockeyes, the money fish. We are ever hopeful.

To a fisherman, every fishing day is like Christmas, every net like presents to be opened. We never know what surprises we might find, only that there'll be something there and that it just might be, this time, the stuff of our dreams. That's why we fish days when we catch just ten fish, and in storms, and on those days when nothing seems to go right, because the only thing predictable about fishing is that we won't catch anything if we don't have web in the water.

This morning our nets are not, however, loading up with fish. Ken blames the weather. It's too good; we need a storm to move fish up the inlet and in against our shore.

We start back through the nets, pulling leads and corks between us across the boat. Ken snaps loose a silver, worth just half a sockeye. The next fish is a silver, too. I slip a finger under one gill to peel away web and then shake the other side free. Every fish is its own puzzle to pull through, spin out of a twist, unbag, ungill, shake off. After years of practice the hands know, but my brain still clicks through its calculations, seeing the patterns. Ken looks glum, but at least we've got fish in the boat. This is another maxim among fishermen: We have to have one fish before we can have ten, and we have to have ten before we can have one hundred. We pull more net and Ken grabs for our first sockeye. "Now that's a beauty," he says.

The fish, still fighting fresh, leaps around the center bin as though it would throw itself from the boat. It smacks against the aluminum, splashes water, dances on its tail, and comes to rest against one of the still-twitching silvers. It is, in fact, a very good-looking fish, with a rounded body and a dainty-featured face, marred only by the gillnet's score across its head. It's the color of distant water, a soft gray-blue that deepens over its back into a metallic, nearly cobalt shine. Mirror-like scales divide into contour lines like shifting plates of antique, tarnished mail.

The fish flops again, spattering blood that's hemorrhaging in thick, tomato-bright clots from its gills.

Wherever this ocean fish was headed, it was a long way from beginning its transformation to spawner. In another week or so we'll begin to catch an occasional wasted-looking sockeye, as flat as if it had been driven over by a truck and rose-colored, with a monstrous green head and hooked snout, all the better to scare its competitors once it reaches its spawning grounds. One will spill eggs like jewels into the boat, and we'll wonder if it lost its way home.

The fish makes a last flop and then lies quietly, its mouth working open and shut as though it's gasping for breath.

I'm well aware that some people think this cruel—killing fish like this, killing anything. They forget—or they never understood—that killing is part of how we live, the fish as well as the fisherman, the fish eater as well as the most committed vegan. Something dies that another may live. To me, the morality lies somewhere else—in what happens after the killing. When salmon are caught as "bycatch" in other fisheries and discarded overboard, or when someone takes a fish but leaves it on the bank or in his freezer to get freezer-burned, that's when behavior must be faulted.

These days, I frequently find myself examining that most basic of Dena'ina beliefs—that all things have wills and give or withhold themselves by choice, depending on whether a person shows respect or is insulting and wasteful. Among Peter Kalifornsky's Dena'ina belief stories is one about a young man who didn't listen to his elders about the proper treatment of animals. He left bones lying all around, and he killed mice cruelly and threw their bodies away. Other mice spoiled his meat, chewed up what was in his traps, and scampered over him in his sleep. At last he dreamed of going to the place where the animals wait to be reborn, and there he saw the ones whose bones had been walked over. They were horribly disfigured by his mistreatment and unable to return to human space.

Such lesson stories clearly helped enforce what the Dena'ina considered proper behavior and served the culture well in the long run. Would that our own laws and practices work so well to feed people within a conservation framework.

What's a better end for a salmon—being chewed on by a seal, rotting to a slow death after spawning, or flopping into a fishing boat? From a salmon's point of view, the question has no meaning. The salmon's brain can't consider the options. The salmon doesn't think; it reacts. Nor does it feel pain as we know pain, not with its simple nervous system. The sockeye in the boat isn't gasping. It only looks that way to people, who know what it feels like to them to struggle for breath.

In the belief that a quick death is a humane one, sport fishermen often club their catch on the head. We knock only the lively kings with the back of the gaff, to keep them from bruising themselves—or us—as they thrash. The smaller fish are difficult to club without damaging their flesh, and they fade away quickly as it is. In any case, most fish we bring into the boat are already dead; once they're in the net, the web caught in their gills prevents them from working water through properly to extract oxygen. In fishermen's language, the fish "drown."

The best way to handle a fish—to be quick and to ensure good quality for whoever's going to eat it—is immediately to slit it gill to gill and drain out the blood and then place it on ice. Some commercial fisheries have moved in this direction, and the better care brings a higher price. Change is slow, though, in those fisheries that have traditionally dealt more in volume than in quality. Our processors still want salmon untouched by a knife, and they won't bring us ice.

We do the best we can. We don't step on our fish. We don't let them go dry on the beach or get beaten into noodles in the surf. We keep them out of the sun.

Our count now is up to eight—four sockeyes, four silvers. There's the sockeye with the metallic shine and another that's smaller and greener, the silver with a thick tail and two lankier ones that took like twins. These are the fish in a "mixed-stock fishery," where salmon headed for a variety of large and small, glacial and clear, fast- and slow-running rivers and lake systems mingle before turning right or left and separating out. Bluebacks belong to one river, bullet shapes to another. That's the beauty and the essential genius of salmon: the custom design that matches each separate stock to color and stream flow, the natural conditions in their different home waters. As the big kings evolved to dig spawning beds below the scoured depths of powerful rivers, the sleekest sockeyes perfected their ability to move through shallows, the strongest to throw themselves up falls, and the greenest to blend into mossy depths.

I soak a piece of burlap over the side and cover the fish, a little brown mound in the center of the boat. Across the inlet, the sky is streaked with rain. The time is 7:40.

"How many?" Ken shouts as he cuts the motor. This is one of our games—to guess the number of fish in a net. Ken has not only much better eyesight than I do but also an uncanny ability to predict what lies under the surface of the thick flour-roux water.

I always make a conservative guess. That way, when there are more, I feel lucky to have them. "Three," I say, leaning from the bow to grab the cork line. I already see two heads.

Ken guesses six.

There's a silver along the lead line right away, and then the next pull of net brings in a big, headless sockeye, all gnashed red meat and dripping eggs. Ken curses and we both look around.

The seal's right there, just fifty feet off the outside buoy, bobbing up to get a better look at us. The way it stretches from the water makes it look as though it's standing on something solid, on tiptoe. Ken and I both yell, and I grab an aluminum post and bang it three times against the boat. I always think this should sound to a seal like gunfire, but it never seems to have much effect. This seal—a harbor seal, the most plentiful of Alaska's seals—merely ducks under and reappears seconds later a little farther downstream.

"Go away," I yell as I might at a dog loitering around a picnic table.

The seal lowers itself to whisker level and stays where it is, watching us. It has a bowling-ball head, dark and shiny, and saucer eyes. Most people think seals are cute; they would have a completely different opinion if seals had hard, little eyes and ferocious fangs—if a seal looked, for example, anything like a bat. Seals, in our modern classification system, are closely related to Bambi, and everybody loves Bambi. As a culture we Americans have Bambified ourselves away from any real understanding of individual species and their importance in the ecological picture.

Sometimes, grudgingly, I, too, will admit to being taken with fawns, bunnies, puppies, the baby seal that once swam to our boat wailing and still wearing its umbilicus—all soft and cuddly animals, cartoon creatures with fluttering eyelashes. *Bambi* was the very first movie I was taken to as a child, and I was struck to the soul with empathy. It was many years before I came to understand that there could be cultural systems even within my own country with beliefs different from and as strong as any I grew up with. This understanding came to me with pinprick clarity the day a Native woman told me about the time *Bambi* played in her village: when Bambi and Bambi's mother came on the screen, all the boys in the audience raised their arms as if to shoot.

At least cartoons were recognized as cartoons then. A more recent movie, about a seal named Andre, stars as Andre not a seal at all but a young sea lion. Every few years we spot a sea lion in the inlet, and even from a distance—with most of the animal underwater—it's easy enough to distinguish it from a seal. Much larger, more brown than gray, a sea lion swims and rolls along the surface, tossing its flippers. It has a pointed, doglike face and visible ears. Out of the water, it has longer limbs and an altogether different, more upright shape. Perhaps it was the sea lion's superior posture that attracted Hollywood, or perhaps they're easier than seals to train or have some other cinematic advantage; I don't know. Hollywood didn't care about correctly depicting a marine mammal, and most viewers, more familiar with E.T. and the Little Mermaid than with either seals or sea lions, didn't have a clue.

Ken keeps an eye on the seal as he works to free the mangled fish. With the head gone, there's no good way to grip it, and the web is tight in the flesh and tangled with bones.

It's not that we begrudge the seals having a meal; it's just that we think they ought to get it on their own. We can only guess how many gilled fish they steal from us. Often there's little evidence—just an empty or near-empty net. Their usual technique is to grab fish by the heads and pull them cleanly through, though sometimes they tear the heads off salmon that are too fat to slide through the web, and rarely, like vandals or epicurean wastrels, they swim along a net and bite out just the sweet bellies.

Ken finally frees the fish and it drops into the boat with a lifeless thud, like a sack of wet sugar. Since we can't sell it, we'll take it home for ourselves. The seal has ducked out of sight, on its way, we imagine, to our next net. We rush to beat it there, though we know our slapping around in a tin boat is no competition to a creature born to the water and shaped like a torpedo. At most, we can try to keep our nets picked clean, to avoid leaving fish dangling like so many buffet items.

Seals—though in recent years they've grown both more numerous and bolder along our beach—have, of course, been a part of the life here for as long as anyone knows. The traditional Dena'ina relied on them for their skins, meat, oil, bladders—all various parts, down to their whiskers. It took twenty seals to make one large skin boat.

After Americans brought the canned salmon industry to Alaska, seals, despised for eating fish that could otherwise be caught by fishermen, were systematically slaughtered. For most of the past hundred years the government paid a bounty on their noses and even, for a time in the 1950s, dynamited seals at the mouths of salmon rivers. At the peak of bounty hunting in the 1960s, seventy-thousand seals were taken in a single year. Not until 1972 were seals protected; the federal Marine Mammal Protection Act prohibits the hunting of seals and other marine mammals except by Natives for subsistence purposes.

Today, although seals are notoriously hard to count, biologists estimate there are about 250,000 harbor seals statewide, a population considered healthy. Alarm has arisen only recently over apparent sharp declines in the Gulf of Alaska and the Bering Sea. Those two areas are, perhaps not coincidentally, the locations of aggressive harvesting of bottom fish by factory trawlers.

When we began fishing, we rarely had problems with seals raiding our nets. Most seals in the area kept to the south of us, to the clearer water of the river sloughs and the easy hauling out along the bars. Whether population growth has pushed them north or they've simply learned how to find an easy meal, I don't know. I imagine the sound of our outboard calls seals to our nets in the same way the grind of an electric can opener calls a hungry dog to a kitchen.

Not too many years ago, Alfred and Ann Topkok, Natives originally from the coast near Nome, fished a few miles north of us. We sometimes saw Alfred 's boat pass our camp as he went to hunt seals, and when we visited them at their camp Ann showed us baby booties she sewed from the spotted silver pup skins.

Alfred and Ann are gone now, and the local seals are probably less hunted today than since before the Dena'ina first arrived on these beaches. Perhaps they are also as fearless as any seals, ever.

When the tide's high, it's time to move nets.

We tear over the flat water at full throttle, the shore alongside us a narrow band, the water everywhere high and capacious, swirling in muddy boils. Darkening clouds make a patchwork of the wide sky. I lift my chin and breathe deeply of the rushing air, lick my lips clean of salt and splashed gurry. We pass under a low-flying flock of gulls, and for a time we neither gain nor lose on them but keep their exact pace, floating with them in the same ethereal dimension. We stare at each other, the birds and I. Their wings sweep up and down. I could be a feather, a barb of a feather, one of the one million fluted and hooked barbules of a single feather. I could be the floating lightness of down.

This, too, is a part of fishing.

We take a break and go ashore, clipping our bowline to a net. The sun has broken through and beams down warm on the sand, rumpled with old bear prints above the tide line. I shed my gloves and vest, peel my Neoprene to the waist, open the lunch box, take a long drink of water. I make myself comfortable against a rock and unwrap a Fluffernutter sandwich—an obscenely high-fat, high-sugar, sticky concoction of peanut butter and marshmallow cream. Ken and I both ate these as children and somehow came back to them for fishing foods even though the thought of eating one in any other circumstance makes me gag.

I've taken just two bites before Ken spots a seal at one of our nets and we rush back out. We pick fish, and then we sit on one net and then another, waiting for more fish, watching for seals. The water's so still we can both see and hear salmon moving past—jumpers behind us, a finner leaving a ripple, small fish squirting through our nets. The jumpers leap elegantly into the light; like dancers or basketball players, they defy gravity to hang in the air, stop time. We watch one launch itself several times; closer, closer, closer to a net, and then we don't see it again. Another, instead of slipping back tail first or landing on its side, traces a high arc, like a diver springing from a board to make a clean, headfirst entry into a pool.

Why fish jump is one of those questions that may forever entertain us with possible answers. Surely one good reason is to escape predators—in this case, the seals that continue to pop up around us. Some biologists, noting more comely females than humpbacked mates among pink salmon jumpers, believe that at least some jumping has to do with females trying to loosen their eggs. I think it's entirely possible that fish may appreciate, on some level, the sensation of leaving the water, of feeling air ruffling through their gills and the blast of all that white light on their eyeballs.

Off to the south, a skiff at Kustatan glides out toward the rising bar. As we pick one fish, two more hit the net, kicking up splashes of water. Ken shouts, "They're really popping now." This is what our former neighbor Lou used to say before he quit fishing and we bought his sites, and it's become part of both our lexicon and our folklore, our ritualistic good-luck chant.

The tide goes out. We pull nets from the beach and reset them between offshore anchors. When we return to pick the first of them, I've only just lifted the cork line and begun to gather web when a huge, purple face floats up out of the murk.

"King!" The word squeaks through my teeth. We rarely see king salmon after the beginning of July. Ken squeezes into the bow, and I let my side of the net go as he studies the way the fish lies against the net and begins to bunch web around it. Kings are too large to gill, and when they don't simply bounce off a net they often only rest up against it or are snagged by a single tooth. They can be gone in a flash.

Ken loves nothing in fishing more than catching king salmon, and he is at his most intense at this moment. This is his art. He works quickly, delicately, wrapping web around the passive fish and then grabbing for the bundle.

The fish comes alive. It thrashes with violent, tortuous twists of its body, spraying water ten feet high that falls on us in sheets. But Ken has hoisted it over the side, and it dumps into the boat to finish beating itself out among the little fish. It's not as large as its shapely head made it out to be—perhaps thirty-five pounds—but it's a fresh ocean fish, still gleaming, its spotted tail unfrayed. It's rounded like an old-fashioned pickle barrel. Near its tail, a couple of scaleless circles the size of nickels mark where lamprey eels caught a ride through a far sea.

On average, our kings are smaller than this, but they can reach Bunyanesque proportions. Earlier this summer, a sport fisherman across the inlet caught an eighty-nine-pounder. A catch like that on rod and reel must surely be a thrill, but the burgeoning sport fishery that's developed around kings threatens those who fish commercially. Across the inlet more than here, commercial seasons have been shortened—targeted to sockeyes and timed to avoid the early- and late-running king. In addition, fishermen there have begun their own campaign of releasing live kings from their nets; they hope this altruism will keep them from losing more fishing time. I try not to be overly pessimistic, but if history is any indicator, the battle over fish won't be won by the commercial side. There are many more of them than there are of us. Already the "sports" get the main allocation of silvers as well as the kings, and now they're casting into the political system for more sockeyes, our money fish.

We head for the scow to make a delivery and lighten the boat. As we motor past George and his crew, bent over a net, I slip hands into our king's gills and hoist it high for them to admire—and envy. George pushes the air with his hands and yells across the water, "Throw it back! Throw it back!"

After we've tied up alongside the scow, Ken and I pitch our salmon. We grip them by their heads, tossing sockeyes into one, silvers into another. We keep our own silent counts. The fish drip slime; stiff and discolored now, they handle like sticks of firewood. Ken lifts the king last, steps up onto the scow, and drops it in on top of the sockeyes.

To our north, Mount Spurr towers whitely over the land. A volcano as raw as the beginning of time, Spurr belched ash and steam and nearly brought down a passenger jet just a couple of years back. Its Dena'ina name, which translates to One That Is Burning Inside, attests to its eruptive fame; of the four volcanoes in the region that have been active in my time, it's the only one whose traditional name refers specifically to its status as a volcano.

Today, as we chase fish in its shadow, scientists are poised on Spurr's rim with a NASA robot, the world's most sophisticated, designed for exploring Mars. The spiderlike machine, named Dante II, will descend into the crater on its computer-programmed legs, and then beam up video and geochemical data to a satellite. I take a minute to marvel at the juxtaposition—fishermen on water as perilous as it's ever been, engaged in the same basic hunt for food that people have pursued since day one, and space technology on the mountain, as state of the art as it gets. What a world we live in, that can accommodate both in the same here and now.

The reason we chose setnetting over other fisheries in the beginning was largely for its simplicity: its basic, low-tech nature. All we really needed was a skiff, a net, and a couple of hands. When the world's oil was drained, we told ourselves, we would row our boat with oars; we would work with the tides. And yet, I'm surely no Luddite. I follow the space program with a keen interest in all its inventions and discoveries. I want to know about the farthest stars just as I want to know about the bottom of the ocean and the inside of a salmon's brain. If the "crater critter" designed for Mars can also totter down into an active volcano and add to our collective understanding of rocks and gases, that's gravy.

Rachel Carson wrote that the picture of the sea that existed at midcentury was "like a huge canvas on which the artist has dictated the general scheme of his grand design but on which large blank areas await the clarifying touch of his brush." That picture, surely, still has plenty of blank space. Why do fish jump? Where do the belugas go when they leave the inlet? What's the reason for the sudden sharp decline in the numbers of seals and sea lions in the Gulf of Alaska? Only recently have marine biologists discovered that the deep ocean floor, long thought to be a biological desert, is in fact home to a diversity of species rivaling those thought to exist on the planet's land surface—somewhere between ten million and one-hundred million different species. Imagine the possibilities for undersea discoveries in light of the fact that a species of large terrestrial mammal—the goat-like saola of Vietnam—escaped scientific notice until 1992. Although I don't doubt that someday humans and their machines will reside away from the earth's surface, I also believe with absolute certainty that no artificial creation or substitute world will ever be as infinitely interesting and lovely—not to mention munificent—as this one and only earth.

We motor past George again, and this time he holds up a fish. It's a pink salmon, we can tell even at a distance—skinny as a knife blade, weighing less than two pounds. If we were closer I'd hear George saying, "I caught one of them spotted-tail fishes, too."

At low water we move nets again, back around the point. These offshore sets we make with regular anchors, whose buoys have popped to the surface now that the tide's out and the current has eased. It takes my whole body to lift each anchor while Ken turns into the current; from the soles of my feet to my aching shoulders, every muscle pulls. For each set, I hook the anchor on the gunnel and tie off the outside end of the net to its buoy. We motor to shore; I hop out and fetch the on-shore buoy and tie the inside end of the net to it. Then we motor out again, net behind us. When the net is straight and tight, I drop the anchor over.

This time, though, we screw up. One of the nets catches on itself, and a lump of corks and web flies out of the boat all at once. Ken slows and tugs on it, but it doesn't come free, and then the current swings us into rocks, where we bang the prop. We pull back on the net to try again, but as we back up with the motor in gear the net flags, and suddenly there's that abrupt clothy sound that's always like a kick to my gut. The prop has caught web and ground to a stop. Ken swears and slams his hand against the boat, then climbs onto the seat and balances over the transom to begin twisting and untwisting and peeling the tightly wound web from the prop. I'm grateful for the calm weather and that we're not caught in surf and having to hack away with a knife while the boat pitches.

All afternoon, seals continue to plague us. We pick nets and find only viscera or telltale catches in the web, and one very large new seal-shaped hole. We break sticks, throw back flounders, and shake out the aptly named jellyfish that roll in the net and fall to pieces like Jell-O taken too soon from a mold. We pause to eat again from our lunch box. I peel an orange with hands that smell as foul as the insides of my leaky rubber gloves. A seal surfaces well outside the net with a flopping fish in its mouth. It bobs high and looks as though it's juggling the fish as part of a circus act, though it must only be trying for a better grip. We continue to pick fish, one by one by one. We're catching more sockeyes than silvers and are glad of that.

Ken chants, "One fish, two fish, red fish, blue fish." I try to remember the words to a Russian peasant rhyme that counts dresses and sacks of flour and magpies. Gulls squabble over something in the rocks and are silenced when an eagle lands in their midst. Eagles are, above all, scavengers, which is one reason Ben Franklin didn't think they were particularly suited to represent our country.

"He is a bird of bad moral character," Franklin wrote of the eagle after it was selected as our national over his own favorite, the turkey: "like those among men who live by sharping and robbing, he is generally poor and often very lousy."

In places with clearer water, eagles are known to dive for fish, but here they rarely even circle the water when salmon are finning or jumping. We've never seen one catch its own fish, though we did once see one carry off a wiggling one.

When the tide comes in, we move our nets back up the beach.

At 6:30 we begin to pick up nets, and at 7 p.m. on the dot we pull the last piece of web from the water and head in to dump the whole pile on the beach. We deliver again to the scow, tossing our afternoon fish into our totes while George and his do the same into theirs. The tender will be by later, sometime during the night; we have only to leave our permit card and some outgoing mail in the "mailbox" tacked to one end of the scow.

While Ken fills our gas tanks from a barrel we keep on the scow, I pour water over the fish and fit the covers back on the totes. I summon a last spurt of energy to wash down the boat, coil lines, rinse the burlap, and stretch it to dry. My legs are bruised and my shoulder creaks. The muscles in my hands are light, and my little finger got squashed between an anchor and the skiff's rail. My chest aches from being pressed into the bow every time I lifted a cork line. I hurt with the hurt of a full day's work, hard work done well.

Before we leave the scow, I take a look into George's totes. We high-boated him again, just barely. We have 262 fish for the day.

Back at the cabin, I strip off my fishing clothes and wash my face and arms. I scrub aluminum stain from my forearms until they're pink, and then I pick off fish scales with a fingernail. Each scale pops off like a brittle flake, leaving a circle on my skin like a slightly gathered pockmark. There's something satisfying in this picking of scales, even in finding a last, crisp scale days later on the back of my arm—better than gold stars, they're the medals that remind us how we live with fish.

"We work hard for our fish," I say to Ken. "We work harder for two-hundred than we do for a thousand." It's been a long time since we caught anything near a thousand fish in one day, but it's true that when there are more fish to pick, we pick more and work our gear less. It's trying to maximize possibility that's so hard.

Ken yanks off his hip boots and drops them with heavy clunks in the center of the floor. He has mud on his cheeks and fish slime glistening in his beard, and his hair is so matted his scalp shows through. The back of his neck has darkened one more shade. He smiles a tired smile and says, "You can expect to find a little extra in your paycheck this week."

The leftover pizza warming in the oven has begun to fill the cabin with its burnt-cheese and tomato smell. Ken asks, "How many sets do you think we made?"

The individual pieces of the day are becoming a blur to me, but I know Ken recalls every set, every circumstance of every set, every pick of every set. He has a memory that can recall the play of a bridge hand six months earlier, and he carries a map in his head for every city he's ever visited and every road he's driven, just as he knows every contour of our beach and its every rock.

"How many?"

Ken lists our sets in order, holding up a finger for each. "Cove, Point, Emmet's, South Point, Eddyset with a short net, Eddyset with a full net, 12K, short net at Point, Eddyset deep, Lou's, Emmet's deep, Point deep, short net at Slide, full net at Slide, Rock, Campset, Emmet's, Cove...."

Eighteen. The recitation is like poetry to me, but it's poetry I want only to wash over me at the bottom of the deepest, absolutely motionless sleep. Eat, then sleep. The next fishing day is four days away. ⚓

NANCY LORD, Alaska's Writer Laureate as this anthology went to press, holds a liberal arts degree from Hampshire College and an MFA in creative writing from Vermont College. In addition to being an independent writer based in Homer, she fished commercially for many years and has, more recently, worked as a naturalist and historian on adventure cruise ships. Lord is the author of three short fiction collections (most recently *The Man Who Swam with Beavers*, Coffee House Press, 2001) and five books of literary nonfiction, including *Rock, Water, Wild: An Alaskan Life*, University of Nebraska Press, and *Early Warming: Life in the Climate-changed North*, Counterpoint Press. She teaches part-time at the Kachemak Bay campus of the Kenai Peninsula College and in the low-residency graduate writing program at the University of Alaska Anchorage. Her awards include fellowships from the Alaska State Council on the Arts and the Rasmuson Foundation, a Pushcart Prize, and residencies at a number of artist communities.

LOST SEASON

Remembering the
Exxon Valdez oil spill,
TOBY SULLIVAN
describes the rage
and immobility of all
who watched oil
take over the Alaskan
waters, a single
thought echoing
through fishermen's
minds: "if but for the
spill..."

IN KODIAK THE NEWS came at eight o'clock on a snowy Friday morning, the barest facts on Alaska Public Radio. A 963-foot oil tanker named the Exxon Valdez was aground on a rock pile called Bligh Reef outside of Valdez. The radio sat on the windowsill of the closed-in back porch, next to a cup of coffee. The herring gillnet I was building hung from a hook in the corner, the green plastic mesh bundled with the corkline, a plastic needle full of white twine in my hand; the Kodiak herring season began in three weeks. Wet snowflakes hit the window, slid down to the bottom of the pane, obscuring the view of Women's Bay. It was March 24, 1989.

According to officials, as of 6 a.m., there were ten-thousand barrels of oil in the water. What did that mean? A soft tremor of distant catastrophe reverberated in the room with me. I went into the kitchen and asked my wife if she'd heard.

The Exxon Valdez had untied from the Alyeska oil terminal in Valdez the night before, fully loaded with 1.2 million barrels of North Slope crude. Third Mate Jeffery Cousins, left alone on the bridge by Captain Joseph Hazelwood soon after departing Valdez, and apparently trying to avoid icebergs, had steered across the inside corner of a dogleg traffic channel and impaled the ship on Bligh Reef just after midnight. Driven by the head pressure of tanks whose tops were sixty feet above the waterline, oil was now pouring out at the rate of twenty-thousand barrels an hour. The response from officials—the Alaska Department of Environmental Conservation, the U.S. Coast Guard, Exxon Corporation and Alyeska Pipeline Service Company (the oil consortium that owns and operates the trans-Alaska oil pipeline and Valdez terminal)—was muddled.

"Did you hear that?" I asked my wife.

She nodded. "Do you think that oil could come to Kodiak?"

"Nah," I said. Bligh Reef was three-hundred miles from Kodiak. "But it'll be bad in Cordova."

Although Alyeska's oil-spill contingency plan mandated that a vessel loaded with skimmers and booms be at the scene of a spill within five and a half hours, the containment barge was dry-docked with a broken weld, and the skimmers and heavy duty boom that went with it were buried under tons of lightweight harbor boom in a warehouse. In the predawn darkness, workers began sorting the equipment using a crane and a forklift. Apparently there was only one man competent enough to run both machines. He drove back and forth from the warehouse to the barge, hopping up and down from the forklift to the crane, to get the boom onto the barge.

After hours of this, and just as the equipment was finally loaded, word came that the barge was needed instead to move fenders and other lightering equipment to the grounded tanker. Another ship, the Exxon Baton Rouge, was being maneuvered to pump off the oil still onboard the Exxon Valdez. An hour went by while workers searched for the fenders under the snow. The boom that had just been loaded on the barge was unloaded and the lightering equipment was craned aboard. People watching the Alyeska workers were appalled at the disorganization. It was rapidly becoming apparent that the response plan was a fiction. Nevertheless, Alyeska spokesman Tom Brennan told the Anchorage Daily News: "Describing this as some sort of Keystone Kops routine is ridiculous. Utter nonsense."

At 2:30 p.m., fourteen hours after the tanker went aground, the barge with the boom and skimmers finally arrived on scene at the Exxon Valdez. By 5:30 p.m., the oil had pretty much stopped pouring from the ruptured hull. Estimates put the amount of oil in the water at 240,000 barrels–eleven million gallons, the largest oil spill in U.S. history.

For three days, in calm weather, the oil slowly spread from the tanker while confusion reigned in Valdez. Alyeska skimmed up several thousand barrels but found it had nowhere to put it. Fishermen from Cordova scooped oil into buckets and ran into the same problem. Officials and biologists and oil industry experts began what would become a protracted argument over the use of dispersants—essentially dishwashing detergent sprayed from C-130 airplanes. Alyeska's contingency plan had claimed one-hundred-thousand barrels would be recovered within forty-eight hours of a large spill, but by Sunday, March 26, less than three barrels had been skimmed off.

"I know these people are upset by what seems a slow response, but they just don't understand that you just can't move that fast in a situation like this," Brennan said. The only good news was that the Exxon Baton Rouge had maneuvered alongside the Exxon Valdez and begun pumping off the remaining one-million barrels.

For three days the oil lay in a great black mass attended by a few skimmers, some boom and the fishermen from Cordova, armed with their five-gallon buckets. And then the wind began to blow. By Monday morning seventy-mile-an-hour gusts and twenty-foot waves had swept the boom away and sent the skimmers scuttling back into Valdez Arm. The fishermen sought shelter in the Cordova small boat harbor.

By Tuesday the wind had spread the oil west across five-hundred-square miles of water and onto the beaches of Smith and Naked islands. Pictures of dead otters and bald eagles were on television screens around the planet. Within a week the wind and the prevailing westerly setting ocean current had carried the oil through the islands of the western Sound and out to the open ocean between the Kenai Peninsula and Kodiak Island.

If the weather is clear and I am sitting on the western side of the plane, I cannot fly either to or from Kodiak without thinking of the spill when I see the Barren Islands (Amatuli, West Amatuli and the largest, Ushagat), steep treeless islets set in the roil of currents between the southern tip of the Kenai Peninsula and the north end of the Kodiak archipelago. In the summer they are as green as Ireland, and look as though sheep would be at home there. But on a calm and cloudless April dawn in 1989, as my wife and I drove past them in the boat we had just purchased in Homer, the hillsides were wheat straw brown with the previous year's grass. The oil lay invisibly a few miles to the northeast.

The day after we passed by, the oil came ashore and killed half a million birds.

Four weeks after the oil seeped out of the western end of Prince William Sound, my daughter turned three. A decade and a half later, she graduated from Kodiak High, the ceremony held in the same auditorium where the morning oil-spill briefings were held. A lot of us spent our mornings in late May 1989 in the auditorium, listening to the weather update and the Coast Guard assessment, the Exxon situation report, the Fish and Game report, the dead-bird count, and the increasingly aggressive questions from the fifty or so people in the audience every day.

How much oil is it going to take to get Exxon to get some kind of cleanup going here? If the situation is improving, then how come Fish and Game is canceling the salmon season opener on June 9? We would come out of those briefings, look across the parking lot at the slicks of sheen in the water off the north end of Near Island, just past Fullers Boatyard. We knew the oil had made the world different out there, and we wondered how long the spill would go on, and when it was over, would we be different too?

Today, when I pick my daughter up after school, I see her coming across the parking lot, her hair in the wind, turning to shout to someone behind her, almost her whole life lived since the spill. Across the tops of the cars the ocean is blue, breaking rhythmically on Williams Reef. To an observer who might not remember that summer, it might seem that the spill had never happened.

My daughter has a memory of sitting in a white plastic fish tote on a beach while my wife and I and our fishing crew and the other fishermen in Uganik Bay shoveled oily gravel into plastic bags. We would put her in the tote with blankets, some crackers, and a bottle of juice. She remembers not being able to see anything except the sky and the high white sides of the tote, and hearing us talking a few yards away. She remembers a blue and white helicopter. I remember the beach, the sand flies and the rain, the helicopters blowing sand in our faces when they landed to pick up our paperwork. I remember it as a rainy summer, a slow-motion stumble through meetings with Exxon, lawyers, fishermen, the mayor, reporters, days of shoveling oily gravel, the dead birds in the gummy tidelines swirling through the bay, the empty rocks off the point in front of the cabin, where the otters hauled out every year but that one.

I remember the constant moral battles over who was cleaner in their dealings with Exxon. There were the general questions: Was it wrong to take money from Veco, the oil-field service company Exxon hired to run the cleanup, to wipe rocks? Would you do it if they didn't pay you? Was it worse to sit in town and let the oil float around killing birds?

And then there were the particulars. Was it wrong to skiff eighty miles into Kodiak to get food on an overnight roundtrip (if the weather was good and you didn't get stuck in town) and not log the trip? Because if you did log the trip, Veco would know you weren't in Uganik wiping rocks and you wouldn't be paid that $600 a day for your skiff charter, which you needed to make up for the salmon season you weren't having. Neither would your crew get $16.50 an hour if the skiff wasn't there to take them across the bay to where the oil was bad, to wipe rocks, and put dead puffins into plastic bags.

On the other hand, if you didn't go to town, you all went hungry. You couldn't eat anything swimming in the bay and the canneries weren't sending any tenders out with supplies because there weren't any fish to buy. A one-hundred-twenty-foot crab boat, the *Arctic Lady,* was anchored a mile away with $100,000 worth of groceries on deck—on contract to Veco to support Veco workers who might or might not show up to clean rocks in Uganik Bay—but the skipper of the *Arctic Lady* couldn't give us anything because Veco had decided the food was for Veco workers, not setnetters who were "working out of their own homes," responsible for their own sustenance. But the skipper was a cool guy. Sometimes he'd let you skiff over in the middle of the night and snag potatoes, steaks, lettuce, and milk after the Veco representative on board had passed out behind a half-gallon of maple pecan ice cream and a pint of vodka. Otherwise, you went to town and lied on the skiff log if you needed food.

The second time I went to town to get groceries, (six hours into the wind, pounding through a jackhammer chop in Kupreanof Passage, wet and cold and dementedly angry to the bone when I came under the bridge and pulled up to the transient float) I went up to the Veco office in the old Captain's Keg restaurant to give them a piece of my mind about being caught between eating a rock or a hard place. The setnetter liaison cut me off.

"Look," he said, "if you write in the log that you came to town to get food, you know we can't pay you 'cause you're off charter, right? But if the log says you're on charter we pay you, right? So the log is the key to the puzzle, right? See that guy over there in that cubicle?" He pointed to a large man with his backed turned to us. "He reads the logs and puts in for the checks. He doesn't go checking to see who's who and who's where. He goes by what's written in the logs. Then he goes back to the Westmark and drinks himself silly at the bar every night, like any sane person would do in his situation. You look like a smart kid. Figure it out. Do what you need to do."

When I told this story to another fisherman that summer, he looked at me like I was a fool.

"Check this out," he told me. "We put three inflatable rafts onboard over at the fuel dock, brand new fifteen-foot Achilles with twenty-five-horse outboards. They told us to take 'em over to Katmai and give 'em to a beach crew over there. Nobody gave us an invoice or a receipt or nothin'. So we put two on deck and stuck the other one down in the fish hold and piled a bunch of shit on top of it—some nets, some groceries, y'know, whatever. When we got to Katmai the next day, we unloaded the two Achilles on deck, and the Veco guy over there goes, 'Hey, where's the other raft? I ordered three of these things.' We just looked stupid and said, 'Dunno, they gave us these two, told us to deliver 'em here, and here we are. You want us to go back and get another one?' He said fuck it and took the two on deck. He never even came down to look around. Now we got us a real nice inflatable for beachcombing. Nobody cares man. It's all cost plus."

These days I work part time in the same building as Jamin, Ebell, Schmitt & Mason, the law firm that represents the Kodiak plaintiffs in the ongoing Exxon punitive damages lawsuit. Matt Jamin, one of the founding partners, flew to the dock of the old Uganik cannery in mid-June 1989 and told the fishermen there that Exxon had promised "to make you whole," that their lost salmon season would be compensated. But it would take lawyers and time to make that happen. And sure enough, by the end of the year, we had gotten checks worth about a third of the 1988 salmon season. The checks were based on a fantastical model of variables and possibilities, of predicted fish runs, Tsukiji fish market trends for salmon, last year's ex-vessel prices, and personal-catch histories as percentages of the fleet catch. The variables for thousands of fishermen's professional lives were plugged into a formula that answered the mantra, "if, but for the spill, how much would you have made?"

Every salmon fisherman from Cordova to Chignik eventually was codified as a fraction of the value of all the salmon that should have been caught in Alaska that summer, a number stretching six places to the right of the decimal, a fractional multiplier that was applied to the sum total of money Exxon paid in damages. That same multiplier will apply to the punitive damage award too, if it is ever paid to the thirty-two-thousand claimants still fighting Exxon.

In 1994, a jury ordered Exxon to pay $5 billion in punitive damages, the amount of profit it had made in the year before the spill. It was a number meant to deter it and other large corporations from ever spilling eleven million gallons of oil again. Exxon has vociferously denounced the punitive damages award, vowing to fight it to the legal death as a matter of principle. And despite ten years of consistent court rulings upholding the plaintiffs' legal points, the suit has stalled in the federal Ninth Circuit Court of Appeals in San Francisco. It could someday end up in the Supreme Court. Last year Exxon cleared $11 billion, after expenses. Since 1989, seven-thousand of the original plaintiffs have died.

Nearly every day I hear the lawyers down the hall talking on the phone to fishermen, cannery workers, and villagers. They patiently review the history of the case, explaining the options available in the same tone a doctor might use to explain the latest tests to a patient who has been fighting cancer for years. If but for the spill…

At first, everyone in Kodiak thought the oil would never leave Prince William Sound. Then they thought it would never get past the Barren Islands, and then that it would never come to Kodiak. In the first days of the spill, we watched the news from Cordova and Valdez, saw the TV footage of dead otters and birds and yellow rain-gear-clad workers spraying beaches with hoses, and we thought the only effect on us would perhaps be a price jump on herring roe, since it looked like nobody would be fishing in

Prince William Sound. Maybe salmon prices would go up too, we thought, if we were lucky and the spill lasted long enough. We were utter fools.

In mid-May, coming back from herring fishing in Uyak Bay, we saw brown objects the size of footballs floating everywhere in Shelikof Strait— mousse balls—in some places one every few feet.

I stopped the boat and we leaned over the rail with a hook. The balls were like underdone egg yolks—soft and runny when we poked them. The brown weathered surface hid a heart of fresh black oil. A month later, at the fish camp, we watched them burst open and run like black lava as the sun warmed them on the rocks.

The oil was the darkest, most beautiful shade of glistening black we had ever seen. The surface of any glove-full was usually so smooth, like liquid glass, that you could see your own curving reflection in it. But beneath the reflection the oil had a spooky blackness, a density of opaqueness and heavy viscosity that was like nothing we had ever seen. Even after being washed through three-hundred miles of ocean, it remained depthless and black and pure as alien blood, the distilled blood of dinosaurs. I still have a glob in a canning jar that I take out and show people sometimes. It's dried out and no longer flows, but it still looks weird, and it still sticks to your finger if you touch it.

We could see oil was the dirtiest thing on earth, that one drop on your pants would smear every part of your raingear while you walked and a little on your hands made the valleys of your fingerprints black for days. It gave you a headache if you worked in a heavily oiled section of beach and the wind died down for more than a few minutes. But one day an Exxon guy on one of the support boats told us about all the hydrocarbons in crude oil, all the complex carbon and hydrogen chains that could be "cracked" and reassembled into plastic and fertilizer and fuel. He got excited talking about the oil, and we could see he was more than just a hired hand for Exxon. He believed in oil the way we believed in fish. It's the most amazing substance on earth. I mean, just look at it!

But the oil seemed to have some strange other quality, a kind of venal stickiness that affected everyone that came into contact with it, from the corporate Exxon guys, to whom every facet of existence seemed to be defined or mitigated or buried with money, down to us, where it tar-brushed some of our secret hearts with greed and envy the same way it smeared our raingear. To some degree we all were corrupted by the money we got, or wanted to get but didn't, and almost no one was revealed to be a better person by their contact with the corruption that followed the oil down the coast. Most people did things they weren't very proud of, but sometimes people did things which almost everyone condemned, things that in a small community like Kodiak remain part of the collective memory. We all knew who let their crew members go and hired their kids as paper deckhands, so the kids got the lost-season crewshare money while the crewmen wandered from office to office trying to explain why they deserved a damaged crewman's share. Some crewmen had actually gone out to a set-net site and worked for a week or two setting things up for a salmon season that never happened, and then been fired and sent back to town. Without any fish to catch, a real deckhand was unnecessary, and Exxon just needed names in the boxes on the forms.

Some people manipulated the boat-chartering system, and there were rumors of kickbacks to get your name to the top of the list, or of not getting on the list at all without paying a kickback. A few really smart folks got Exxon contracts first, then found boats (one guy bought a boat lying in a Louisiana bayou sight unseen, flew down and sailed it up through the Panama Canal), then got bank loans secured by the contracts and paid the boats off in three months with Exxon money. The two brothers who owned the *Arctic Lady* and the *Frances Lee*, both one-hundred-twenty-foot Bering Sea crabbers, had crewmen hanging off the sterns three days after the spill, painting "Kodiak, Alaska" over the old homeport "Depoe Bay, Oregon," just in case it turned out boats registered in Alaska got hired first, or exclusively.

In the end, Exxon didn't care where a boat was from, but the rules of engagement were arbitrary and capricious. The salmon boat owners who got charters used the money to get bigger boats the following year, which got them bigger catches thereafter, which allowed them to claim bigger damages, because damages were calculated on your percentage of the catch for the whole fleet for the four years after the spill. All of this just lowered the damage settlement shares of those who hadn't gotten charters.

A woman, who had run her own boat for years, got pregnant that winter and leased her boat to a guy with a permit. She caught plenty of fish in the qualifying years following the spill, but when the numbers got crunched she got six zeros to the right of the decimal–nothing–because Exxon compensated only permit-holders who could show they had a boat and were planning on fishing in 1989. Another woman showed up at a morning Exxon spill briefing in July and asked which official at the table up front was going to pay the house payment, the boat payment or buy food for the kids, because she and her husband owned a boat but not a permit, and they couldn't get a charter.

A woman who worked in the Veco charter-contract office that summer watched fishermen coming into the office. At first they were their usual cocky selves, then after days of no contract, no check, no sympathy, they got angry, and then they began pleading – the ones who were above bribery or couldn't afford it. The last phase, the worst one to watch, was when they just sunk into utter despair and began believing there was no hope for them.

All of this made people flip out in very public ways–in bars, in banks, in the middle of the street, but mostly in the Veco offices where the new reality first set in. One deckhand without a job went into the Veco hiring office and started throwing computer monitors against the wall. "I'm born and raised in this fucking town and I can't get hired? I gotta eat too!" When the cops came, they told the Veco guys, "Just sign this kid up on a boat and get him out of town."

In the inverse of the sacred ethic of fishing, working hard had nothing to do with success during the oil spill–scamming had a lot to do with it, and the rest was simply luck. You could show up at an office moments after they decided to let contracts to the first five guys who walked in the door, or like me, you could arrange to have your new used boat re-wired that summer, and have the old wiring torn out and the electrician skipped off to Katmai before you wised up to what was happening around you. And the level of corruption was something few people in Kodiak had any experience with. There was talk about the lawyer from the Kodiak Veco office who fell off a dock in Homer in the middle of the night and drowned, maybe not accidentally, maybe after making noises to the FBI about the kickbacks. The Sealand vans ran up and down Mill Bay Road every day all summer, loaded with steak and lobster from Safeway to load onto the tenders and crewboats.

One morning in the charter contract office, I walked by a fifty-year-old fisherman in tears, his salmon-tendering contract evaporated, talking to the man in charge.

"I don't get it Jack," the fishermen said. "I was two from the top of the list the other day, and now you're saying I'm on the second page."

Jack barely glanced at the man as he picked up a ringing phone. "Don't worry, Coogan, you're still on the list, just not on top. Things will work out. Check back next week." A secretary caught my eye, but said nothing.

There was no way to be a winner. If you made money, people questioned your motives and your methods. If you didn't make money, you could hold your head up, but then you might end up at the morning briefing, begging for a handout.

If, but for the spill!

In Uganik Bay in early August, the tender that was supposed to be picking up dead birds hadn't come around in a few days. Roger Benney and his two crewmen were burning oil-soaked cormorants on the beach in front of his cabin. It required nothing but a little newspaper and a match to get them going. While they were staring into the little pyre of burning wings and webbed feet, a helicopter with a Veco "beach-assessment" team landed and a fat Texan walked over. He asked how things were going:

Did they need any more absorbent towels, any boom? How was their fuel situation? Benney said they had enough equipment, but the problem was the whole thing itself – the oil–the dead birds–the not fishing.

"We're really not having much fun you know," Benney said.

The Texan, who'd been hearing that kind of thing for two weeks ever since he got off the plane from Houston, squinted at him. "Y'all have joined the real world now, boy."

Still, there were a few shining moments when we were proud to be Alaskans, where we behaved honorably, when we were still outraged, before we started getting paid. Before the money started, we were possessed of almost religious scorn for the line that Exxon had been talking in the weeks before the June 9 salmon season was supposed to start.

"We want some answers from Exxon but all we're getting is rhetoric," said a big red-headed setnet fisherman named Stan Ness on May 24. "It's boring. Exxon is boring. We want some answers."

The Exxon guy who was standing up in front of the morning briefing crowd at the auditorium was a man from Houston named John Harrington. He had a receding hairline of frizzy hair, wire rimmed glasses, a plaid shirt, and sneakers. He looked more like a mandolin player in a college town bluegrass band than Exxon's public face in Kodiak. Every morning he came out from behind the table, where the Mayor and all the other officials remained, holding the mike like he was a talk-show host. He never lost his cool, was always respectful, even when people were rude. He said things like, "We're monitoring the situation, and we expect to have a better assessment of the situation by next week."

The Exxon guy was calm, but the other people on the stage—the Coast Guard liaison, the Fish and Game official, the manager from the Kodiak National Wildlife Refuge, the Kodiak city mayor who was now working for Exxon in some capacity— all were getting spooked by the steady animosity, the hard stares, the arms folded across chests, the snorts of derision at almost anything John Harrington said.

As the mood worsened, the mayor tried to maintain some civility between the crowd's unfocused anger and Exxon's arrogance, or distract people from the fact that Exxon had closed down the boom material shop out at the Coast Guard base, and was talking about handing out plastic bags to clean up fifteen-hundred miles of coastline. "I see your point Stan, about thinking that all you're hearing is boring rhetoric, but maybe we all need to take the long view here."

And every day for two weeks, Exxon's John Harrington said, "We're doing the best we can, we're monitoring the situation on a daily basis, you have to be patient." On May 24, when Harrington said, "We plan to distribute plastic bags to all the canneries around the island and pay volunteers $50 a bag for oily debris," one fisherman called it the "Rome wasn't burned in a day" speech. Some people even remembered what Tom Brennan, the Alyeska spokesman in Valdez, said two months before: People just don't understand that you just can't move that fast in a situation like this!

But by then it was too late. On May 22, some setnetters had flown to Uganik and Viekoda bays in a chartered floatplane to see how much oil was really out there. They found oil everywhere; not thick sludge like in Prince William Sound, not even much more than a colossal bathtub ring on the high tide line of all the beaches inside the bays. But there were huge sheens eddying in all the bays on the west side, and the rocky capes up and down the Shelikof were a mess of mousse and oily seaweed and dead birds. The night they got back, the setnetters had a meeting to mull things over. Thirty people showed up and began the usual ranting about Exxon as an evil force in the universe, about how it looked like there might not be a salmon season at all, about paying their bills if they couldn't fish, about making some money, goddammit!

And then Janet Axell stood up, a woman in her forties with long hair in a braid down the back of her Kodiak Oil Sales sweatshirt. She fished a setnet site every summer at a wild place called Cape Uganik, fifty miles from town by skiff. In winter, she lived in a cabin in Anton Larsen Bay, at the end of twenty miles of bad road. Janet told the room how she'd just been out at Anton Larsen and there were a few dead otters, lots of dead birds, and a bay full of sheen. She started crying. She talked about the affront of having oil smothering what had been pristine, even holy places to her. She never once mentioned the financial aspects of not fishing due to oil. She sat down. Nobody said anything.

A tall thin intense man in his forties, with a trim mustache and a leftover British accent, shook his head. Roger Benney fished every summer at Miners Point in Uganik Bay and spent his winters in New Zealand. "Well, I don't know about you, but I've heard enough of Exxon's bullshit. I think we should have a protest march. It's the only thing that will get their attention."

By the next day there was a committee and a plan. The day after that, on May 24, right after Harrington put out his volunteer bag and bounty system, a woman in her early forties, in a black dress with a white lace collar, stood up at the morning briefing. In a sometimes halting voice, she read a speech written the night before.

"I am Ann Barker. I've been fishing on Kodiak for eighteen years, running a local business, and Kodiak is my home," she read in a high, clear voice that got stronger as she went on. She spoke about the dying wildlife, the increasing despair and confusion in the community, and the fact that, in the Kodiak archipelago, "there is no serious cleanup operation and one is not planned. In reviewing all this, we the people of Kodiak will wear black armbands and clothes of mourning, and on Friday May 24, we will march in protest."

Barker went on about the duplicity of Exxon and the lack of regard for the island of Kodiak, "and we will march," about Exxon's corporate mentality in a community that lived by fishing, "we will march," about Exxon's constant refrain, file a claim for your financial loss, "we will march," about the lack of moral responsibility, "we will march for cleanup," about the fact that two months since the Exxon Valdez hit the rocks—three weeks since oil had hit the beaches of Kodiak, less than two weeks before a salmon season was supposed to start—there was no cleanup plan.

The mayor thanked Ann for her "comments," and started in with an update on the governor's conference the following Tuesday. People stood up and walked out while he talked.

"And we will march!"

By that afternoon, there were flyers taped to store windows and stuck under windshield wipers. The day after that, fifteen-hundred people with signs and banners marched from the high school parking lot down the hill to the boat harbor in a driving rain. Roger Benney got up on the back of a truck and led the crowd in chants.

CLEAN IT UP, EXXON, CLEAN IT UP!

Every business in town shut down for an hour, and Exxon evacuated all of its Kodiak personnel to Valdez for an "organizational meeting." One of the brothers who owned the *Arctic Lady* and the *Frances Lee* stood in front of his house on Rezanof Drive and taunted people in the crowd as they marched by—"Get on the clue-bus folks, this ain't how it works."

On Monday, May 29, Exxon reopened its offices and rolled out a blueprint for a cleanup program on Kodiak. Boats started getting hired, the setnetters got contracts to clean up their beaches, and Veco took over the absorbent-boom project and started paying people. The irony, eventually lost on no one, was that from the passion and altruism of wanting to clean up the oil, came the uneven distribution of cleanup contracts, the bribery and the profligate expenditures of fuel, labor and materiel—no one cares man, it's all cost plus!—that may or may not have made a difference in removing hydrocarbons from the environment. Y'all have joined the real world now, boy. We ended up with as much oil on our hands as Exxon.

Early in the summer we were thrilled with the helicopters. They were everywhere, and they were beautiful. Once, when I flew into town in a chartered Cessna to get supplies, a guy in the Veco office told me they'd be happy to fly me back out in a helicopter if one was going that way; just show up out at the airport at 8 a.m. to do your safety briefing. The next morning, I waited with a crowd of fishermen, Coast Guard officers, lawyers in suits, and various federal and state officials. It was like a taxi stand. Twenty Bell Jet Ranger helicopters sat at the end of the runway, shiny as new toys. My pilot explained the procedure if we lost power (who's he kidding? I thought) and then we strapped in and took off.

The ride was like sex, the pilot streaming us tight between mountains, his face exquisitely expressionless behind his wraparounds, the cliffs, and vegetation at one-hundred fifty knots like skin sliding against the window. We landed on the beach in front of my cabin. I stepped out in front of my wife and crew members like a god. The high lasted all day.

Every day helicopters landed on the beach where we worked to deliver edicts from the contractor, take the logs and crewmember time sheets back to town and to monitor the progress of the cleanup. One of the pilots told us the Veco guys were using the helicopters to count skiffs on the cleanup beach to make sure we were all working. One day my wife took our daughter back across the bay to our cabin to feed her some lunch. A helicopter hopped over the hill behind the cabin and hovered in the front yard like an insect, the pilot and an observer staring in the kitchen windows while my daughter stared back over a spoon full of macaroni and cheese. A few days later another helicopter swooped around the cabin trying to take pictures of my crew members while they ran behind the corners of the building, gulping sandwiches and beer. One morning a helicopter landed at a setnet fish camp across the bay and blew a tent with a couple of kids down the beach into the water.

By July, the crew members were getting edgy and bored, tired of watching for helicopters whenever they snuck back to the cabin for lunch, tired of wiping rocks all day in the rain. My wife was growing unhappy about keeping our daughter on the beach all day. The mail wasn't getting through on the Veco boats. (Once they dropped a sealed postal bag over the side and two weeks' worth of mail for the bay disappeared.) Driving eighty miles in an open skiff for food was getting old. The helicopters flew down our beach at eye level four or five times a day, the sound of the turbines arriving like tearing metal, the grass flattening as they went by forty feet from the cabin windows. One night I dreamed about all the Jet Rangers parked rotor to rotor at the end of the runway in Kodiak. I was standing with two five-gallon buckets of gasoline and a Bic lighter. There was no fence to stop me. The beautiful machines had become carriers of the plague.

We stood in the yard next to the cabin—myself, my wife, our daughter and our three crew members—watching for a glimpse of the helicopter that hovered just out of view, clattering invisibly just below the other side of the trees a hundred yards beyond the front yard. A white and blue Jet Ranger rose slowly into sight, the cockpit facing us, two men in sunglasses staring through the Plexiglas windshield, their faces like masks, the leaves on the birch trees around the helicopter thrashing in the rotor wash. One of my crew members, a nineteen-year-old kid named Frank, stepped out of the cabin with a rifle. He raised it and sighted down the barrel at the helicopter, his right index finger curled around the trigger.

"I'm pretty sure I can pop that pilot from here." He was serious.

I raised my arm to push the rifle away just as the helicopter swung around and dove behind the trees, the sound of the rotors fading as it ratcheted away into the inner bay.

In early August, during the week that would have been the peak of our salmon season, we stood in oil-blackened raingear while a Veco manager informed us that Uganik Bay had been downgraded from "moderately oiled" to "lightly oiled."

"It looks pretty clean, don't you think?" the Veco man said. "You guys have done a great job!" He seemed pretty happy about things. He had a Coast Guard crewman with him, an acned boy barely out of his teens. We knew the Coast Guard had to sign off on all status changes for oiled beaches before any cleanup could be suspended. The fishermen argued, holding up oily pieces of kelp and gravel. The Coastie kid looked at his boots. The Veco guy gave the kid a pen and held the clipboard while he signed.

"You can turn in your shovels in the morning, and get the vouchers to have your skiffs sanitized when you come into town. Have a good one!" They got back in their helicopter and flew away. The cleanup was over.

On a recent sunny afternoon, a view of blue winter ocean between the trees, I talked to John Devins by phone. Devins was mayor of Valdez in 1989, still lives there, and for a long time after the spill was President of the Prince William Sound Regional Citizens Advisory Council. "RCAC," as it is known, is the organization that tracks oil regulation and spill contingency plans and tries to keep accidents like the Exxon Valdez from happening again.

"Well, as far as another spill goes, it was Riki Ott who said 'not if, when,'" says Devins. " She said that six hours before the spill in '89 at a task force meeting in Valdez. In the model today, we'd have lots of secondary storage, plenty of boom, more equipment, a much better organized incident command system. But still, worldwide, only ten percent of oil that gets spilled gets recovered. I think they do better than before, but that's the number, about ten percent, even now."

Not if, when...

"An eleven-million-gallon spill would not be a good thing, obviously," says Tom Cirigliano, spokesman for Exxon Mobil in Dallas. "As far as how a cleanup might be done now, well, it's hard to generalize. Quite frankly, from a public perception standpoint, a company would have to do some kind of cleanup. I don't have an answer to the ten percent recovery number. We have a lot of natural degradation and a lot of weathering. There are natural seeps in Prince William Sound and bacteria that eat that oil. A lot of oil gets lost to natural causes."

When I asked about "the legacy" of the spill after fifteen years, a faint tone of righteousness came into Cirigliano's voice. There was a trace of the same indignation that had once been in the voices of the people of Kodiak at the morning briefings and on the beaches wiping rocks. It was the sound of someone who felt they'd been wronged, and as affable as he was, it was strange to hear it now coming from Mr. Tom Cirigliano of Exxon Mobil in Dallas, Texas. Apparently, Exxon considers itself the occupier of whatever moral high ground might be left fifteen years after eleven-million gallons of crude oil have been spilled in a marine wilderness.

"Exxon made a commitment from day one to stay until the state and the Coast Guard said the spill was cleaned up," Cirigliano said. "We did that. We stayed till 1992. We paid $300 million to eleven-thousand Alaskans and Alaskan businesses, and another billion dollars in damages to the state and federal governments. We spent $2.2 billion on the cleanup. We don't think any other corporation in the world could have done as good a job as Exxon Mobil in trying to make people whole again. If adversity doesn't build character as much as reveals it, then our response to the spill revealed the corporate character of Exxon Mobil."

When I told Cirigliano that many people in Kodiak believed 1989 was as much a moral disaster as an environmental catastrophe, that the money had been unevenly distributed and often contingent on playing a certain kind of game most were not suited for, that the experience, and the money, rather than making them "whole," had cut deep divisions within the fishing community, Cirigliano paused.

"I don't know how to respond to that," he said. "I'd never thought of it like that. I guess I'd have to be in a fisherman's shoes to understand."

There are days when the spill seems like a very long time ago, and other times, as if it were last weekend, or even, in some strange way, like it is still happening somewhere, still in the process of arriving from just over the horizon north and east of the Barren Islands or lying outstretched in the forests of our minds where certain dappled moments of the past live brightly forever. Like all great events, the oil spill created its own weather of effect, perception, memory. Even now at this fifteen year remove, I sometimes feel a certain sensuous echo of that lost season.

Frequently when I asked people if there was a thing they considered part of the central experience of the spill for them, they grew quiet, paused, audibly inhaled. In that pause the meaning of the story they were about to tell me would always come somehow before they said it, like the sound of a helicopter's rotor wash rattling a hilltop stand of birch trees before the machine itself rises into sight from the other side. I was struck with the familiarity of the landscape of that time as described by other people, the different remembered particulars of detail always orbiting the same nexus of emotional experience I recalled myself.

It may be that the images of the most intensely lived parts of our lives reverberate and sometimes outlive us in the memory of those who knew us and heard us tell the things we saw. It may be true that these images infuse our deepest moments of sharing or understanding, when the space between us and the particulars collapses. Such moments become the place both speaker and listener inhabit when we hear someone tell us something important about themselves. When I asked people about 1989 they would pause and then tell me their story, the underlying reality of which was almost always the same. If, but for the spill…

That last day of the cleanup, we skiffed back across the bay to the cabin in an evening drizzle. Streaks of sheen lay in great swathes across the water. Oily sticks and kelp and the occasional dead gull lay in the sheen. The bay was quiet; the helicopters were gone. We picked up the birds and put them in a plastic bag. Veco left us lots of those bags after they pulled out. They were great bags. We used them for years afterward to keep our things dry whenever we had to make long runs in our skiffs. ⚓

TOBY SULLIVAN lives in Kodiak, Alaska, where he has worked as a commercial fisherman since 1974. He began writing in the mid-1990s, received a minor in creative writing from University of Alaska Anchorage in 2002 and an MFA in creative writing from Antioch University Los Angeles in 2005. His work about the lives of commercial fishing people has appeared in the Anchorage Press, *We Alaskans, Alaska Magazine, Xtra-Tuff, Mary,* and *Moving Mountain* as well as several anthologies. He has appeared at the annual Fisher Poets Gathering in Astoria, Oregon most years since 1998. Between December 2004 and April 2006, Toby made four trips to Iraq as an embedded journalist and as this book went to press was at work on a book about his experiences there. He fishes commercially for salmon each summer on Kodiak Island.

A DROP IN THE BUCKET

MOE BOWSTERN
comes into her own
as a deckhand,
balancing
self-confidence and
grit with learning
how to "toss a
bucket over the
side and fill it up just
enough to haul
it aboard."

THE BOW OF THE BOAT curved up my back, exerting an insistent pressure between my shoulder blades. I felt around with my arms and encountered nothing, just darkness I kept trying to feel. I was surprised that I was not more startled; I knew from the wind against my face that I, that we—the boat and me in front—were sailing forward in the pitch black.

By the time I realized that I was strapped to the bow as some kind of living figurehead, glimmers of light had begun to reveal the interior of a vast cave. The boat floated forward in the cave, then angled down and plunged into a deep pool. I braced myself for an icy shock, but the water was warm, the same temperature as the air. Diving downward, I thought my lungs would burst; when I finally shuddered against all better judgment and inhaled, I found I could breathe under water.

I shed all fear at once and gave in to the joyous porpoising of the boat. I merged with the twenty-two tons of aluminum that drove me, and allowed myself the delight of frolic.

At some point my bladder pounded at me, and the motion of the boat gradually ascended to a side-to-side slosh. The buoys squeaked against the hull. I opened my eyes. I was under my damp sleeping bag in the dim fo'c's'le of the *El Tigre*, the same boat in my dream.

The boat I so proudly led was not some steel swan, sparking wanderlust in the soul of the staunchest earthbound landlubber; no, it was "The Tiger," who, despite her fierce name, was about as sleek as a bran muffin.

She was built in 1982 to fish salmon in Bristol Bay, where regulations limited vessel length to thirty-two feet. Boat builders found space for the bunks and the galley by building wide; at sixteen feet in the beam, by twenty-seven and a half feet from bow to stern, the *El Tigre* was a squat aluminum cube with a slightly tapered bow. Her twin screws granted her agility in tight corners, but you couldn't call her quick. She wallowed forth from the dock like a piglet in the tall grass. She would have fit right in among the tough little boats of Bristol Bay, but she never made it west of the Shelikof, and instead lived among the slender hulls of Kodiak's seine fleet, a true ugly duckling.

In 1990, a cod fisherman excited by high salmon prices persuaded the boat owner to convert the *El Tigre* to join the local seiners and the skipper began a brief experiment in salmon fishing, which resulted in me landing my first seine job. How I ended up somehow lashed to the bow of the boat after this was beyond me, but most things were beyond me that first summer.

Half-awake now, the dream fading, I pawed the bag off, swung off the bunk and shoved into my boots, then stumbled out on deck in a fog of sleep. I could still feel the bow of the boat bruising the length of my spine. My bladder ached. Where was the deck bucket? I found it and clambered up to the relative privacy of the top house, where I erected an invisible electric fence around myself, yanked down my pants and covered the bucket, quietly chanting "Invisible, invisible" while I relieved myself.

I paused on the bucket for a drip dry, closed my eyes, and lifted my face to the sun. Two months ago, before I became a real live Alaskan deckhand, I might have called this a beautiful day. Sun high in the sky, some clouds, no rain, and a breeze nudging at the damp sweatshirts hung out in the rigging—glorious, even, a fine day. But now I knew those wisps in the sky to be cirrus clouds, known locally as mare's tails that accompanied high winds. In wind like this there was no fishing for the *El Tigre* and her crew.

I shook my head, took a reflexive scan about me for other boats, then stood up and pulled up my sweats in one motion. I thought about dumping the bucket from the top house, and then imagined it being a moment when our skipper, a predictably unreasonable maniac, decided to peer out the window. Opting for safety over inconvenience, I made the awkward climb down the ladder with the bucket. I tried not to splash the bucket, but was too tired to care, already covered in fish slime, salmon scales, jellyfish snot, seaweed, sweat and dried seawater. What were a few drops of my own pee on top of that lively bouquet?

At the rail I scanned again for neighbor boats and tipped the contents of the bucket over the side, then, holding the line tied to the handle, tossed the bucket itself with a practiced flick that sent it open-ended into the sea. I hauled the bucket back to the rail in a single motion, and dumped it out again. Bucket flushed.

If someone had told me earlier in the spring, when I announced my intention to head north and join the bloodthirsty ranks of deckhands in the commercial fishing industry, that safe bucketing would be an important job skill I would need to master, I think I would have laughed. I would have laughed that automatic, airy giggle that I now recognize as the response of greenhorns and urban know-it-alls.

We city people, we college people, we seek the secret, the trick that will unlock the mystery and provide us with the cloak of experience without us having to go through the inconvenience of thrashing about in our own ignorance. Really, what I needed to learn about fishing was how to toss a bucket over the side and fill it up just enough to haul it aboard. Our boat lacked both a bathroom (which I learned to call a 'head') and a deck hose, and we dipped the bucket countless times in a day. Throw in the complications of traveling on the boat at six knots (yes, the *El Tigre* was a sleepy cat) and it was a feat deserving of pride, hauling back a bucket and not following it overboard as it caught the speed of the boat's passage.

I stowed the bucket and stepped into the galley. My crewmates sat at the table. Both of them gave me a look which I have since learned to interpret as one that young men give to female crewmates the first time they witness the crewmate doing something the women in their lives, in the movies or on TV, have never done in front of them. I call it the "alien" look. I've gotten it for having hairy armpits, expressing lust, and, with two young men from Indiana, for preparing food that contained no meat.

I looked back at them. "Good morning?" I hazarded, though it was well past three in the afternoon.

"You were snoring!" one of them blurted out, as if he had caught me committing an illegal act and felt obliged to inform me before he called the police. I opened the fridge and pulled out some lunch meat.

"Yeah, I bet," I said, "That's the first time I've had more than four hours of sleep in a row since we left town. Hungry?"

They shook their heads no, and I made a sandwich in silence, wondering if I was supposed to apologize. Every night after we delivered our fish and wolfed down our midnight supper, I raced to my bunk to try and calm myself to sleep before our skipper began his hull-rattling nightly roar. I have never since heard any snoring so loud, and it was a big reason I was so short on sleep. His chainsaw serenade started up about fourteen minutes after he hit the rack—I timed it—and I never heard my crewmates comment on it to him, and I never heard him apologize. I was too sleepy to pick a fight. I stowed my sandwich makings and took my snack to bed.

"Lemme know if anything happens," I called from below, "I'm gonna saw some more logs."

My crewmates never mentioned my snoring again, though others have. I now tell people I snore when I am really tired, and finally dreaming. My dream as the figurehead on our stubby little boat has stayed with me, far beyond that long first season. Being part boat, part fish really taught me a lot about the best ways to think about being a good deckhand, or a good anything at sea. Let go at just the right time—like letting go of the bucket and bringing it back clean. Snore, because if you can't be yourself when you are at rest, who are you? Breathe underwater; I learned that I could do things people told me I could never do. Other fishermen had predicted I would never make it on a boat, and yet I was a fine deckhand.

I could breathe underwater, and even if it was only in a dream, that was more than enough. ⚓

MOE BOWSTERN is editor of *Xtra Tuf*, a 'zine that chronicles the experiences and adventures of commercial fisher-folk in Alaska and beyond. Moe performs annually at the Astoria, Oregon Fisher Poets Gathering; she has also appeared at the Sea Music Festival in Mystic, Connecticut, the Working Waterfront Festival in New Bedford, Massachusetts, and Tony's Bar, "Kodiak's Biggest Navigational Hazard," in Kodiak, Alaska, among other places. Moe has worked on fishing boats since 1986 when, as a miserable eighteen-year-old boat cook, she once inadvertently threatened the lives of the crew by serving pasta tossed with shards of glass. *Xtra Tuf* #5: The Strike Issue won the 2007 Lilla Jewel Award. *Xtra Tuf* #6: The Greenhorn Issue featured contributions from more than twenty other writers, all on the theme of initiation into the rough world of commercial fishing. Find her at www.moebowstern.com

TROUBLE ON THE INSIDE PASSAGE

JOE UPTON rides the crab boat *Flood Tide* through Seymour Narrows and other icy straits, amazed at the raw, terrible beauty of the Alaskan seas, their danger and their power.

"HEY, KID, IT'S SEYMOUR, you gotta see this..."

Russell's voice intruded into my dreams, but the words instantly registered in my brain: SEYMOUR NARROWS! The place where the tidal current ran almost twenty miles an hour was legendary among Northwest mariners.

I pulled on my clothes and went up the steps into the wheelhouse. When I'd taken my eight-to-midnight wheel watch for the first time in my new job as deckhand on a Bering Sea-bound king crabber, we'd been steaming up Georgia Strait, a wide inland sea north of Vancouver, British Columbia. But now, in the thin light of the February dawn, the shores had drawn closer, the dark forest, clad in wisps of fog and low clouds, pressing in from both sides. And most alarmingly, there were whirlpools in the channel around us—from the tide, I assumed—and our heavy boat lurched from side to side. I'd seen Seymour once before in daylight, the summer I'd worked on a fish-packer, my first Alaska job. It wasn't a sight you forgot.

Off our port side, in a clearing in the dark and thick forest, a great sawmill emitted steam or smoke from every opening and stack, surrounded by stacks of freshly cut lumber. Barges laden deep with yellow sawdust lined its docks. To the starboard side was a small cove with fishing boats lying peacefully and the lights of cabins in the forest around it.

Our new steel crabber, the 104-foot *Flood Tide*, swayed slightly in the current as we swung to the port and entered a steep-sided canyon where the dark walls seemed to press in around us even more. For a moment, it looked like we were headed for a dead end, there didn't seem to be any exit. Just then, on the right, a misty and forbidding passage through the mountains opened unexpectedly ahead of us, giving me a glimpse of a different landscape. Behind had been settlements and lights on the shore; ahead were wild, impenetrable forests growing right down to the water's edge, the hand of man nowhere to be seen. I stepped out onto the deck behind the pilothouse to see it more clearly and the cold, misty air seemed to wrap around me—the smell of the sea and the forest. At the same time, the first snow we'd seen began to swirl softly around our little ship.

An invisible hand seemed to grab the *Flood Tide* and swirl us sideways. I grabbed the rail to hold on and looked down as we maneuvered between whirlpools the size of baseball diamonds, their vortexes choked with kelp and driftwood, spinning faster and faster. Suddenly, I felt uneasy out on deck alone and stepped back into the comforting warmth of the pilothouse. George Fulton, our skipper, was steering by hand. He had switched off the automatic pilot and was moving the short jog stick back and forth, trying to keep us out of the whirlpools that were swirling down from the channel ahead.

"That's the kind of crap you don't want to hit, kid." He pointed with his chin to what looked like the top of a phone pole that had appeared out of one of the whirlpools just to our port. As I looked, it disappeared out of sight. As far as I could tell, it didn't come up again

"You get these big logs, we call 'em deadheads, and they get waterlogged, and settle in the water so just one end is sticking up, three or four feet in diameter; they might weigh tons, sometimes they're so waterlogged that they might bob up only every few minutes. It would only dent our hull, but if it came up under our propeller, it'd mean a trip to the shipyard. And where we're going, there aren't any shipyards..."

I looked back to where the log had been. Just before the spot disappeared into the mists, I thought I saw something, but then it was gone. How could you see something like that to avoid it? An upwelling of current erupted suddenly from the water ahead of us, seeming to boil and surge, full of driftwood logs that obviously had been sucked under just a few minutes before, and George moved the jog stick all the way to starboard this time to miss them.

"It used to be worse." It was Russell this time, George's brother, a hard-bitten but kind-hearted fisherman of about fifty, who nudged me to the window as George steered us over to the east side of the channel. It was truly a canyon there, the walls rising steeply from the churning water's edge, and so narrow that just ahead power lines crossed the channel high in the air.

"Look right there." Russell pointed ahead and to our left. "See that big swirl, that's 'Old Rip,' Ripple Rock, or what's left of it." I peered into the gloom and saw what he was pointing at, a place where the biggest whirlpool yet was rotating, taking up at least half the width of the channel, where the surface of the water very clearly dipped down at least six feet at the center of the whirl. "There used to be a rock right there, just below the surface. It would sink one or two big boats each year, sometimes even a big steamer that got swung into it by the current. And that wasn't the worst of it—Old Rip would make whirlpools large enough to suck down fifty- or sixty-footers if they weren't careful."

The somber sight of that huge whirlpool and his words chilled me. And I knew, from previous conversations, that we had timed our departure from Seattle to arrive at Seymour around the time of slack water.

I knew the story of Old Rip; it was part of the lore of the northwest waterfront, one of the first things greenhorns heard about from other young men, proud of their Alaska season or seasons, proud of having been "through Seymour."

Each year Old Rip had claimed at least one large vessel and numerous smaller ones, whose operators misread their tide books, underestimated the power of the currents, or were careless, stupid, or both.

As vessels grew larger and traffic increased to Alaska and farther up the B.C. coast, it became an intolerable situation, and attempts were made to drill and blast the rock from big barges anchored with four concrete moorings, each weighing two-hundred-fifty tons. It didn't work. Despite the moorings, the barges moved so much in the current that accurate drilling was impossible. A work crew drowned when their boat was caught in a whirlpool and the effort was abandoned in favor of an ambitious scheme to tunnel from the east shore of the Narrows.

Crews sank a shaft some five-hundred feet vertically, then tunneled under the bottom of the Narrows, and very carefully upward again, exploring with small-diameter, diamond-tipped drills until they broke through into the water, plugging the holes, measuring, creating a three-dimensional map so that there was always at least thirty feet of rock between the tunnels and the angry rushing water of the Narrows.

They honeycombed the insides of Old Rip with tunnels and side "drifts" like coal miners. Tugboats pushed barge-loads of Dupont Nitramex 2-H dynamite packed into fifty-pound canisters to the loading dock, where cranes lowered the heavy pallets into the shaft to be packed into the tunnels. Finally, on the morning of April 17, 1958, patrol boats pushed fishing boats and spectators a mile back. No one knew how far the rock would be flung by such an immense quantity of explosives.

And in a dramatic moment, watched by thousands on TV all across Canada, Ripple Rock disappeared, filling the air above the Narrows with its remains. What was left, forty feet under the Narrows, was renamed Ripple Shoal.

We passed under the big swooping power lines just then, strung from the top of the cliff-like sides of the Narrows, and I looked behind. You could still see a few houses half hidden in the trees in the shore a half-mile back from where "Old Rip" had guarded the channel. Ahead, in the increasing swirl of the snow, I could see that the land was very different—dark and wild, even unfriendly. I remembered what another old-timer had told me about Seymour, Yuculta Rapids and the other places where the tide raged through the narrow passages between the islands. He said that the waterways to the south were all busy with homes on all the shores, with a friendly twinkle of lights at night. He said that anyone traveling to the north coast of British Columbia, or on to Alaska, big boat or small, had to proceed cautiously, waiting for slack water, before going on to the wilder land beyond.

"It was beyond them rapids, beyond Seymour and the Yucultas that I always felt the true North began," the old-timer told me. "Where there were hardly any towns, where a fellow was really on his own. But it was like this: It was as if nature had set these obstacles, right in that place where the busy south coast ends and the true North begins. It was like a warning to the traveler to be careful of the very different land and water that lay beyond."

It was February, 1971, and what would turn out to be the biggest commercial fishing boom in recent American history was just starting on the remote, cold, and windy waters of the Bering Sea between Alaska and Russia. I was twenty-four, with just a year of commercial fishing under my belt, and felt lucky to have been hired for the king crab season. Already, stories had begun to filter down from Alaska to the Seattle waterfront about the big money to be had by king crab fishermen in the remote Bering Sea.

For myself, and for many young men in those days, the lure of Alaska was a powerful elixir and the atmosphere was electric along Seattle's Fishermen's Terminal. Wintered there, on the shores of several interconnected lakes, separated by a set of locks from the salt water of Puget Sound, were many of the thousands of vessels of different sizes and types that headed north each spring for the Alaska salmon, crab, and herring fisheries. Seattle winters are mild, and even in February, as we had prepared the *Flood Tide* for her long Bering Sea battle, salmon and herring crews had been starting to stir, beginning to fit out, paint up, and get ready for what was for some a seven-month season along the wilderness waterways of the Alaska coast. Already, young men, including greenhorns who had never touched a salmon or been to Alaska were beginning to walk the docks, trying to find a moment when the busy skipper or boat owner might be approached about a job "going Up North."

I'd been one of those young men a few springs earlier, living on a friend's fishing boat by night and "beating the docks" by day. It had been June when the preseason Alaska fever was at its height, the activity along the docks, machine shops, and marine supply houses frenetic. Each night friends and family would come to drink noisily to the long season ahead aboard a freshly painted fishing boat that would be gone, through the locks and up onto the Inside Passage, in the morning. "Happy Are We Who Fish on the Sea" said the banner across the flying bridges of three gleaming fifty-eight footers the evening before they were gone.

My heart cried for each boat that left without me. Finally after three long weeks of despair, a garrulous man hired me as engineer on his fish buying boat—sort of a mother ship that transports fish from the remote fishing areas to the canneries—and my new life began. When, after a busy week of loading supplies and freight for the cannery, and learning about the engine-room systems, we slid through the locks and down into the salt water on a shining Puget Sound morning, I was about as full to bursting as a young man possibly could be.

That first season, in 1965 when I was just nineteen, was ALASKA in capital letters. We worked for a cannery in an Indian village. There were totem poles on the docks, bald eagles in the trees, and icebergs in the channels. The mate, Mickey Hansen, was an old Alaska hand—a Norwegian with fifty seasons "up north," having fished for about everything that swam or crawled in the waters of Alaska. Mickey took me under his wing, showed me the intricacies of fish-buying, navigation, diesel mechanics, and refrigeration. But most of all, he shared with me a lifetime of fishing in Alaska. Hardly a bay or a cove would we pass without Old Mick telling me a story like: "We picked our way into there in a snowstorm in '39 aboard the old *Patty A*. There wasn't no radar then, so we used the steam whistle, listening for the echo off the rocks."

That first season in Southeast Alaska filled me up in a way nothing else had and when it was over all I wanted to do was to get up there in my own boat.

Finally, in 1970, I had my chance and leased a very tired thirty-foot salmon gillnet boat in Fishermen's Terminal for the Alaska season. I should have taken a tip from the husky fisherman on the handsome boat in the next slip.

"Kid," he said, nodding at my boat with his chin, "I wouldn't let my children swim off that boat."

It didn't work out. The engine I'd had rebuilt threw a connecting rod through the side of the block, and the mechanic, aboard for the test ride, said, "Every engine I've rebuilt lately does that..." By the time I found another engine that I could afford, I didn't have the time or the money for the six-hundred-mile trip up to the Alaska salmon grounds and instead spent a discouraging season fishing in the very northern part of Puget Sound, along the border with Canada.

Then by a stroke of luck, I got a job aboard the *Flood Tide*. George was known to be a "highliner," a top fisherman, and I saw the job as a way to make enough money to get my own salmon boat and return to the waters of Southeast Alaska, where Old Mickey Hansen had showed me so much.

Our cook was Missouri Bob, a Southerner with a slow drawl and seemingly endless stories about his years working on shrimpers on the Gulf of Mexico. Our engineer was Johnny, a feisty redhead, who'd been an amateur boxer, and fished with George on other boats for years. Russell, our skipper's brother, was the mate, and I, the youngest, was a relative greenhorn.

No wives with children in arms came down to the dock to wish us well the night before we left Seattle, to drink to our luck in the long season ahead. Except for George and Russell, we were all single and childless. And this: there seemed to be an air of tension about our departure. In June, when the salmon fleet leaves, the days are warm and long, the trip up through the winding waterways of the Inside Passage something to be savored. But I sensed from George and the MARCO shipyard staff, which had built the *Flood Tide,* that a winter passage up the coast, even in a vessel as well built, fitted out, and crewed as the *Flood Tide* was not to be taken lightly. And we were traveling alone; if we got in a jam, there would be no one to help us.

The second to last day of February had come nasty, a cold rain turning to sleet. By mid-morning, the last, last things had come aboard, and I went ashore to call my parents on the East Coast, and to tell them that we were off finally. They wished me luck, but I sensed anxiety in their voices. Their friends' children had regular jobs and phones at home, where they could be reached at night. This business of going to Alaska, to the Bering Sea, in winter, was out of their realm of experience, and they were uncomfortable with it.

A day out of Seattle, I was focused on the job at hand and on the exciting season ahead. Russell and I worked on the deck, in the narrow rectangle of space between the back of the pilothouse and the first row of the huge seven-hundred-fifty-pound crab pots that filled our back deck. These huge, heavy wire and steel pots were rectangles seven feet by seven feet by three high.

Our job was to drill dozens of holes in each of the hundreds of screw-top plastic quart containers that were to be filled with chopped herring to attract crabs. Each had to be rigged with a short piece of heavy nylon twine tied to a stainless steel spring clasp that would be clipped inside our crab pots. There was little conversation between Russell and me. At cruising speed the sharp bark of the engine exhaust over our heads was loud enough to discourage all but the most important exchanges of information. The snow squalls came and went. When they came, we traveled in a white cocoon that swirled around the boat, chilling us, even wearing long underwear and insulated heavy coveralls, boots, and gloves. When they went, we peered out beyond the spray flung by the bow to a steep forest shore, unbroken by the hand of man—no roads, phone poles, docks or settlements.

The next day brought even more snow. By mid-morning, the wind had heaved up such a nasty sea that it was no longer possible to work on deck, so we retreated inside to the refuge of northern seamen—a comfortable bunk and a good book. At noon, I took over for my four-hour steering watch—essentially monitoring our position while the automatic pilot steered our heavily laden craft north before a southerly gale. The seas were large, and getting larger, but they were behind us so we had an easy ride.

George was asleep in his stateroom. I'm sure this was the first time he had been able to get in a good sleep since the frenzy of last-minute preparations for our season had begun a month or so earlier.

We were then traveling up thirty-mile-wide Hecate Strait in northern British Columbia, about sixty miles south of the Alaska border. If the *Flood Tide* had been a smaller boat, like one of the several thousand thirty- to sixty-footers that traveled up the coast each spring from the Puget Sound ports to Alaska for the salmon season, we would have taken a route through the much narrower and winding channels forty miles farther east. They were a series of water-filled canyons that penetrate the steep coastal mountains deep into the interior of British Columbia and make for delightful traveling in almost totally sheltered waters. It was those sheltering channels that comprise the Inside Passage—the thousand-mile route from Seattle to the historical Klondike Gold Rush port of Skagway, Alaska—that allowed even the smallest craft, by carefully watching the weather in the wider sections, to travel safely up the coast.

Threading through narrow channels and among numerous reefs however required the highest level of diligence from a vessel's crew. Rarely was a course leg more than a few miles long, requiring that the position of the vessel be monitored constantly, or a turn not made at just the right time might put the vessel in peril.

Our parallel route up Hecate Strait allowed our skipper to relax without worrying about whether the person on watch was making the myriad and precise course changes required by a passage up the narrower channels. The strait, however, exposed vessels to the wind from any direction, and was a notoriously nasty place except in summer.

At around 3 p.m. alone in the wheelhouse as the rest of the crew slept, I noticed an odd, blotchy-looking target on our radar, where no land was supposed to be. Outside the thick windows that stretched all the way across the wide front of the pilothouse I saw nothing but swirling white. I fiddled with the radar controls, and again studied the chart carefully. But there was only open water. Yet, the radar showed something–something that was growing closer as we swept northward, pushed by the growing seas of the building storm behind us. Inside the wheelhouse all was peaceful and quiet except for the muted hum of the engine. But I began to feel very uneasy, and finally pulled the engine throttle controls to the half speed position, a move that I knew George would quickly react to.

The skipper was out of his cabin in an instant, quickly scanning the radar display and the chart, pulling the throttle back to an idle and speaking into the intercom, all in an instant, it seemed. "Johnny, flood both crab tanks... quick as you can." We had been traveling with our two big holds or crab tanks, empty, to give us a bit more speed. Filling them would make us travel a bit slower, but most important, it would lower our center of gravity, making the vessel more stable in heavy seas—an important factor, considering the heavy load of crab pots we were carrying on deck. A minute or so later, we could hear the big diesel generator in the engine room change tone as the massive crab pumps came on line.

While the crab tanks filled, we idled slowly ahead. Sensing something was happening, the rest of the crew filed up into the pilothouse, peering forward into the snowy dusk. Finally Johnny came up and gave us the word—the tanks were full and overflowing, the condition for maximum stability. George throttled up to two-thirds, and we moved toward whatever was out there.

For a long while we saw nothing but the big grey-bearded seas marching past us in the thickly falling snow. Then there was what seemed like a lightening in the snow and gloom ahead, and we all peered intently, pressing our faces into the thick glass, trying to get some glimpse of what the radar was seeing, now less than a half-mile ahead of us.

Then, briefly, a frightening sight, glimpsed quickly through the gloom and as quickly gone—the backs of great seas, breaking, the spume from their crests thrown back like the manes of wild horses, covering a wide area ahead.

"Shit ... hang on guys," George swiveled to look out the back window at the seas behind us, then throttled up, and in a break between seas, pushed the steering lever all the way to starboard. As we swung into our turn, our boat, which had seemed so big tied to the dock in Seattle, dropped suddenly and rolled alarmingly to port for what seemed a very long moment as a huge sea plowed into our side. Time seemed to stand still. Dishes crashed in the galley below, an alarm bell rang shrilly, and only then did we finish our turn, slowly come back upright and the alarm stop ringing.

George stood at the chart, shaking his head, and pointed to the north end of the strait, where it narrowed slightly.

"Lookit this ... breaking here, in a hundred feet of water ... breaking, for Christ sake... I heard about it once before, but I never really believed it."

What was happening was that the seas created by the gale blowing from the south were meeting the tidal current flooding in from the north, producing breaking seas all the way across the relatively shallow shelf that was a hundred-feet deep at the north end of the strait. Given the conditions, these were seas that we'd be foolish to risk, even in our very rugged and new 104-footer.

Somewhere there was a narrow gully of much deeper water, where we thought the seas wouldn't be breaking. But if it were there, we couldn't find it as we jogged back and forth in that windy wasteland of angry churning water and hissing snow. Finally, the wind came on stronger still, and it began to get dark. The seas grew even larger as the tidal current increased. It was rapidly becoming a bad place to be, so we reluctantly headed east, looking for a way through a maze of islands and breaking reefs to the sheltered waters of the Inside Passage.

However, we had no detailed chart, relying only Russell's hazy memory of a passage through, several decades earlier, in good clear weather. The area we had to transit was full of islands, winding channels, and hidden rocks—no place to be on a night like that without a chart.

Then, we felt something unexpected, unspoken, but something that settled over us all the same—fear, even in the pilothouse of the finest and most rugged boat that the best shipyard in the whole Northwest could put out.

The daylight fled away to the west and the windy, snowy, blackness swallowed us up. The flying snow and spray were so thick that our radar could barely penetrate it. Three times Russell said, "That way..." and we proceeded cautiously into a narrow channel bounded by rock and snow-blasted trees. This led to three dead ends as our crab lights high on the mast turned the night into snow-thick day and revealed only the sea beating violently on a rocky cul-de-sac. One dead-end was so narrow there was not even room to turn around. We had to back out ever so cautiously. No one spoke.

Finally, the fourth channel opened into another, and yet another after that, and the sea died away, and the water stayed deep, and sometime after midnight, we found our way into the sheltered and calm waters of the Inside Passage. It was still snowing hard and inky dark, but we were back on our charts. Still my confidence in our powerful boat and experienced skipper and mate had been shaken, something I hadn't expected on just the third day of our trip, and I slept uneasily.

In the early dusk of the next day, as we transited Wrangell Narrows, a winding channel between two large islands, we passed a Norman Rockwell scene that tugged strongly at my heartstrings—a single cabin, in a little clearing on the shore with two small outboard boats drawn up on the bank before it. Wood smoke rose from the chimney. The snow covered trees stood all around. And from each window shone a cheery warm light that pierced out into the wild landscape. Even though I was excited and proud to be on the *Flood Tide* and headed north into a fishery that already was becoming a legend along the waterfront, I yearned for the kind of fishing and living that could be had among those islands of Southeast Alaska.

My summer of fish-buying among those forest-clad islands and remote towns had filled me with the desire to go back. Now, it was my dream to make enough money on the *Flood Tide* to purchase a more modern boat in better shape and try again.

As a crew, we had no illusions about what the months ahead held. None of us had fished the Bering Sea, the vast storm-breeding body of water between Alaska and Russia, yet we'd heard enough tales to know that it didn't take kindly to those folks and boats that came to wrest a living from her waters.

In the dark, a few hours later, we met the first ice—just small bergs, perhaps the size of a dump truck—drifting west with the current and the wind from LeConte Glacier, the most southerly place on the coast that the great glaciers meet the saltwater and break off icebergs. The earlier snow had blown off to the west, and a half moon illuminated the bergs with an eerie glowing light. We stood out on deck, taking in the sobering sight—the inky water, the eerily lit icebergs, and beyond, the snowy ice and rock spires of the coast range. We were humbled. We were then some eight-hundred miles north of Seattle. Ahead of us lay almost another twelve-hunded miles of an increasingly brutal and unforgiving landscape.

"Hey guys... listen to this:" The next morning, we'd been in the galley, taking a warm-up and coffee break from the deck work, when George came over the intercom, switching the speaker over to the single sideband radio (a shortwave radio with long range capabilities, favored by mariners).

" ... position ... west of ... Spencer ... iced up heavy, antennas broken ..." The transmission faded in and out and then faded out entirely.

The Coast Guard with its higher antenna must have received the signal more clearly.

"Roger, we understand you are fifty miles northwest of Cape Spencer, have suffered broken windows and have lost your main antennas from icing and sea conditions, but require no assistance at this time. Please call every hour with your status and we will be standing by on this frequency."

The speakers went silent and a moment later our somber-faced skipper came down the stairs from the pilothouse to fill us in.

"It's a Martinolich boat, a year old, smaller than us, an eighty-six footer, but husky, built for anything the Bering Sea and North Pacific can dish out. She'd been fishing south of Kodiak when it started to blow cold from the Northwest, blowing down off the glaciers and icy mountains and valleys of the Alaska Range. She was headed back into town, and blew out two pilothouse windows bucking into the seas and making ice so heavy their only hope of survival was to turn around and run with the wind behind them, away from the land. By the time the storm blew itself out, they'd been blown all the way across the Gulf..."

Ice. No one said much as we nursed our coffees. "Making ice" was the single greatest danger that boats working the Alaska coast faced in winter. When the air temperature dropped into the twenties and below, sea spray thrown up by the waves froze instantly upon contacting the cold steel rigging and hull of any boat. For crab boats, traveling with their loads of heavy pots stacked many layers high, it was a double whammy; the pots offered a huge amount of surface area on which ice could form, and with such loads boats had a reduced capacity to survive heavy icing as their center of gravity was raised by the weight of the pots.

By 1971, enough boats had had close calls with icing that fishermen and mariners were just beginning to become more aware of the problem. But for the unsuspecting, especially at night, the effect was sinister. A boat with a high level of stability, meaning a low center of gravity, would have a quick, almost uncomfortably quick, motion in a seaway. But when such a vessel began to accumulate ice on her decks and rigging, her center of gravity would rise. This would have the effect of making the vessel's motion easier—the rolling and pitching occurred more slowly. To the uninformed, the change in the vessel's motion might bring a sense of security. In reality, the vessel's stability was diminished and was having a harder and harder time bringing the vessel back upright after each roll because of the increased weight of the ice. If nothing was done to break the cycle and the ice kept accumulating, the rolls would become slower and slower and more and more "comfortable," and eventually the vessel would, without warning, roll completely over.

In the afternoon, we worked on deck preparing for the next phase of our journey—the Gulf of Alaska. Following our incident with the breakers two evenings before in Hecate Strait, we'd been traveling among the sheltered waterways of Southeast Alaska, where our route passed among hundreds of islands and sheltered bays and harbors. This route offered many places for a vessel to anchor up and wait, safe and secure, until the weather improved. But once we passed Cape Spencer in the evening, our route for the next two-hundred-fifty miles would be along an unforgiving coast where most harbors were shallow river mouths, guarded by breaking seas, accessible only to small craft in good weather. If a storm found us along this coast, we would have many miles of hard traveling to get to a safe harbor. If the weather had been more settled, we might have elected to take the straight route from Cape Spencer to Kodiak, saving several hundred miles of following the long curve of the coast. But in winter, the prudent fishing vessel traveled along the coast, a few miles off.

If a storm caught us along that coast, it would be hard for us to go out on deck to tighten up the lashings on the crab pots, so we retightened the chain binders that held our pots securely to the steel rails on the bulwarks.

We were passing then through Icy Strait, with Glacier Bay and the austere 12,000- and 15,000-footers of the Fairweather Range (definitely not named for the weather...) to our north. Now and then we would pass an errant iceberg, and the ice and the more and more unforgiving landscape were a sobering reminder of what lay ahead.

The wan afternoon sun had worked its way to the southwest and we all were up in the pilothouse with our coffees when a strange sight appeared in the water. At first, as we scanned it with the binoculars, we thought we were seeing some odd ice creation, spawned from the bowels of the great tidewater glaciers to our north, perhaps an iceberg with odd shining protrusions. Then, as we got closer, we realized what it was, shining in the last rays of the setting sun—the iced-up king crabber we had heard on the radio talking to the Coast Guard.

That she had survived her battle with the ice was incredible. She was truly sheathed in it, from the stubs of her broken radio antennas to the dark water streaming along her iced hull. As she got closer, we could see her crew, breaking the ice off the anchor winch and railings around the bow with baseball bats, and shoveling it over the side. Two others were on the back deck, breaking ice off the few remaining pots. A single pilothouse window had been cleared of ice, and two plywood patches on the others showed the battle scars of a storm at sea. As we passed thirty or forty yards apart, the back door of the pilothouse opened and a figure emerged, waving. Humbled by the sight, we waved back. Probably she was headed to Juneau, fifty miles to the east, the nearest town with good marine supplies, to lick her wounds before heading out again.

The mood in the pilothouse after supper was subdued. Astern was the sweeping beam of the light at Cape Spencer, the entrance to the sheltered waters of the Inside Passage. Ahead lay the immense Gulf of Alaska. The night was hazy, black, and cloudless. The bow rose and fell with the long Pacific swell, and there was neither star nor horizon to guide us.

Just before midnight, I rose, made coffee, and went up into the pilothouse to take the "graveyard watch," my midnight to 4 a.m. watch, relieving Russell Fulton, the skipper's brother, whose hazy knowledge had guided us through that difficult passage from stormy Hecate Strait into the sheltered waters of the Inside Passage. The pilothouse was dark, illuminated only by the dim numbers from the Loran, radar, and instrument displays. A half moon had come up, shining starkly on the wall of ice and snow that rose from the shore ten miles east of us.

Russell's stubby forefinger punched down on the chart and he spoke: "Lituya Bay. You don't want to go in there unless you really have to. All that water in them fiords and this bay has to pour in and out through that narrow entrance. You can go in if the tide's flooding or slack if it's not blowing heavy, but on the ebb that current stacks up the seas and it's a boat-killer. That's the hell about this part of the coast." His finger traced the entrances to some other bays: Dry Bay and Dangerous River, "You get in a jam with some engine problem or bad weather and you need a harbor, and there's no place to go. I've seen breakers out here, two full miles from shore … you want to give this coast a good berth…"

Twenty miles north of Yakutat, one of the few good harbors along that coast, a wind came up. After five minutes it was blowing seventy. The temperature was fifteen degrees. The first spray over the bow froze instantly on the wheelhouse windows. George Fulton turned around the *Flood Tide* with hardly a discussion.

In the outer part of Yakutat Bay, a sobering sight had us all up in the wheelhouse. The 140-foot trawler *Deep Sea,* pioneer of the king crab fishery, lay at anchor with a big covered barge in tow. She had iced up bad, as had her barge, all the corners and sharp angles softened by the smooth and sinister contours of thick ice. But the sobering part was the barge. The whole front of the structure built on it, a long metal warehouse of a building, was crumpled in, the top and sides mangled for a third of the way back and in places the aluminum sheeting had been ripped off like paper. George got the story over the radio: the barge was a floating shrimp cannery, headed for Kodiak, four-hundred miles to the west. They had gotten within ten miles of the shelter of Cape Saint Elias, one-hundred-thirty miles north of Yakutat, when the wind came up. Two hours later, the seas had punched in the front of the barge, forcing the *Deep Sea* skipper to turn around and run before the storm, icing as they went, all the way back to Yakutat.

We tied with frozen lines to a silent cannery wharf, and I walked up to the village with Johnny and Missouri Bob in the blowing, drifting snow. In all of Yakutat, we saw only two lighted windows, and nowhere a footprint or car track. We trudged back to the boat through the knee-deep snow. Our boat, with the bark of her diesel generator filling the night, seemed like a visitor from another planet.

A blizzard swept in from the Canadian Yukon after midnight. At the head of the harbor, in the lee of the great mountains, we lay sheltered from its force, but morning showed a grey and eerie world. Outside the windows of the pilothouse, a steady plume of snow settled down on us, drifting down from the wharf above. By noon, what little free deck we had was drifted rail to rail, almost waist deep with snow. It was as if we'd come to the edge of the world as we knew it. And we still had some one-thousand miles more to go.

That night, sometimes even over the reassuring hum of our diesel generator, we could hear the wind, screeching through the trees and cannery buildings above us. But at 4 a.m., when we got up to sniff the air, to see if it was "a chance," as mariners sometimes call a window of good weather, the storm had blown out to sea. So we drew in our stiff lines, and headed out of the still bay, into the Gulf of Alaska.

The dawn, when it came, was truly awesome—first a faint yellow line, then a dozen peaks tinged with pink. The sun, when it rose, was red and angry, lighting up thousands of square miles of bleak ice and rock with its eerie long-shadowed light before it disappeared into a strange, thin, hazy, cloud cover.

All day we steamed northwest, a few miles off the beach. The wind was off-shore and light, our ride easy, but there was something about the day and place that made us all somber. The land to the north and east was a strip of beach, rising to ice fields and mountains as far as the eye could see, range after range of cold, white peaks. The coast was broken here and there by little bays, all ice-choked and shallow, offering no shelter.

The night came early and inky black, but without a breath of wind. It seemed as if we were traveling through a featureless void. We ate early and then gathered in the darkened pilothouse, anxious to make Cape Hinchinbrook, the end of the most exposed passage. The tension in the air was something you could feel, and finally I went below to an uneasy sleep. ⚓

After a white-knuckle season fishing for king crab in the Bering Sea in 1971, JOE UPTON purchased a thirty-two foot gillnetter-trawler to pursue his dream of fishing in the sheltered waters of Southeast Alaska. He wrote about those years in his memoir, *Alaska Blues,* which won a Pacific Northwest Booksellers Award, and later wrote about crab-fishing in *Bering Sea Blues,* both published by Epicenter Press. When salmon fishing in Southeast went through one of its cyclical slumps in the mid-1970s, Upton headed to the coast of Maine, purchasing a 1917 seventy-one-foot sardine carrier to operate in the lobster bait business. But Alaska always called Upton. He and his wife, Mary Lou, returned to Alaska to operate a fish-buying vessel, the *Emily Jane,* in Southeast Alaska for several seasons. After eleven seasons in Bristol Bay, Upton retired from commercial fishing in 1998 to start Coastal Publishing, which produced guides for Alaska cruise-ship passengers, the *Alaska Cruise Companion* and the *Alaska Cruise Handbook.* Upton and his wife live in Bainbridge Island, Washington, and Vinalhaven Island, Maine.

THE STORMS AROUND US

W HEN I WAS NINE and started fishing every day in our salmon setnetting operation, I thought I knew most of the rules of the water. Obey without question. Work hard, never complain, and when you are most miserable, make a dumb joke. But every year I learned more.

The best way to pick a salmon out of the net is to hook your thumb and forefinger inside its gills before you yank it free. Clear jellyfish are harmless; colored ones sting. Tuck your pants into your socks and your sleeves into your plastic gloves and your hair into a bandana if you want to stay dry. Acting like a girl means crying when your father yells or dancing too wildly in the bow—both should be avoided. Sharks that look dead probably aren't.

At nine, I never went out in storms, but at thirteen I knew more than the crewmen who were five years older and ten times stronger than I am. So when the first storm of the season blew in my thirteenth summer, there was no reason to stay onshore with my mother and my younger brothers. With my father, fear never counted as an excuse.

NAPHTALI FIELDS relives moments from a childhood of fishing, including a terrifying moment in the skiff, and tries to find her elusive place on the ocean and in the work that has defined her life.

No one fishing with us had died during a storm, but I knew how it would be. A wave would sweep the net under the moving prop and it was hopelessly tangled. The wind would push the bow towards shore and the stern would swamp in a minute. The crew, desperately reaching for floating tote lids, would be smashed against the cliffs by the surf before another skiff could save them. Though it sounds terribly melodramatic now, I imagined walking through my freshman year of high school shadowed by their ghosts whispering, "Why weren't you watching? Why did you let us drown?" They would not be the only ghosts to walk these islands. One winter two Native fishermen disappeared close to our beach. The villagers say the boy fell into the ocean first then his grandfather after him, but no one really knows for sure. They only found the empty skiff, drifting aimlessly with the wind and tide.

My favorite storm scenario was less morbid and got more vivid every summer as I longed to know the mysterious crewmen who lived on another island and worked with us each day. I imagined fishing with one of them, a handsome, kind one with hair that wasn't too shaggy and a beard that was still scruffy but not intimidating. Our motor would suddenly quit and the wind would push us out to sea before anyone noticed we were gone. We'd land, completely disoriented, on a far-away beach. We'd make a fire, huddle together for warmth, and await rescue. Neither of us would sleep so he'd ask, "Naphtali, what do you think about life?" I'd talk for hours and he'd listen, smiling and twirling my hair around his calloused, fisherman's fingers. When morning came we'd be rescued. My dad would leap towards me with a bear hug and thick, wool blankets for the ride back to the islands while the other crewmen would surge around my scrappy companion with backslaps and relieved grins. I'd look back at him in the commotion and he'd wink at me before turning to join his friends. My father would usher me away, but I'd smile: I'd made my first conquest.

That particular daydream would never come true, because the crewmen were off-limits. Stuck with Dad and my brother Noah every time the skiff left shore, I admired them from a distance. It was only during storms that he approved of me watching them. I was his lookout, staring at the seven skiffs behind us, ready to yell if one of them stopped and started drifting towards the rocks or got hit by a huge wave. We work close to shore, so one moment of hesitation might bring injuries or death. Every storm day, as my Dad's skiff led the others to the nets, I felt it was my eyes alone that would be keeping us all from disaster.

This storm was spectacular. On the walk down to the skiff that morning, the wind hurled sand at us like driving rain. The skiff bobbled on the water like a long, metal cork, the motor's prop dipping in and out of the waves. We pushed off from shore into the boiling sea, doubt and fear already knotting my stomach. I sat beside

Noah, my younger brother, both of us in identical green raincoats, two sizes too big, our backs to the wind as the skiff crashed heavily into each swell. We faced our father, who was standing, leaning and squinting into the wind. He'd later teach me about driving in waves this high, how to ride the waves to keep the wind from flipping the skiff. He scanned the water, watching for the other seven skiffs in the fleet to join us the five-mile run out to the nets. Noah calmly tucked his chin into his lifejacket and napped while I stared, transfixed at the swelling waves pushing against each other for control.

That morning, my dad drove like a sea captain on a sailing ship. His legs braced wide apart, his mouth open, he tasted the wind and the spray with his tongue. Now I am older, twenty-two, and drive in storms like the one that began my thirteenth summer. I sing loudly and open my mouth and spit saltwater until my lips crack and bleed. Now I am older and stand like my father, boots braced against the floor, hip pushing on the outboard handle, chest leaned into the storm, but I pretend a calm I do not feel, a knowledge I do not have, an occupation I'm never sure I really want. I've learned the ocean well, but my place in it evades me.

That long-ago morning, full of images of shipwrecks and catastrophe, I didn't eat my breakfast. It was ham and eggs because Dad believed in hearty food on difficult work days, but my stomach started twisting when I woke to the storm outside. As Noah methodically cut his ham and gulped his milk, I spooned my food into the compost, hiding it under grapefruit peels while Dad was in the outhouse. The three youngest boys slept through our preparations. They too had to fish, but not as much as me and Noah and not in bad weather. Mom hadn't been sleeping well since her pregnancy, so she got out of bed to hug us as we put on our grimy sweatshirts with hoods stiff from salt.

"These are awful," she said, "Don't your hoods scratch you like that? Look at them; they've held the shape of your head all night. Why don't you wear another one?" She grabbed a handful of the shirts drying in front of the oil stove and held them up for my inspection.

I shrugged. "When they get wet, they loosen up. It's my best shirt. Either way, you can't switch shirts in a storm."

She nodded knowingly and put the other shirts down. She hugged me once more and watched us as we marched down the path, her arms crossed above her growing belly.

We fish from a setnet site that perches on the edge of the Shelikof Strait. In the summer, our islands are as green as jewels, snugly surrounded by the sea. It is the most beautiful place in the world. My grandfather came here to fish for salmon in 1961, bringing his wife and three sons to a wilderness cabin on Bear Island. Its previous occupant had been an alcoholic who, as he descended into madness, swore that people were coming and cutting steaks off his cows as they grazed.

My grandfather passed fishing on to my uncles and father, who taught me to pride my work on the sea, our strength as a family, our enduring legacy. I was told we were one of the biggest setnetting operations in Alaska, that we worked on some of the roughest water for setnetters, that our season was one of the longest. I believed all of these things because I could not imagine another family having the audacity to fish in waves so big you couldn't see over them to the other skiffs, wind so hard it whipped williwaws into our stiff backs as we kept picking. I believed what I was told, and I imagined more.

The ocean changed my family. It transformed ranchers and farmers into fishermen; it carried land-locked Southerners to isolated, Alaskan islands. Some of us it alienated; others, it freed. Visually, the transition from the beach to the water is obvious. We layer on filthy sweatshirts, cut-off sweatpants, wool socks, hip boots, raingear, life jackets, and gloves, kneepads sometimes. When crewmen first get their gear, they waddle like penguins down the beach, unaccustomed to so much bulk. Other changes are less photogenic. I learned both fearlessness and terror on the ocean; it fostered my family's pride and gave us reason to ignore each other when the flood of fish was a more pressing priority.

Dad was cheerful that day until we met up with the rest of the skiffs by Bear Island. My Uncle Weston divided the crew without radioing us. Normally he and my dad worked together, sorting each guy based on their original rubric, "strong, clueless, with-it, too-much-attitude, green" and the skiffs faced the storm with equal ability. That morning, Weston inadvertently put two green guys in a skiff and we joined them on the water too late to say anything. Dad contained his initial frustration, but I could see it under his clenched jaw and his tight eyebrows as he navigated through the waves.

On good days, Dad peddled corny puns and bellowed classic country songs with laughter. On others, he brimmed with fury, yelling at every mishap. I either feared or admired him on the water, depending on the day. But I did not pity him.

Feeling sick, full of dread, as we made our slow way to the nets, I hummed my favorite hymn into the echo of my raincoat hood, the splash of spray against the skiff my only accompaniment. Noah sat unmoving. After an especially big wave threw spray against my back until it dripped down my neck, I peered around his raincoat's floppy hood to see his face. His eyes were closed; he looked calm. Then, Noah's passivity seemed like maturity, which wasn't fair because he was younger. I tried to picture him watching the sunsets like I did, twirling around in their light, sighing at their romance. I couldn't do it. If he wasn't excited by a storm, what could solicit a reaction from him? I was tired of being the only one who, according to him, "freaked out all the time."

The motor interrupted my thoughts. It suddenly roared and we lurched forward at full speed into the waves. "Hey! Hey! Hey!" Dad shouted. Noah sat up with a jerk. We both turned around and faced the bow, but we couldn't see the crisis. With one hand steadying the outboard's handle, Dad inhaled deeply before he yelled again. It was blowing thirty-five miles an hour and the sixty-horsepower motor thundered. No one outside the skiff could possibly hear him. We were going faster than I could ever remember, riding in between the rollers, my dad leaning into the disaster ahead that I had yet to see. And then, there they were, the greenhorn skiff on one of the nets.

Drifting helplessly on the swells, the skipper, Dan, was desperately trying to start the motor. He was yanking at the pull cord with quick jerks, choking it, yanking again, only stopping to look up with huge eyes as we drove as close to them as we could on the waves.

"Throw me your bowline!" my dad shouted at the bowman, Travis, who hesitated a second before he remembered where it was and how to untie the simple clovehitch against the side. The decibel of my dad's yells increased. "Naphtali, go catch it!" I stumbled up to the bow and stood, Noah beside me, holding onto the rail for balance, praying that I would get it before both skiffs were carried to shore.

In the bow, I realized my hands were sweating; my stomach rumbled. I counted seven seagulls riding on the waves around us. Everything was so distinct and clear, it felt like death. Dad was stiff with frustration as Travis fumbled with the rope. Every second the swells were pushing us closer and closer to the crushing surf on the beach. The heavy skiff would flip and no one would be close enough to help. Noah and I couldn't swim; I would be the ghost following my cousins and crewmen asking why they let me die.

Dad cupped his hands and boomed across the waves, "Cotton-picking nincompoop, throw it!"

On the top of another wave, Travis threw the rope and I reached, leaning my torso as far over the rail as I could, trying not to let my legs swing up into the air, praying, "Come on, come on, come on!" My gloves were inches away from the line when we were carried off on a separate wave. I missed it. I immediately glanced back at the stern, but Dad's favorite, original expletive turned me back towards the bow.

"For Pete's sake! Stop pansying around and get the rope! No margin for error here!" he shouted. I cringed; Noah stood closer in what I imagined to be camaraderie. We were only two-hundred feet away from shore, getting closer with every wave. Travis and Dan's faces were pale, their eyes huge. Dan kept trying to start the motor and Travis rushed to pull the line back in.

Dad yelled again, "Throw it!" and the line snaked out from the skiff in a beautiful loop that all of us could see would fall short of my hands. I was still reaching over the side when Dad lurched the stern at a right angle. Both Noah and I fell backwards into the skiff against the floor. Dad caught the line and tied a clovehitch against our skiff's side in one motion, then revved the engine as hard as he could into the surf. "SIT DOWN!" Dad screamed at Noah and me as we stumbled from the floor to stand. We staggered back to our original position on the seat and watched the skiff we towed behind us. Dad looked straight ahead into the swells, his jaw locked. My cheeks flushed. It was my job to be the lookout, but I neither saw the guys nor saved them; nothing depended on me.

That afternoon, as we sat around the lunch table, my mom asked how the morning had gone. Noah and I were silent. Dad grunted before saying, "Couple of bunglers out on Bill's set almost got us killed this morning. Maybe if Naphtali concentrated more during softball practice it wouldn't have been such a close call." I didn't smile at his joke; just kept burying my fork in the rice pilaf. He didn't notice because he was laughing with my little brothers who loved teasing me about my lackluster attempts at softball.

Mom interrupted them to ask, "Well, how was the storm for you, Noah?"

"Fine," he answered quickly, his mouth full of food.

I kept mashing the pilaf and pictured the crew, eating lunch on their own island, telling the story at the crowded table. If I figured into the story at all I would be the comic relief, the wide-eyed girl in the bow who couldn't catch a rope.

After the storm, the summer unfolded as it always did. The hills of the island purpled with lupine then exploded in the hot pink of fireweed. The salmon began to swarm the nets, and Noah and I worked like the grownups to keep up with the fish. The prison of the skiff relaxed in the frenzy, and I worked with crewmen for the first time. My fantasies of a companionable shipwreck never came true, but I now had faces, eyes, and voices to piece into my daydreams. The work wore us down; I lost feeling in my arms when I slept, my pillow was covered in incandescent scales. Though my body slumped under the strain of the work, I couldn't say anything about it. My exhaustion began to harden into bitterness as the summer ended and another continued and still I was trapped by the island and fishing.

And so it went, each summer that passed fading into the last one's memories until now at twenty-two I can barely distinguish year from year. They blur together into images of massive waves, thousands of salmon, and floating bull kelp. I carry the weight of fishing always: my first day of high school my hands were too swollen to hold a pencil; I dream of coiling rope; I evaluate men based on their ability to weather a storm. The rules are different now than my thirteenth summer. Acting like a girl is not a bad thing. Passivity, like freaking out, is a way to cope. The ghosts that follow me are often alive, and I don't have to listen to them. And ropes, if they are missed once, can be caught again. ⚓

NAPHTALI FIELDS has been salmon setnetting off the Shelikof Strait every summer of her twenty-two years. In 2010 she driftnetted both the Bristol Bay salmon season and the Kodiak season, working until late September.

Fields spent four months in southern Chile in 2009 interviewing commercial fishing women and wrote a theatre piece based on their lives. In 2010 she graduated from Wheaton College with a degree in bilingual theatre, and will spend 2011 in Central America with Artcorps, facilitating community theatre in rural villages.

CATCH AND RELEASE

DEBRA NIELSEN recounts her struggle for survival in the sinking of *The Wayward Wind* in the Bering Sea, and her struggle afterward to reconcile her losses.

THE VIVIDNESS OF the flowers floating on the dark gray water rivets the eye like bright balloons in a cloudless sky. Sprays of delicate baby's breath, burgundy roses, and purple iris entwine a pale blue ribbon that reads, "Beloved Son." A breeze brushes over the wreath, trembling its petals.

A large woman stands dockside. Beside her is a wheelchair, next to which a man peers into a video camera. Occasionally he utters an explanatory narrative, or makes a quiet observation.

As the woman fumbles with her camera, her ragged breathing mingles with the cries of circling sea gulls.

"I can do this," she says.

I can't.

I don't want to be here. I don't want to be standing here on this dirty dock, splattered by sea-gull droppings and smudged by creosote, staring at a ten-year-old tribute, floating on a monochromatic sea. I'd rather be anywhere else. I'd definitely rather be fishing, maybe casting a net over sparkling salmon, or reefing a halibut from the fathomless deep. I'd rather be feeling the hope of the hook, the anticipation of the baited pot, or unloading a deckload of dreams.

Instead, I am here, an honor-bound captive of two flatlanders with a need to float their flowers.

One week ago, the woman called to tell me they were coming. She didn't say she could barely walk. She didn't say the man would be with her. She didn't say that she smoked nonstop, or that she was dying. Years ago, I met her briefly when we went to Wisconsin to see his folks.

"This is Connie, my younger brother's wife. She can clear out a barroom all by herself."

She seemed nice enough, but I had different criteria for friendship, and I wasn't in the market for Barroom Betty.

As a matter of fact, the entire factory mentality of Kenosha, Wisconsin, left me cold. Pickled eggs? Retirement? Not for me. I had my eye on an entirely different horizon.

Now, she tells me she has a rare neurological disorder, something called reflex sympathetic dystrophy. Originally, she says, it was associated with farm women. It seems that occasionally, while canning produce, a heavy jar would accidentally drop sharply onto a woman's foot. The signal sent from the foot to the brain would somehow arc due to the distance of the extremity. Apparently, this uncompleted circuit reacts like a live wire, continually sending a message of pain to a mystified brain, and, consequently, plays havoc with the nervous system.

"The doctors didn't want me to come," she says, "but I told them I'm going. 'I'm going to Kodiak, Alaska,' I said. And I told Ma, 'I'll buy you that memorial wreath you want and float it for your red-headed Billy.'" She shakes her head.

"Ten years—I just hope it brings her some peace. If it brings her some peace, it's worth every step I have to take."

The wreath is drifting into the dock. I bend to give it a gentle nudge toward the center of the stall.

I think about shocks to the nervous system: Arcs of pain ricocheting about, endlessly seeking solace from a recoiling brain. Do the aftershocks ever cease? Or are these unquelled sparks of harm snuffed out only by death? As I straighten, the woman draws me into her arms.

"I'm so sorry to cause you more pain," she says. "I wouldn't cause you pain for anything, and I know I am and it hurts me. It hurts my heart to do it. You don't know how it hurts me." Her face is contorted with emotion. I nod into the smother of her shoulder and she tightens her embrace.

As soon as I can, I pull away, cross the dock, and face the open ocean.

It is January, the sky clenching snow, the iron sea below—no wind, only the push of our passage through the icy stillness. The harbor has begun to freeze, and our props churn through a blended margarita of iced pewter, chilled mercury, and bits of silver. The ocean steams where it touches the frozen air and ice fog smudges the horizon.

We wear thick neoprene gloves and heavy raingear as we secure the deck for travel. Each movement realized through resistance, like working under water. Lines are stowed below; left on deck, they would freeze to useless lumps of ice. Even as we coil, they begin to stiffen.

I take the lines and go below, shedding my raingear and gloves before descending into a well-lit laboratory-clean engine room. It did not always look like this. We spent five years of nonstop effort and a small fortune on her refitting. After stowing the lines, I check the gauges on the main. The stack temperature on the port exhaust is running a couple of degrees high, but everything else reads normal. I wipe a seep of oil from the forward head of the auxiliary and wait. It does not reappear. After securing the toolbox to the bulkhead, I wipe a three-quarter-inch wrench with an oily rag and hang it in its silhouette against the hull. The wrenches make metallic music to the rhythm of the engines. I stow a wooden box of hydraulic fittings in the forward compartment before ascending once more to the galley.

Thick white mugs hang from evenly spaced hooks above the sink. There is enough space between each mug to keep them from colliding in heavy seas, but all of them are chipped. One has black electrical tape wrapped tightly around its hand. I grab our mugs, fill them with fresh coffee, then balance the three steps up to the bridge. Red receives the smooth porcelain heat into his hand.

The skipper, Red, has spent over twenty years on the water most of it on the bridge. His jaw is square, his eyes the color of the winter sea, and his hair a banner to his temperament. He can run a boat with a bit of spit, a paper clip, and a few choice words. Red's praise is as rich as his rage, the copper fire of his haul surging equally hot through his veins. In his rough, capable hands, equipment comes to life. In his sure, calloused hands, I do also.

For fourteen years, we've powered through the seasons, netting herring in the spring, chasing salmon in the summer, harvesting halibut whenever we could, and risking everything in pursuit of lucrative crab during the worst of winters. This season, we have a first-class boat and a great crew. Confidence is running high.

Outside Ugak Island we set three strings of pots at different depths just to get a feel for the movement of the crab, then run till we get a little protection from the island. We anchor up to get some rest. I awaken as Red crawls out of our bunk and fumbles for his clothes.

"Go ahead and sleep for fifteen minutes more," he says to me, walking out and closing the door. The engines rumble and the anchor winch growls as it seizes the chain. There is a high-pitched whine as the hydraulics tug at the firmly entrenched anchor, then a clanking rush as the anchor lets go. We head out to check our pots.

Rising from the bunk, I pull on dry clothes and go to the galley to start breakfast. If we eat before we hit open water, it won't be as rough, so I hustle to prepare scrambled eggs, fried potatoes, bacon, and toast. Coffee is already making and the breakfast smells draw the guys to the galley. Red eats in the wheelhouse, adjusting the jogstick or checking position between bites.

"Mornin' dear," Mike says, grabbing a mug and filling it with black coffee. Mike, his brother "Little Dave," Jay, and I are the other crew members aboard. In the summer, Mike and I run salmon seiners, Jim has a charter boat business, and little Dave works a beach seine operation. Jay, also a seasoned mariner and longtime friend, rounds out the crew. The guys suck down their food, inhale their coffee, and don foul-weather gear within ten minutes.

"Great grub!" Mike calls cheerfully from the companionway.

"Yeah, like you Hoovers tasted it!" I scoot everything into the sink and am out on deck before the first long swell of open ocean lifts the hull.

Now it's "boat time." Every move at triple speed. No mistakes. No hesitations. There's an adrenal quality to it, an indefinable satisfaction in its execution. You learn to tie a bowline with your eyes closed so you can do it in the dark. You learn to leap, in just about any sea conditions, from boat to skiff and back again, both vessels under power, careening wakes adding interest to the calculation, split-second timing the only alternative. Greenhorns discover firsthand that for every action there is an equal and opposite reaction. Speed and precision often come at a painful price.

Looking out over the water, I can just make out the bobbing pink of the first string of gear. Red idles up to the first buoy and Mike throws the hook, snags the trailer buoy, and lays slack over the top of the hauler. Dave coils. Rapidly the line snakes upward till the coil stands knee-high. At twenty-five fathom shots, we slow the hauler slightly for knots, flip the line, and keep coiling.

"Bridle!" I yell as the pot begins to emerge. I hook it and the whine of the deck crane accompanies it over the side. Several long-legged snow crabs cling to its webbed sides—spider monkeys of the sea.

I unhook the door and we pull the crab out carefully, measure their carapace, then toss them into the tank. All but three are keepers. Meanwhile, Red is jogging to another pot. Mike throws the hook.

Overall, the catch around Ugak is disappointing. Red decides to head toward Sitkalidak, at the south end of Kodiak Island.

Once more we are underway, steel hull creasing a silver sea, sky darkening to soot as it begins to snow. We are tanked pumping fresh seawater on our crab to keep them constantly aerated. Water pushes out from under the main hatch, sloshes over the dock, then finds the sea through scupper holes cut in the base of the railings. All other deck hatches must be securely bolted down to prevent flooding. The pots are stacked on the stern, securely tied, lines and buoys inside.

In the Gulf of Alaska, storms brew up with little warning. Lines are triple-checked, rigging cinched until hydraulics squeal, and eyes are always moving. You look for slack or fray or leak; you listen to the cadence of the engines, the auxiliary's high whine, the deep throb of the main. You watch and you listen for any sign that something's not quite "right." Seasoned fishermen call it "running a little scared."

Up in the wheelhouse, I put on Elvis Presley's Greatest Hits just to rag the guys about being older than me. Once in a while, Red gyrates his hips or pantomimes slicking back his hair.

"I'm going to be violently ill if you don't quit that," I say.

Apparently, any attention is encouragement because he starts singing off-key, wailing along with the music.

"Love me tender, love me true ..." He's really getting into it now and I cover my ears as he closes in all dreamy-eyed: "Never let me go-o-o-o."

"Somebody save me!" I yell. Nobody looks up. "You guys even care if I get drooled on?" I push Red toward Little Dave. "Sing to him," I say. Little Dave's eyes brighten with amusement as Red leans in his direction. "Don't come one step closer," Dave warns.

The snowflakes have fattened to heavy cartwheels. They do handsprings against the portholes before the wind blows past. Beyond the momentary vision of the snowflakes, we can see nothing. Inside, the wheelhouse is also dark. It makes it easier to see the luminous radar screen, read the sonar, scan the numerous neon gauges, and watch the plotter guide us south. Radio chatter punctuated by static interrupts the silences. The wheelhouse is a cocoon, womblike in the vastness of night.

"We'd best get some rest, Angel," Red says to me, untangling his long legs from the chair where he's been draped. "I'll wake Jim." As the watch switches, I go below to the engine room for a quick inspection. Everything looks fine.

Back in the galley, I get a couple of bowls of ice cream and join Red in the stateroom. We eat, stretched out on the bunk, pillows behind our heads, cold sweetness on our tongues.

When our bowls are empty, we reach out for each other, then asleep, lulled by the hum of the engines and the rise and fall of the hull pushing through the waves.

"Get up!" Jay yells, slamming his fist against our door as he runs past. "The back deck's under!" He shouts it over his shoulder as we tear open the door and run out. From there it is dark mayhem—survival suits pulled and donned, Maydays sent and repeated, Red in the engine room, water to his waist, starting Emergency pumps, me urging him up and out, fear in my voice.

"Do you need any help?" So many other times, he has been my help.

"No, Angel. Get your suit on. Get mine ready." He yells it to me as the emergency pump kicks in.

With my survival suit on, I can barely function. The suit is big for me. The mitts are cumbersome as lobster claws. I make my way back to the engine room hatch. Red is still working frantically, trying to save the boat.

Everyone else is outside, standing on the bow. The deck is slanting sternward at a forty-five-degree angle and I know we won't bring it back. Red knows it too and makes his way down the ladder to grab his suit from me, already soaked and shivering. He goes out on the back deck after ordering me to get to the bow. I make my way, shakily, clinging to the walls as the boat lurches forward into the swell and settles deeper astern. Water is halfway up the back deck now, and I cannot see Red.

I pull myself out the wheelhouse door. The wind is cold on my face, the men silent as statues.

This frozen moment, I realize the degree of danger in every cell of my body, and my mind searches frantically for insulation from the yawning fissure opening at my feet. Adrenaline floods my blood. I feel like I am running, leaping just ahead of jaws or hanging miles above a void—the crack of the branch I cling to the only sound in the stillness of the sheerest terror one can own.

My voice is snatched into the wind as I find a small handhold in sanity's cliff. "Does anyone have a line?" I shout. No one answers. "Does anyone have a line?" The men stir but do not respond. "We need a line to stay together!" I yell again.

"There ain't no time, girl," Mike says.

"The lines are right here—we're standing on them!" I shout back, feeling tremendous relief as I remember the extra coils of crab line we stored on the port side of the vessel toward the bow, and then dismay as I recall that it is sinking line. We'll just have to hang on to it. Mike is galvanized into action and quickly sees a shot of line in the darkness, unties it, and threads it among us.

"Does anyone have the EPIRB?" I ask. No one does. By now, the boat is sliding seaward, the bow trapping air, and I have to hold on with all my might to direct my motion back into the boat. The floor slants downward and only my arms keep me in place. Inside, the wheelhouse is dark and still. The neon gauges of the electronics are like eyes, open in the blackness. The radio spits our name again and again into the stillness . . . "*The Wayward Wind*, calling *The Wayward Wind...*"

I lift the EPIRB carefully from its receptacle and hang on to it as I make my way back outside. It is a twelve-inch-tall cylinder about six inches in diameter. It is capable of signaling our position via satellite to the Coast Guard personnel in Kodiak who will be trying to find us. I muscle my way out, the EPIRB tucked under one arm, so that I can use both hands. My feet are practically useless, and I press into the wall to get to the door handle. I grasp it in one hand as the floor suddenly disappears completely from beneath me. Clinging to the door, clutching the EPIRB tight to my body, I swing for a moment, regain footing, then pull myself outside.

Red is on the bow. His suit is on, but the hood is not up. His hair is tangled and wet with sweat, his eyes tender and quiet.

"Are you zipped up, Angel?" he asks.

"I'm fine," I say. He goes to the stern to check, maybe to see. I do not see him after that.

The wind and waves are increasing, or maybe it only seems that way as we get closer to them. I am concerned that I will lose the unwieldy EPIRB as I enter the water, so I try to hand it to the person next to me. He does not respond. I tuck it tightly under one arm. Now, the water is midway up the house, the back deck several feet under. One by one, we slip silently into the sea. The man beside me is suddenly gone and the sea rises up to meet me. I attempt to propel myself outward, hoping to get as far as possible from the pull of the ship's hull. The line is wrapped once around my right arm. Both my hands are clamped tightly onto the EPIRB.

I am immediately dragged beneath the water and thrust deeply into a wave. It bursts against the hull and my face scrapes steel. Plastered against the curve of the hull, the sea slides me toward the surface. My chest, then my knees, bounce off the boat. I push backward with my feet. I push hard. The distance gained allows a wave just enough room to curl around me and throw me once more into the hull. This time, I am upside down, and my head hits hard. I am desperately trying to protect the EPIRB from impact; twisting, I manage to get my feet against the hull once more, and kick off with all my strength. At some point, I am floating free.

The swell of the ocean seems calm after the surging rush of the sinking boat. A trailer buoy is bobbing beside me. I grab it and slide it under my neck, elevating my head. Someone bumps into me.

"Hang on to me!" I shout, "I have the EPIRB!" He drifts by without response.

Now, I am all alone. I can see nothing but darkness. After a time, the black ocean looks slightly darker than the blackness of the sky. More time passes, and I can distinguish the breaking brightness of waves. Large white snowflakes define the sky. Sea gulls appear like apparitions of light. They look like luminous angels until they extend their feet. None land.

As I float, buoyed by the massive sea beneath me, looking upward at an inverted bowl of sky, a mighty calm pervades me for the first time in my life; I understand my place in the universe. I understand fully the privilege of life—I absorb the precious fragility of that privilege. I feel a part of everything—selfless as seaweed, rimed by salt and slime, storm-tossed or becalmed at the whim and will of the waves; a bright blob of orange on a blackened expanse of ocean; Poseidon's small plaything, a momentary diversion from designing beaches or escorting migratory whales. I do not feel fear. I feel everything else.

From time to time I call out for Red. I want to tell him that I'm okay, that I'm not afraid, that I have no regrets. I'd like to thank him for the experiences we shared, the way he taught me to absorb the layers of our combined humanity, to enjoy the manifestations of our abilities and to savor the saturation of our days. Together, we became so much more than the sum of our parts that now, facing obscurity, I am undaunted.

A strong wind parts the clouds high above me, revealing small shimmers of light. I've often watched sea otters float like this, toes scuffing the sky, bright eyes reflecting the stars. They have more hairs per square inch than any other mammal, silken armor to guard them from the piercing cold. My back is numb where it touches the sea.

Only the waves and the occasional cry of a gull can be heard. The blackness is a shroud.

"Red!" I cry out again, "Red!" Someone yells out in the darkness off to my right.

"Over here! I'm over here!" I strain my ears. Probably only a gull.

It is uncertain how long I float before something bumps into me in the water and I am pulled close to a large rubber body.

"Hang on to me!" I yell, "I've got the EPIRB!" He holds me, but I cannot make out what he is saying. He's trying to tell me who he is; Jim or Jay.

"I'm Jay!" he yells again. It is such an overwhelming comfort not to be alone.

I rest for longer than I should.

The cold has begun to weaken me and when I rouse myself, I maul the EPIRB with awkward mitts. All night I have been trying to activate it. The recessed toggle switch is about half an inch high and approximately the diameter of a chopstick. I know where it is located, but with little feeling in my extremities, the mitts seem slightly more dexterous than boxing gloves. Each wave rumbling toward us interrupts my efforts as I am flung about or tumbled under. Each struggle to right myself, re-position the EPIRB, and commence once more the frustrating search for the elusive switch takes its toll. Each fight to the surface weakens me as the freezing water seeps into my suit. After the waves break us apart, it takes fatiguing effort to find each other. Somehow, we keep managing to find each other.

Now the waves are growing larger. A big one tells us it is coming by the pull at our bodies and the resulting crescendo off its tumbling waters. Our recovery takes longer as the waves get rougher. At some point, I realize I am becoming hypothermic and try to tie the lanyard of the EPIRB around Jay's leg.

"What are you doing?" His voice carries above the waves. I am too tired to reply, and my attempts are unsuccessful anyway.

I want to close my eyes. It has been hours since the boat went down, and I can feel my body losing purpose. Only the outside chance that I might be able to influ-ence our survival keeps my efforts alive. As my systems begin to shut down, my brain narrows its focus. I keep trying to direct my mitts over the puzzling surface of the canister.

I feel stuck with the frustration of the uncooperative EPIRB. If not for it, I could just go to sleep. Now, I'm angry as I fumble with the damn thing. I yank and puff and push and jerk at it and suddenly, I snag something and a tiny red light comes on in the darkness. It blinks off, then on. I yell out in amazement and relief.

"It's on!" The EPIRB is on!

"Try turning it off, then back on again, just to make sure!" he yells during a lull in the wind and waves.

I reject this idea without reply, holding the EPIRB carefully, almost warmed by the blinking red light and the hope surging through me.

"It's on!" I yell back.

Now that my goal has finally been achieved, I remember the line wound around me; I had completely forgotten it in the shock of entry, in the stunning unfolding of events, and in my intense focus on the EPIRB.

"Help me pull in the line; we need to tell the others!"

We began pulling on the line. It is a Herculean effort to reef it through the waves. It takes a very long time. Finally, we get to the end of the line.

I hold it—empty—in my hand as we float in the darkness.

Sometime later, I hear the sound of engines. A plane is overhead. Homing in on our signal, the C-130 makes several passes before a rescue helicopter arrives on scene. Now there are blades whipping the snowy blackness above us, then piercing light and deafening noise. A steel-framed basket is lowered. Pulled by the chopper, it jerks and pitches erratically, buries itself in a wave, then yanks free and is gone. The next time it comes close, Jay tries to stop it and heave me in. The basket hurtles past.

This time, I am ready. I swim hard when I see it lowered, wait for it to settle in the belly of a wave, then grab on to the metal web and curl myself into a tight ball. I am pulled sideways, dragged deep beneath the waves and nearly drowned before the lift begins. Suddenly, the sea no longer holds me. There is a moment when I become sky.

Kneeling beside the dock, I memorize the curls and peaks, the variation of hue, the balance of color of the memorial wreath. The man and woman have begun their journey up the dock. She insists on walking, and he pushes the empty wheelchair behind her, shaking his head at her stubbornness. I admire her courage. She does not succumb to pain. She makes it wait its turn when she has living to do.

"I'll be there in a moment," I call after them.

I stare at the dull gray water. It reflects nothing; it absorbs everything.

I think about pain.

For too many years, I've carried their deaths in my thoughts, the weight of their dreams on my heart. For over a decade, I've polished their memories, fondled their faces, and smoothed back their hair. Leaning as close as I can to the memorial wreath, I touch my fingers to my lips and place a farewell kiss upon the waters. Closing my eyes, I stay for a bit, then stand and start to walk back up the dock.

Ahead of me, the woman rests against the man. They talk for a moment, but I do not hear what they are saying. I fall in step behind them, walking slower than I have ever walked on the busy conduit of a dock. We push our way forward as if the air itself were a cushion of resistance. She pauses as the ramp begins its steep incline. The tide has fallen and the ramp may as well be a mountain. Inexplicably, she begins to sing as she places one wobbly foot on the ramp.

"There were ten in the bed and the little one said, 'Roll over! Roll over!'" She takes a step, "They all rolled over and one fell out...."

The man and I exchange concerned glances.

"There were nine in the bed and the little one said..."

The man shrugs his shoulders and joins in: "Roll over, roll over! So they all rolled over and one fell out..."

I realize I am gritting my teeth. They sing louder as the incline steepens. Other people pass us on the ramp. They give wide berth to the crippled woman stoutly singing as she struggles with her pain—"They all rolled over and one fell out, there were four in the bed..."

I feel slightly foolish as they avert their eyes. A couple of guys I know are starting down the ramp when I finally let go.

"Roll over," I sing. "Roll over!" A sense of joy washes over me at the release and I sing out loudly. Connie hears me with her entire being and shoves herself upward with renewed purpose. We look at each other. "They all rolled over and one fell out, there were two in the bed and the little one said...."

She takes a final step to the top of the ramp. She is soaked by rain and sweat. She is shaking with fatigue and pain, but her eyes are bright with triumph and her face looks almost beautiful. ⚓

DEBRA NIELSEN lived in the Alaska bush for ten years earning a living by salvaging sunken boats and fishing. She began as a cook and deckhand and worked her way up to skipper, running her own boat for five seasons, until the tragic sinking of the Wayward Wind that killed her husband and three others. Debra now divides her time between delighting in the way light falls on objects and trying to find a way to keep a few coins in the fountain.

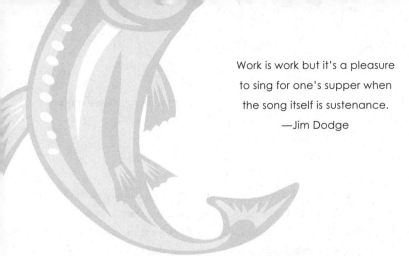

> Work is work but it's a pleasure
> to sing for one's supper when
> the song itself is sustenance.
> —Jim Dodge

THREE YEARS OUT

I'M SURPRISED THAT she's calling me at work. I wonder if she even knows what day of the week it is. I never did when I was a deckhand. Days were distinguished by what we were doing on the boat: fishing, running, unloading. Those were the three days of the week. But she's a skipper this summer; it's her job to know what day it is. I smile and keep my thoughts to myself. As I listen I realize she doesn't care what day it is, she needs someone to talk to, someone who understands a summer spent chasing salmon.

She was working for me at the college last winter when she landed this job. I was skeptical; I don't think she has the experience to be a skipper. I admire her tenacity but like any greenhorn, she doesn't know what she doesn't know. Now she's complaining about the cannery expecting her to run all night to Ketchikan. I find myself irritated thinking that's part of the job. I remember hundreds of nights running between Noyes Island and Petersburg. We took three-hour watches dodging logs in Warren Channel, avoiding gillnets at Point Baker, nego-

ERIN FRISTAD tries to reconcile her white-collar job with her desire to fish, her memories of being a deckhand reminding her that "fishing alters you, forever."

tiating with cruise ships at Wrangell Narrows. There wasn't time to complain, it was a race
to get unloaded and back on the fishing grounds.

"It's forecast to blow like hell tonight," she adds.

"You can go the back way," I offer.

"Zimovia?"

"Yeah, and that big sound." I pause, hearing my heartbeat in my head when I can't
remember the name of the sound. I close my eyes and picture the chart. I can see the sur-
roundings. I remember a trip south following an orca bull in the fog through Zimovia. He
had a notch missing from his dorsal fin. I remember crossing that sound reading an essay
by Barry Lopez about the forty-one sperm whales beached near the town of Florence on
the Oregon Coast. I read with urgency because it would be too rough when we turned
south into Clarence Strait. When I still can't remember, I realize my irritation isn't with
her but with myself. I've lost my edge: I'm no longer part of the fishing fleet.

"Ernest Sound!" I blurt it out with a note of triumph that shocks both of us.

Truth is, I'll never leave fishing. Forgetting the name of a sound or a headland won't
change this. Fishing lives in my cells. It appears when I coil the garden hose as though
it's a three-stranded poly tie-up line, in the way I secure a tarp over the bed of a pickup
truck, or that I still insist on cooking two boxes of pasta. My real fear is where I'm going.

August 1: I arrive in Juneau. No one meets me at the airport. I catch a cab to Auke
Bay and wrestle my two large bags to the end of the dock where the boat is tied up. I see
a crewmember. He tells me we're leaving immediately. The skipper arrives. I give him a
hug that makes him uncomfortable. His cell phone falls out of his pocket and is broken
for the rest of the season. He informs me that I won't be the cook: "You're better than the
one I've got but it would hurt his feelings too much." I shrug and tell him I'm flexible.
He seems relieved and takes us out to dinner. I do my best to boost everyone's energy,
which is the unspoken expectation of having a woman on board. I've performed this role
fifteen years: I ask questions, listen, smile, and laugh often. I slug two glasses of the house
wine and remember that wine tastes terrible in Alaska: this land requires beer and whiskey.

I had left fishing three years before for a job I was offered at a cocktail party. I was
hired to set up a satellite college campus in the small town where I live. I had four months
before students arrived. I appeared to be the ideal candidate because, as a graduate of the
college, I understood its mission, but I wasn't burdened by knowing the rules of the bu-
reaucracy. Fishermen make things happen quickly. Everything on a fishing boat is urgent.
Fish don't wait for Academic Services, the Business Office, and the Registrar to make a
decision. In fishing, you act quickly or you don't make a living.

August 5: We run all night to new territory. The other boats are anchored up when
we arrive. The skipper decides we'll jog to get the first set. He posts a watch schedule on

a small piece of paper tucked behind the mirror in the passageway. We look at it and go to our bunks in silence. There is nothing to say. Our sentiments are mutual. Deckhands hate jogging all night. But we're too professional to complain. Jogging is old school. Now it's common for boats to wait in line on the anchor so everyone can get some sleep. The old-timers think we're lazy.

The skipper points where he wants the boat and heads for his bunk. It's dark, raining and I can't see beyond the bow chock. I create a position mark on the plotter. I put the boat in gear and nose into the westerly swell. The skipper pops his head in: "Where are you going?"

"Trying to keep it out of the trough so you guys can sleep."

"We don't do it that way." And he disappears. I'm not sure how to translate this comment. I guess these guys are accustomed to sleeping in the trough. We drift an eighth of a mile off our mark. I put it in gear and move back toward the beach. He reappears out of the dark "Don't use the throttle. That wakes us up." His tone reveals irritation. "Idle in circles," he says, and disappears again. I'm relieved when the hatch opens and my replacement appears. I point to the mark on the plotter. He nods. We don't speak.

As a college administrator, I wear mascara, lipstick, four-inch heels and carry a black leather briefcase. I spend most of my days in meetings or communicating by email. I sit a lot. I do good work. I hold a place for adult students to reach their potential, many are pursuing a dream they put off for twenty years while they were busy with careers and families. At graduation they cry, hug me, take my photo, and thank me over and over.

I earn more money now than I did fishing, but it trickles into my bank account like a drip feed of methadone: there is never enough to live high or quit. I miss the satisfaction of being gainfully unemployed at the end of every season. I had one skipper who loved to hand us our paychecks and say, "Here, you're fired … until June 1st of next year." The check equaled freedom. I paid cash, avoided debt, visited friends, lived in different cities, traveled to different countries, studied poetry, earned my master's degree, and slept late the entire month of February.

The previous summer, I had a ritual: Every morning before work, I walked along the bluff and looked out at the Strait of Juan de Fuca. I would judge the tide and wind, seeing if the strait looked fishable. I'd imagine fishing in Alaska: chum at Hidden Falls, pinks in Chatham, sockeye at Noyes Island. Then I would return home to dress for work. As I walked, I wondered, asked myself questions. How important are memories? Is my identity a collection of memories? I kept a journal my last year fishing; I knew a day would come when I'd wonder why I left. Now I flip through it for recollections, answers.

August 9: The sockeye hit the west side of Noyes Island. It's rough out but we're hungry. So are the sea lions. They seem more aggressive than usual. We have one in the net who pops up every ninety seconds with a fish in his mouth. Our skipper becomes insane with anger. He yells, swears, jumps up and down, then throws the ring bar leaving a giant gouge in the wooden deck. The other deckhand and I keep our heads down and pile gear. Our skipper disappears into the wheelhouse and returns with his rifle. Just as he fires the boat is tossed in the swell, he loses his balance and the bullet ricochets off a cable. The other deckhand and I collapse into balls and cover our heads. My ears are ringing, then it's silent like the whole ocean is holding its breath and then there's yelling from the skiff driver because the block is still running and net is falling off the stern. Our skipper laughs hysterically.

August 15: The fishing is good and we're going to deck load the boat. The skipper directs us to unbolt the hatch cover before we get more fish on board. It's rough and the cover breaks free, slams into my leg knocking me down. I swear loudly and point out how stupid it is to unbolt the hatch in rough weather. Everyone stops and looks at me, horrified. The skipper asks if I'm hurt. "No, I'm pissed off." He looks like he's going to cry. I quickly smile and make a joke and everyone returns to work. They'll talk about how I "lost it on deck" for the next week. I avoid shorts until the bruise on my leg heals.

August 17: This is the first boat I've worked on in fifteen years of fishing with issues of Playboy scattered all around the galley. There is also a calendar showing a naked woman half hidden behind potholders above the diesel stove. I watch her while I have my first cup of coffee, before the sun comes up, and take comfort in thoughts of her being cozy and warm while we prepare to go out on a cold deck. I'm not bothered by her nudity; instead it's the vacant look on her face. Her eyes remind me of the trophy elk hanging over my neighbor's fireplace.

We're plugged with fish by noon, tie to the tender, unload, and start scrubbing the boat. I'm in the fish hold hosing down gurry and foam. The tendermen have finished cleaning their deck and stand at the rail visiting with my crewmates. I hear excitement in their voices and realize that they're trading issues of *Playboy*. Our cook trades his much beloved *Playboy Brazil,* which wields extra leverage in these dealings. I hear the talk turn to pubic hair: too much, too little, and it goes on. I'm content to be below deck where my facial expressions are concealed.

Unfortunately, I complete my task, climb out of the hold, and discover the tendermen remaining at the rail like three seagulls. The boat is too small for me to hide behind the side of the house so I'm forced to take off my raingear with them watching. I wonder if they're thinking about my pubic hair. I pretend I didn't hear their conversation, hang up my raingear and smile. They stare and don't speak. We're picking the skiff. I focus on this project, hustling to the stern to guide the tie-down straps for the skiff driver. He claims I've twisted them. We tease like deckhands do. I make an exaggerated show of flipping him off. We laugh. Our skipper pauses and says in a loud voice: "Please excuse Erin's behavior, she's not usually so crude," and then he continues across deck with an armload of magazines and places them on the galley table.

Later, looking over my fishing journal, I wonder why I thought these notes would ease my departure from fishing. Now I find these situations funny. What I know is that three years ago there was something I needed to follow. I also know that now, when I walk along the bluff in the morning, I think of fishing.

I don't have a journal from being a college administrator.

Last spring, I asked the college for a raise. It took all summer to get a response, and I found myself angry over money. I was never guaranteed money fishing. But the longer the college waited, the more I thought about fishing. When our summer session of students was most stressful, I told a story about a tugboat captain who quit when he got off wheel watch, right in the middle of Chatham Strait. The mate took the wheel and was confused by a floatplane circling the boat. Next thing he knew, the engineer had launched the skiff and was taking the captain to meet the plane. He was done and he left. My co-workers stared at me, disturbed.

When a dramatic departure wasn't an option, I started making phone calls. I used the excuse of needing money. The second call resulted in a job offer. I can go run hydraulics, pot fishing for cod. It's a good boat; I've worked on it before, and am well adapted at ignoring what the skipper calls his "Tourette's at Sea Syndrome." I told him to call me when the boat arrives in Kodiak and he knows what they're paying for cod. Truth is, I don't really care what they're paying for cod, and I don't really need the money. I'm looking for the song. I realize that I made a mistake. I left fishing because I expected the song to always be beautiful.

I don't know where this story ends. I'm sharing it with you because this is what happens: fishing alters you, forever.

ERIN FRISTAD followed a childhood friend to Alaska for a summer adventure and was forever altered. She fished fifteen years from Togiak to Columbia River, chasing herring, crab, and salmon, and worked five years on a research vessel. Eventually, the tide brought her to Port Townsend, Washington, where she continues to write, teach, and work at Goddard College. Fristad has performed at the Fisher Poets' Gathering, Sea Stories, Kodiak Out loud, Seattle Folklife Festival, and the Seattle Green Festival. She was a subject in the documentary film, Fisher Poets. Her poems have been published in anthologies and journals, including: *Rosebud, America's Review, The Blue Collar Review, Hanging Loose, The Seattle Review, Mute Note Earthward: a WPA Anthology,* and *Working the Woods, Working the Sea: An Anthology of Northwest Writing.*

READING RECOMMENDATIONS
for those interested in sea stories

ALASKA BLUES
*Story of Freedom, Risk,
and Living Your Dream*
Joe Upton
Memoir, paperback, $14.95

**ALASKA CRUISE
HANDBOOK**
Joe Upton
Travel, paperback, $19.95

BERING SEA BLUES
*A Crabber's Tale
of Fear in the Icy North*
Joe Upton
Memoir, paperback, $17.95

**FISHES & DISHES
COOKBOOK**
*Seafood recipes and Salty Stories
from Alaska's Commercial
Fisherwomen*
Kiyo Marsh, Tomi Marsh,
Laura Cooper
Cookbook, paperback, $19.95

A FISH OUT OF WATER
Arlene Lochridge
Memoir/Journal, paperback, $22.95

**SALMON PATTIES &
ROSEHIP PIE COOKBOOK**
*Art, Food, and the Coastal Life
in Halibut Cove, Alaska*
Marian Beck
Cookbook/Artbook, hardbound gift
edition, $24.95

SPILL
*Personal Stories from the
Exxon Valdez Disaster*
Sharon Bushell & Stan Jones
Anthology/History, paperback,
$17.95

SUNKEN KLONDIKE GOLD
How a Fortune Inspired an Ambitious Effort to Raise the S.S. Islander
Leonard H. Delano
History, paperback, $24.95

**SURVIVING THE ISLAND
OF GRACE**
A Life on the Wild Edge of America
Leslie Leyland Fields
Memoir, paperback, $17.95

EPICENTER PRESS
Alaska Book Adventures™
www.EpicenterPress.com

AFTERSHOCKS MEDIA
www.Aftershocksmedia.com

These titles can be found or special ordered from your local bookstore, or they may be ordered at 800-950-6663 day or night. More Epicenter titles, including many with historical themes, may be found at www.EpicenterPress.com.